A Trekk

Ma Tsum Valley

Lower Manaslu & Ganesh Himal

Siân Pritchard-Jones and Bob Gibbons

© Siân Pritchard-Jones and Bob Gibbons and Himalayan Map House, 2016

First edition March 2013
Second edition January 2016

All rights reserved. No part of this publication may be reproduced or transmitted in any form or by any means without the prior written permission of the copyright holders.

ISBN: 978-1522814641

Text & photos: Siân Pritchard-Jones and Bob Gibbons

Front cover photo: Manaslu from Lho
Back cover photo: Nuns at Rachen Gompa celebrating the Buddhist religious ceremony known locally as Sendang
Cover photos: Lopsang Chhiring Lama

Concept: Pawan Shakya
www.himalayanmaphouse.com
Design: Santosh Maharjan
Maps: Era Shrestha, Rikesh Maharjan, Pravin Shrestha, Nirjan Maharjan, Shree Krishna Maharjan

Tips

Discover the cultural heritage:

1 Bhaktapur Nyatapola temple
2 Bungamati Square harvest and mandala
3 Vajrapani
4 Guru Rinpoche
5 Mani festival at Samagaon

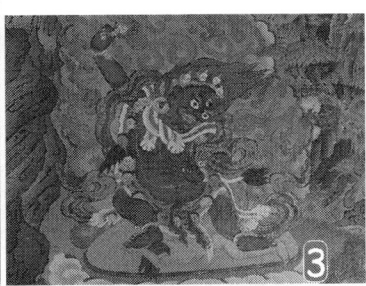

Meet the people:

1 Collecting dung near Chhokang Paro
2 Curious kids in Arughat
3 Novice monks at Lho
4 Daily chores
5 Baby snoozing at Gho

Enjoy the trails:

1 Climbing to Chhokang Paro
2 Steep steps to Lapubesi
3 View of Shringi Himal
4 Where is Bihi Phedi?
5 Trail from Samdo to the
  Larkya La
6 Golden harvest

Keep left of the sacred stupas, kanis and manis:

1 Chortens near Chumling
2 Mu Gompa, Tsum Valley
3 Typical kani gate in Upper Manaslu
4 Chhule stupa

Highlights

1 Ganesh II from Tsum Valley
2 Village house in Chumling
3 Chorten at Pungyen Gompa, Kutang Himal behind
4 Yak attack in Nile
5 Siyar Khola bridge

1 Himlung & Cheo Himal, seen on the descent from the Larkya La
2 Mu Gompa
3 Langpo
4 Himlung sunrise

1 Manaslu from below Bimthang
2 Manaslu North from trail near Larkya Phedi
3 Samdo village below Pang Phuchi
4 Manaslu North sunrise from Lho

1 Ganesh I from Domje
2 Manaslu glacier from trail to Samdo
3 Ganesh Himal
4 Baudha & Himalchuli from Chhokang Paro
5 Approaching the Larkya La
6 Gonhgye Gompa, Tsum Valley

Acknowledgements

Thanks to Pawan Shakya at Himalayan Map House and all the team for allowing us the pleasure of bringing the fabulous scenery and colourful people of the Manaslu and Tsum regions to a wider public through this new publication. Thanks to Sonam Lama and Lopsang Chhiring Lama (co-authors of the Manaslu and Tsum coffee table book also published by Himalayan Map House) for their information about the side trips, both in their native Tsum Valley and beyond. For help on our trek we are forever indebted to Sange, our guide, for all his translations and background knowledge, and our amazingly fast, strong, but sadly partially deaf porter, Tenzing. And of course our two valiant pony men and sure-footed ponies from Samdo. The information concerning Lower Manaslu was written with the kind help of 'Jit' Sane Gurung, Sunar Gurung and Harka Gurung. Thanks also to Bishnu Adhikari and Kate Hargadon at Choice Humanitarian. For the second edition, special thanks to Mr Dhir, one of the best local updaters in Nepal.

Thanks to Uttam Phuyal at Hotel Moonlight for his superb hospitality. We are also grateful to Pasang Dawa of Sherpa Adventure Treks, to Ravi Chandra of Ama Dablam Trekking, and to Niraj Shrestha and Tony Jones of Himalayan Encounters for our stay at the Famous Farm in Nuwakot and much more. Thanks also to Sohan Shrestha at Hotel Pilgrims. Thanks to the Kathmandu Guest House, Rama Tiwari, Mingma Sherpa of The Everest Equipment Shop for the great sleeping bags and jackets, Bhandari's Photo Shop opposite and KC's restaurant for the superb pumpkin pies. Thanks to Damien Francois for information about Ganesh I, which he had been attempting to climb. Last but not least, to David Durkan for his humourous interventions.

Thanks to the lodge hosts, trekking staff and porters who struggle daily through such grand scenery, looking only at the trail underfoot. And finally, thanks to the reader who can help to keep this book updated.

Please send your suggestions and updates to sianpj@hotmail.com, www.expeditionworld.com.

Warning

Please remember that walking in high, remote mountains is potentially dangerous. The publisher and authors have taken every care in producing this guide, but readers must take ultimate responsibility for themselves. Trail and weather conditions can change suddenly and readers must understand these natural risks. Trails in the Manaslu area are particularly exposed and narrow, and unsuitable for anyone who does not have a good head for heights. Those who are unsure and inexperienced should relish the additional safety of taking a fully trained and experienced Nepalese trekking guide, as indeed is required by current Nepalese trekking regulations for Manaslu and Tsum. Those unsure of their abilities or on their first trek in the Himalaya should do the Annapurna Circuit instead.

Neither Himalayan Map House nor the authors can accept liability for damage of any nature (including damage to property, personal injury or death) arising from the information in this book, directly or indirectly.

Although there are now some local mobile phone networks throughout most of the trekking routes, foreign mobile phones may not work. Local lodges will always be able to help and call a helicopter if necessary, but this will be expensive.

Health posts are few and far between and at the time of our research we did not see a single one open and functioning. Apart from the marijuana growing freely alongside many of the trails, drugs are not available on this route. Take a supply of all the medicines you are likely to use, as well as those you do not expect to need!

Banks are also nonexistent, so take more rupees than you need, and then a bit more again.

In other words, be prepared to help yourself in any eventuality. It may be the only way.

Contents

Preface	7
Introduction	8
BEFORE THE TREK	**15**
Country background	**15**
Geography	15
Climate	15
Natural history	16
Brief history of Nepal	21
Religion and festivals	25
Cultural aspects	29
Practicalities	**34**
Getting to Nepal	34
Visa information	36
Money matters	37
Trek planning	**40**
Trek permits	40
Maps	43
Budgeting	44
Style of trekking	45
Independent trekking	46
Fully supported group treks	48
Accommodation	52
Food	54
What to take	55
Staying healthy	**56**
Altitude sickness & precautions	61
Mountain safety	63
Weather	64

Security	65
Kathmandu – Gateway to Manaslu	**65**
Pokhara – after the trek	**69**
Using this guide	70
Pre-Trek checklist	72
THE TREKKING ROUTES	**74**
Manaslu Circuit	**74**
Tsum Valley Trek	**128**
Other Treks	**158**
Lower Manaslu Region	**158**
Gorkha Pilgrimage Trek	158
Gorkha Cultural Trail	160
Lower Manaslu Trek	162
Dharche Danda Trek	163
Rupina La Trek	164
Ganesh Region and Ruby Valley	**167**
Lamjung Region	**168**
Gurung Heritage Trail	169
Khudi - Pokhara via Baglungpani	170
Besisahar - Ramgha - Pokhara	170
Kalimati - Chowk Chisopani - Pokhara	171
Appendices	**173**
Appendix 1: Trek summaries and suggestions	173
Appendix 2: Bibliography	182
Appendix 3: Glossary	185
Appendix 4: Nepali language hints	189
Appendix 5: Useful contacts	191

Preface

> It is impossible for any thinking man to look down from a hill on to a crowded plain and not ponder over the relative importance of things.
>
> *The Mountain Top*, **Frank S Smythe**

From almost any vantage point, the Himalaya seem to defy reality. Standing aloof and dominant, the great shimmering ice spires and gargantuan rock bastions of the mountains float above the fluffy clouds like a painting of the gods. Located between the famous Annapurna region to its west and the whimsically named Ganesh Himal to its east is the great peak of Manaslu (8163m), with its dramatic twin-summits. Guarded by the sublimely majestic summits of Baudha, Himalchuli and Ngadi Chuli, Manaslu hides its best faces for those who seek to reach its inner sanctuaries. Only by trekking for two weeks can one truly appreciate its fantastic secret north walls and mind-blowing glaciers. From Kathmandu the mighty range of Ganesh Himal glitters in the morning sun, while hidden away from civilisation on its northern flanks is the lost valley of Tsum. Closed to the outside world for centuries, apart from a few salt traders, the Tsum Valley is surprisingly fertile – but only for a few short weeks in summer, when monsoon clouds and mist roll up the great gorge of the Budhi Gandaki. Manaslu and the Tsum Valley are proving to be increasingly popular frontier regions to be discovered.

> The power of such a mountain is so great and yet so subtle that, without compulsion, people are drawn to it from near and far, as if by the force of some invisible magnet...
>
> *The Way of the White Clouds*, **Lama Anagarika Govinda**

This fabulous quote is so encapsulating that we have used it in several books over the years, so come and discover for yourself the simple things that nature has bestowed.

Introduction

The Himalaya of Nepal extend for over 800km from the Indian borders of Sikkim in the east to the Indian Garhwal in the west. They divide the often hot, sultry plains of India from the lost horizons of the windswept icy Tibetan plateau. The highest peaks – Kanchenjunga, Makalu, Everest, Lhotse, Annapurna and Dhaulagiri – are located along the northern borders of Nepal. All exceed 8000m in height. One other peak exceeds 8000m and that is Manaslu, whose name derives from the Sanskrit word *manasa,* meaning 'mountain of the soul.'

Nepal was isolated for centuries, a forbidden land, almost a paradise on earth. Hidden below the Himalaya behind rugged foothills and impenetrable ridges was a lush and plentiful kingdom, locked in a time warp until 1950. The rhythms of life remained intact; the daily rituals, the bonds of religious beliefs and the pace of life rolled on with an imperceptible motion. Today villages still echo to the sounds and chants of a Hindu Brahmin priest; festivals dictate the never-ending rhythms of rural life. Farmers plough their small terraced fields while women keep a watchful eye on inquisitive children, intent on new daily discoveries. At higher altitudes the people eke out a hardy living in harsh conditions, where the even the vegetation struggles to survive. Buddhism is a great comfort to these Tibetan-related peoples.

Situated between the Himalayan peaks of Langtang and the Annapurnas are the less-visited regions of Ganesh Himal and Manaslu Himal. These two massive ranges encompass the trekkers' paradise of both the Manaslu Circuit and the hidden Tsum Valley. The Manaslu Circuit offers stunning views of the great peaks of Himalchuli, Ngadi, Manaslu and the Larkya Himal, as well as the eastern giants of the Annapurnas – Lamjung, Annapurna II and Kang Guru. A myriad of lesser known, but equally spectacular, peaks add to the fiesta of snowy summits. East of Manaslu is the knotted collection of the Ganesh peaks, a region so close to Kathmandu yet very little visited. Hidden behind this range is the lost fiefdom of Tsum, so isolated that virtually no outsiders have trodden there. It hosts Buddhist communities living secluded lives, devoted to their traditional way of life and their iconic Buddhist deities.

A number of picturesque monasteries provide the main focus for the communities in these isolated pastures. Dominating the whole Tsum region are the stupendous faces of Ganesh Himal, Shringi Himal and their spectacular, tumbling glaciers.

Any visitor to the Manaslu and Tsum region will enjoy an amazing variety of geographical landscapes and cultural differences below the great peaks of Manaslu and Ganesh. Finely fluted faces and gigantic, jagged rock spires defy the senses, while placid, cool blue lakes lie gracefully below the glaciers that speak to the gods. On the southern slopes of the great Himalaya, the countryside is lush, fertile and alive with life, both human and natural. Passing through impossibly sheer-sided gorges, the deep rivers of the Budhi (Buri) Gandaki and Marsyangdi provide vital access to the high uplands beyond the main Himalayan chain.

Visitors come to Nepal for many reasons. For the majority it is the magical Himalaya that are the great magnet; some come purely for the challenge of climbing the peaks. Others seek a more intimate connection with the country – meeting the people, exploring the architectural wonders of the Kathmandu Valley, where history and fairytale images stare the mesmerised guest in the face. Discerning travellers come to learn about the mystical religious life of the country, where a myriad of surprising sights will baffle and intrigue even the most non-spiritual soul. Some will venture in search of the fabulous diversity of the flora, while others, with endless patience, seek out the fauna – the fleet-of-foot Himalayan tahr or the elusive snow leopard. The birds of the Himalaya are legendary, with beautiful but skittish kingfishers along the riverbanks, colourful Danfe pheasants in the mountains and ravenous carrion-eating Himalayan Griffons and Lammergeyers in the skies. Whatever the reasons for a visit to Nepal, no one will leave disappointed.

The Manaslu and Tsum region is one of Nepal's last Himalayan jewels to behold; a glittering array of panoramas, peaks and peaceful valleys awaits the adventurous explorer. However, as magnificent as the mountains are, it is perhaps the people of Nepal who are its greatest asset. They are hard-working, boisterous, industrious, endearing, brimming with humour, versatile, vibrant and hungry for change, just like most people across our planet. Progress will surely begin to change the region as new dirt roads begin to snake along the deep gorges. Trekkers visiting Manaslu and Tsum are sure to be smitten by these magical places. All will leave with a renewed inspiration for life – as the tourist posters say: 'Inspiration Manaslu – Nature's Call Destination' – perhaps not quite what they had in mind!

Inspiration Manaslu – Nature's Call Destination

The trails are varied and enticing, some criss-cross the intricately sculptured terraces and hillsides, while others head into cool, refreshing forests of bamboo and exotic rhododendron. Just a few of the trails contour gently along, but it seems that the majority of them soar to the skies and dive to the depths with increasing frequency and gradient. One begins to lose count of the metres gained or lost. Wispy lichens and goblinesque woodlands give way to pine and larch, disturbed only by the gentle breezes. Higher trails lead to silent alpine glades and rugged, high mountain desert. All life is encountered along the trails in the villages. In the lower hills you may glimpse a Hindu god worshipped with fervent devotion at a wayside shrine. Higher up, the mesmerising chants of the monks and the intoxicating roar of a Tibetan horn at dawn may be your early morning call.

Manaslu Circuit

Shortly after leaving the Kathmandu Valley rim, there are magnificent views of Ganesh Himal and the Himalchuli/Manaslu range, as well as the more distant Annapurna peaks. For the first few days hikers can luxuriate in the warmth of the low riverside trail along the Budhi (Buri) Gandaki river. The trail meanders, scrambles, soars and dives its way along the confines of the valley. In places the river cuts through very narrow towering cliffs, graced by fairytale waterfalls. Beyond Jagat the colourful Hindu culture is replaced by the more contemplative Buddhism. Mani walls, kani gates and chortens dot the byways.

Heading northwest from Philim through Deng, the Manaslu Circuit trail continues its relentless climb to the upper reaches of the Budhi Gandaki, a river now of diminished stature but of tremendous scenic delights.

The villages of Lihi, Sho, Lho and Shyala are fascinating – a window into the secluded Buddhism of the wild valleys. Meanwhile, ever more imposing and spectacular vistas of Himalchuli, Ngadi and Manaslu cast magical spells on the trekker.

The geographical and geological transition to the arid upland of the Tibetan plateau beyond Samagaon is astonishing. Beyond Samdo is the high, wild pass of the Larkya La, the highest point of the trek at 5160m. The fabulous panorama from the pass encompasses the beautiful massif of Cheo Himal and Larkya Peak, then the giants of the Nar-Phu region – Himlung, Kang Guru, Nemjung and Annapurna II.

The Bimthang meadows provide a welcome respite from the high altitude, the winds and the harsh dry air. This is a paradise of elegant peaks, quiet forests and bubbling streams. From here the trail descends rapidly to Dharapani, where the trek meets the popular Annapurna Circuit route and the new dirt road. Alas, all too soon the trek concludes near Tal, or further down at Bhulbhule for those trekkers who take the Bahundanda trail.

Tsum Valley

Tsum is magical and mysterious. The region was once so remote that almost nothing was known about it. This wild, rugged and exotic valley is located north of Ganesh Himal and just east of Manaslu. The landscapes and mountain vistas can only be described as superlative, as befits another real Shangri-La of the Himalaya.

The main architectural features of Tsum are the distinctive mani walls, chortens and kani gateway chortens, built to ward off evil spirits. The rich cultural heritage includes stirringly located monasteries, lively festivals and historic treasures. Picturesque villages, quaint stone houses with hazy blue wood-fire smoke billowing from the rooftops, mysterious alleys and colourful people add to the mix.

Soon after Philim the trail climbs east to Lokpa in the Tsum region. Dense forest and sheer-sided cliffs almost bar the way. Above Domje a side valley leads up to the great Torogumba Glacier that gives access to the wonderland of Ganesh Himal's rarely seen north-western faces. Also high up here is the Gumba Lungdang monastery. The jagged peak of Ganesh II has particularly impressive icy bastions and glaciated ramparts. Beyond Chhokang Paro are the famed nunnery of Rachen, the mystical monastery of Mu, and Dhephyudonma, the oldest gompa of the Tsum Valley. Continuing further north are the barren mountains of the Tibetan plateau. Eventually a trail leads to the Ngula Dhojyang pass, which enables traders to cross into the Kyirong district of Tibet.

The Tsum Valley has only recently opened to visitors and, as yet, trekking here is in its infancy. Trekkers will be pioneering the way for a few seasons to come, with a degree of basic comfort unimaginable to earlier explorers.

After the momentous earthquakes of the spring of 2015 the region suffered badly, especially some of the Lower Manaslu areas north of Gorkha. However, trekkers are already returning to the main areas of Manaslu and Tsum. Trails and lodges are being improved all the time and soon most of the physical horrors of the quakes will have been repaired.

***

It's a dangerous business, Frodo, going out your door. You step on to the road, and if you don't keep your feet, there's no knowing where you might be swept off to.
***The Lord of the Rings*, J.R.R. Tolkien**

Of course any venture into untamed and wild places presents some risks and dangers. A trek to the remote Himalayan regions needs careful preparation and informed planning. Part of this guide is devoted to the aspects that need to be brought to the attention of any prospective visitor. That 'once-in-a-lifetime' trek to Nepal is likely to be habit-forming and life-changing! The aim of this guide is to inspire readers to go beyond the familiar, to discover the treasures of Nepal – its mountains, its people and its culture.

***Siân Pritchard-Jones and Bob Gibbons**
Kathmandu 2016*

Earthquakes in Nepal: April – May 2015

In 2011 Cicerone commissioned us to write a new guidebook to the Annapurna region of Nepal. Since then we have also been working with a local Nepalese publisher, Himalayan Map House in Kathmandu, producing a series of trekking guides that cover all the main trekking areas of Nepal. It's been a superb job, as we never had the opportunity before to trek in the more off-beat regions like Manaslu, Ganesh Himal, Rolwaling and Dolpo. We were all set to head to the western region when our plans were aborted cataclysmically.

In April and May of 2015 two powerful earthquakes struck Nepal, causing massive disruption to the country. Although many older houses and some historic temples were left in ruins across Kathmandu, the majority of buildings and infrastructure remained intact. Sadly the rural areas adjacent to the two quakes suffered more serious damage.

The main areas affected were below the peaks of Manaslu, Ganesh Himal, Langtang, Gauri Shankar and parts of the Everest region. In the autumn season following the quakes quite a number of trekkers have already been doing the full Manaslu Circuit trek and the Tsum Valley despite the landslides that have damaged the trails. The makeshift trails and important bridging places are continually being improved. Lodges have been repaired and some hydro plants have restarted generation.

Lower Manaslu took the brunt of the first quake and that was much more badly damaged. However, already work is being done and hopefully the region will be open for some business in the spring of 2016. Check with local operators about conditions if planning a trek in the Lower Manaslu region. In any case trekkers always had to camp in the region before homestay and lodges were built, so that option still remains.

Elsewhere, trekkers have already returned to the valleys of the Everest region despite some localised damage that has rapidly been repaired. The Annapurna region, including Mustang and Nar-Phu, was virtually unaffected. Trekking here is continuing as before, where lodges and dirt access roads remain in place to service trekkers' needs. Further west, all of Dolpo, the Rara Lake area and the far western trails of Saipal and the Limi Valley also remain open for trekkers. The routes for trekkers to Kanchenjunga and Makalu were unaffected by the quakes. Apart from the areas mentioned above, the villages, lodges, trails, roads and hillsides are functioning normally; only a few isolated houses suffered. Transport links between Kathmandu, Pokhara and the Terai as well as along the main valleys of the unaffected regions were not affected by the earthquakes.

> **Earthquake Diaries: Nepal 2015**
>
> We were in Kathmandu during the month of May. Having becoming instant aid workers (buying up rice, tarpaulins, tin sheets and warm, locally made clothing using generous donations) we witnessed a remarkable few weeks in the country. After the initial days of shock, thousands of local people, both young and old, engaged in the relief and rebuilding process with amazing energy. There is no doubt that the resilient people of Nepal will be back on their feet well ahead of expectations.
>
> The country certainly needs the tourism sector to blossom again as soon as possible. Your trek will help this to happen more quickly.
>
> Anyone wishing to know how 'amateur' aid works can read our **Earthquake Diaries: Nepal 2015**, published by Expedition World and available on Amazon websites worldwide, in colour, black & white and Kindle.

Above Goldhunga village, Kathmandu Valley

BEFORE THE TREK

Country background

Geography
It is believed that a sea existed about 100 million years ago in the region of Nepal. According to the theory of plate tectonics, India and Tibet began to collide at least 50 million years ago. These plates within the earth's crust create mountains where they collide. Approximately 40–45 million years ago, the northbound Indian plate began to force up the Tibetan plateau. The Himalayan chain was formed some 20 million years ago and continues to rise to this day.

From the Hindu Kush ranges of Afghanistan and Pakistan in the west to the Indian states of Arunachal Pradesh in the east, the Himalaya form an unbroken chain of over 2500km that divides the plains of India from the Tibetan plateau. The country of Nepal is approximately 800km long and 250km in width, with some variations from east to west. Kanchenjunga, Makalu, Everest, Lhotse, Cho Oyu, Manaslu, Annapurna I and Dhaulagiri, all exceeding 8000m in height, are the country's highest peaks.

Rising abruptly from the plains of India are the steep but fragile Siwalik Hills. The forested Mahabharat Hills, rising to over 3000m, mark the southern edge of the middle hills of Nepal, where most of the rural population live. The rolling hills are characterised by impressive terraces and dotted with quaint farmhouses. The valleys of Kathmandu and Pokhara are in this area. The main Himalayan range is not a watershed but is cut by raging, fast-flowing rivers that allow access to the higher valleys. The watershed is north of the Nepal Himalaya in Tibet. The altitude range of the Manaslu region is roughly from Arughat 608m–8163m, the summit of Manaslu.

Climate
The climate of Nepal is influenced heavily by the Himalaya, a natural barrier that divides the main weather systems of Asia. The Indian plains to the south are generally hot and dry, although north India has

cooler, high pressure-dominated winters. During the northern summer, the humid monsoon brings life-sustaining rains to India. North of the Himalaya, the mountains create a rain-shadow, making the climate in Tibet sunny, but harsh, cold and windy. Manaslu lies between these two extremes of climate, making the approach trek in the south very different from that experienced north of the great peaks. This amazing contrast in climates ensures a wide variety of conditions during the trek. As a general rule, throughout autumn and spring, the temperatures on the southern slopes of the Himalaya range from 10°C to 30°C. North of the great mountain barrier, the temperature will range from 15°C down to -10°C or colder at night. The spring season after early April will have generally higher temperatures and more wind. During the monsoon, temperatures rarely dip below freezing, except in the highest meadows.

> "Regard as one this life, the next life, and the life between," wrote Milarepa. And sometimes I wonder into which life I have wandered, so still are the long nights here, and so cold.
> ***The Snow Leopard,* Peter Matthiessen**

Natural history

Plants

With so many climatic zones, Nepal is a paradise for botanists – no one can be surprised by the great variety of plants, recently estimated to exceed 6500 different types of grasses, plants, flowers, and trees. In the 19th century the noted botanist, Joseph Hooker, visited the Himalaya of Sikkim and eastern Nepal and discovered many of the plants now familiar to gardeners the world over. The plants found in Nepal are naturally similar to those of neighbouring Sikkim.

The lowland slopes and hot moist jungles of the Siwalik foothills bordering the Indian plains are home to sal trees, simal, sissoo, khair and mahogany. Behind these rapidly eroding sandy foothills are the sheer and abruptly rising Mahabharat ranges. Here are the ubiquitous pipal and banyan trees that offer shade for the frequent porter rest-stops (*chautara*). Chestnut, chilaune and bamboo are found here, while in the succulent cloud forests are an amazing variety of weepy lichens, ferns, rattans and dripping lianas. The prolific orchids, magnolia, broadleaf temperate oaks and rhododendron (locally called *Laliguras*) drape the higher hillsides. Further up the hillsides are spruce, chir pine, fir, hemlock, blue pine, larch, cedar and sweet-smelling juniper. Poplar and willow are found along streams in the higher reaches of the arid zones and in the highest pastures are hardy berberis and stunted juniper. Amazingly hardy flowers and plants, such as colourful gentians, survive even in the most windswept or icy meadows.

Animals

Nepal is home to an incredibly diverse population of mammals, reptiles and birds. The plains of the Terai are home to the endangered Asian one-horned rhino, a tough and rugged beast that hides in the tall grasses of the plains and sal forests. Elephant are rarely wild but are used to ferry tourists about the National Parks in search of the elusive Bengal Tiger, as well as the sloth bear, from a safe roving vantage point. Spotted deer and sambar deer scurry about in small herds to avoid their predators.

Crocodiles, alligators, the smaller related gharals and marsh mugger lurk in the murky waters of the marshes and rivers that drain into the Ganges River further south. These jungles, once dense, impenetrable and infested by malarial mosquitoes, still host an amazing number of semi-tropical birds. Beyond the lowlands in the middle hills, almost all the hillsides are either covered by undisturbed, dense, spooky forests or are highly developed and extensively cultivated. Yet a great number of animals call these areas home, especially the ones most easily observed, such as the monkeys and langurs that abound in the forests.

Across the more open high pastures and at higher elevations the observant trekker will see marmots, pika (small mouse-like animal, related to the rabbit), weasel, ermine, Himalayan hare, Himalayan tahr (a species of large deer) and more often – the blue sheep. Tibetan sheep, wolf, wild dog, brown bear and the famed musk deer (a prized trading item) are rarely seen. Increasingly fewer wild yaks still roam in isolated, remote valleys, but most are now domesticated. Yak (Nak) milk is also used by nomads to produce cheese and yoghurt as well as the infamous butter tea. The dzo – a cross between a yak and a cow – is commonly used as a pack animal. Herders keep sheep and goats, as well as yaks. The snow leopard is virtually never seen even by herders. Hunting blue sheep at dawn, or in the twilight hours, they are extremely wary animals. Big budget television crews have waited years to get any pictures of these beautiful creatures. Let us know if you see a yeti!

Trekkers are almost never likely to encounter dangerous animals in Nepal, although domestic guard dogs can be a menace and quarrelsome yaks should be avoided.

Birds of the Nepalese Himalaya
by naturalist Rajendra Suwal, WWF Nepal

Nepal is a fabulous paradise for birdwatchers and those keen on sighting the elusive fauna. Because of the devout Buddhism encountered, particularly in the Tsum Valley, where for many decades there has been an active 'no killing' ethos, both animals and birds are plentiful and unafraid of humans.

The Manaslu and Tsum area encompasses the Palaearctic in the north and the Indo-Malayan realm in the south. It represents ecological regions including Colinean, Montane, Sub-alpine, Alpine and Nival. Rare forest types include Larix griffthiana growing at timber line. The unique and varied habitats shelter a fantastic diversity of over 400 species of bird species – from the stunning Satyr Tragopan to the spectacular migration of Demoiselle Crane over the Larkya La during the autumn and occasionally in spring. Birds move mostly in flocks, hunting insects at different levels in the forest. During quiet times you might spot up to a dozen different species, depending on the season. There are diurnal, crepuscular, nocturnal, seasonal and altitudinal migrants; birds such as the cuckoo visit during the spring for breeding.

At dawn in the **forests**, the insects stir into life and the insectivores, including the colourful long-tailed minivet, and fire-capped, green-backed, black-lored and black-throated tits, begin their daily foraging. Nectarine, fruit- and berry-eating birds are active soon after dawn. Berries or flowers are tempting magnets for multiple species, namely whiskered, stripe-throated, rufous-naped and white-browed tits.

The dense **forests** of Lower Tsum and across Manaslu are good places to observe the great parrotbill, spotted laughing thrush, and the velvet, rufous-bellied and white-tailed nuthatch. Try to catch a glimpse of the golden-breasted, white-browed and rufous-winged fulvetta. The forests are full of red-tailed, rufous-tailed and blue-winged minla. The tapping of the rufous-bellied, crimson-breasted and pied woodpeckers invariably interrupts the silence. The forests are alive with the beautiful scarlet, spotted and great rose finch, along with the spot-winged grosbeak. Keen birdwatchers will be amazed to see tiny warblers, including the chestnut-crowned, Whistler's, black-faced, grey-hooded and ashy-throated warblers. Nepal cutia is found in forests of alder.

The **flowering trees** host smart sunbirds as well as the black-throated, green-tailed, fire-tailed and purple sunbird. Fire-breasted flowerpeckers are found near settlements, in the flowering trees and mistletoe. Large-billed crows scavenge on kitchen leftovers or raid village crops. Flocks of red and yellow-billed chough forage around farms or high above the passes. The olive-backed pipit, magpie, robin and common tailorbird are found near farms, along with the common stonechat and the grey, collared, white-tailed and pied bushchat.

The idyllic, quiet, often dreamy **riverbanks** and side streams are teeming with frisky birds. The pristine environments are very rewarding habitat for river birds, including white-capped water redstart and plumbeous redstart; little, spotted, black-backed and slaty-backed forktail; brown dipper, grey wagtail and blue whistling-thrush. Other common birds are the red-vented, black bulbul, great and blue-throated barbet, and also coppersmith barbet in the lower reaches. On the overhanging cliffs below places like Prok are the rarely seen honeycombs made by the world's largest honeybees, where you may spot the oriental honeyguide.

Ravens are acrobatic birds, seen in the **alpine zones**. The abundant blue pine forest of middle Tsum and the Budhi Gandaki above Ghap and up to Shyala is a typical habitat of the very vocal spotted nutcracker, while orange-bellied leafbirds prefer the upper canopies. More treasures are the tiny Nepal, scaly-breasted and pygmy wren babblers, feeding under the ferns, with their high-pitched territorial calls. With its high-pitched sound, the jewel-like, tiny chestnut-headed tesia is a wonderful bird to see in moist undergrowth.

The **mountains** near Samagaon and above Chhokang Paro harbour pheasant species found in Nepal, namely the Danfe, kalij, Satyr Tragopan and Blood Pheasant. Shy by nature, one can hear them before dawn. Despite the wilderness of the Manaslu trek, few pheasants show their colours. In the rhododendron and oak forest, just below the tree line, look out for ringal, and in cane bamboo watch for the satyr tragopan and blood pheasant. The Himalayan munal (known as Danfe in Nepal, where it is the national bird), favours the tree line and more open pastures.

The Tsum Valley is an important **flyway** for migrating birds of prey. Eagles (Steppe and Imperial) and Cinereous Vulture, small birds of prey, pied and hen harriers and common buzzards may be seen flying past in the first two weeks of November.

The **skies** of Manaslu host the Himalayan and Eurasian Griffon and majestic Lammergeyer (with 3m wingspans). As they soar, they lift every onlooker's spirit. Some ethnic groups of Mustang practise sky burial and believe the vultures pass the spirits to the heavens. Cliffs are breeding sites for vultures and lammergeyers. All the vulture species of Nepal, including the Egyptian vulture, the endangered white-rumped, the red-headed and the globally endangered slender-billed vulture, are found in the foothills. A formidable predator of the high mountains is the Golden Eagle.

In the **caragana bush** habitat of Samagaon and below Mu Gompa, look for the white-browed tit-babbler, white-throated, Guldenstadt's and blue-fronted redstart, brambling and brown rufous-breasted and Altai accentor. Rock bunting and chukor partridge inhabit areas between the upper forested zone and the drier regions. In the air you can observe the speedy insect-hunter white-rumped needletail, Nepal house martin, red-rumped swallow and Himalayan swiftlet.

Finally, in the areas below the **Larkya La pass**, particularly around Samdo and in Tsum, above Mu Gompa, look for lively Himalayan snowcocks and flocks of snow pigeons foraging near trails, oblivious of passing trekkers.

Brief history

Nepal is one of the most diverse places on earth, its culture and people as varied as its scenic attractions. Kathmandu, with its long history of isolation, is the country's once-mystical capital. Its ancestry is an improbable cocktail of magical make-believe, exotic folklore, intriguing legend and historical fact.

The Kiranti people were probably the first recognisable inhabitants of the Kathmandu Valley. However, the first facts of history in Nepal relate to the formation of the Buddhist religion. Around 550BC, in southern Nepal close to modern-day Lumbini, a prince, who would have an amazing impact across the Indian subcontinent and as far away as Japan, was born to a rich king. This prince, Siddhartha Gautama, who would become the earthly Buddha, lived a sheltered and indolent life in his comfortable palace until he left his wife and newborn son to search for the meaning of life. Seeking out sages, sadhus, priests and wise men, he found no answers until finally his meditations brought a ray of light. He discovered that the end to earthly suffering was achieved through adopting a middle path in all things and thus he found inner peace – nirvana.

Ashoka, one of the first emissaries of Buddhism in India, travelled to Nepal in the third century BC, building the four ancient grass-covered stupas of Patan and the pillar at Lumbini. After about 300AD the Licchavi dynasty flourished, but Buddhism declined in the face of the popular rise of the Hindu religion, a faith that had been born, but not nurtured, much earlier in India. Much later, as new trade routes and ideas developed between Tibet and India, Kathmandu became the most important Himalayan hub.

On the religious front, the decline of Buddhism in India and Nepal forced its diehard adepts to seek sanctuary across the Himalaya in Tibet. After hundreds of years, the version of Buddhism that came with those refugees adapted and absorbed Tibetan Buddhist themes and, ironically, slipped back once more into Nepal to mix with Hinduism, Shamanism and other animistic ideas. The Tibetan version of Buddhism, now known as the Vajrayana path, provides an astonishingly colourful and exotic aspect to daily rituals and festivities in Nepal today. In the eighth century a sage and Buddhist master, Padma Sambhava (Guru Rinpoche), travelled across the Himalayan region. His exploits in promoting the Tibetan Buddhist philosophy are recorded widely throughout the region as both myth and historical fact.

During the following period there are few records of life in Nepal. However, through the annals kept in Tibet, a great amount of historical fact can be found about the regeneration of the Buddhism found in Nepal. These facts centre on the ancient Tibetan region of the lost Guge Kingdom, located around Toling and Tsaparang. Many Indian masters came here to study and escape persecution from Hindu zealots in the 11th century. Records of Nepal's history come to life again in the 13th century, when the Malla kings assumed power.

The Malla Period is often said to be the golden age of Nepal, and especially of the Kathmandu Valley, with its astonishing array of art and architecture. The Malla dynasties are admired for their vast concentration of elaborate and superbly executed multi-tiered palaces and pagodas. Although the ordinary people lived in much less privileged conditions, their brick houses were also decorated with intricate wood designs. One of the more powerful Mallas, Jayasthiti Malla, adopted the Hindu faith and consolidated his power in the Kathmandu Valley. He even declared himself to be a reincarnate of the Hindu god of preservation – Vishnu, a practice that was continued by the monarchs of Nepal until 2007. Jyoti Malla and Yaksha Malla were rather more benign dictators, who enhanced the valley with more spectacular temples and religious structures. Around 1482 the three towns of Kathmandu, Patan and Bhaktapur became independent cities, with each king competing to build the greatest Durbar Square, parts of which remain to this day.

Like all dictatorships, the Malla reign declined, as debauchery and corruption took hold. In 1769, from the hilltop fortress above the town of Gorkha (Gurkha), came Prithvi Narayan Shah and his forces, who rode in to capture the three cities of the Kathmandu Valley. In so doing he succeeded in unifying Nepal. In 1788 Nepalese armies moved on Tibet.

In 1816 the Gurkhas, attempting to expand their domains into the colonial-ruled hills of northern India, were defeated by the British. Through the treaty of Segauli, Nepal ceded Sikkim to India and the current borders were delineated. The British established a resident office in Kathmandu. Soon after Gurkha regiments were integrated into the British army.

In 1846, a soldier of the court, Jung Bahadur Kunwar Rana, hatched a devious plot. After a massacre in Kathmandu's Kot Square, the king was dethroned and the queen was sent into exile. Jung Bahadur Rana took power and became the first of the infamous Rana dynasty, who held power in Nepal for the next 100 years. Although the Ranas called themselves Maharajas, they were despotic rulers, remembered for family intrigues, murder and deviousness. The Ranas built the sumptuous neo-colonial white colonnaded palaces seen around Kathmandu today. Until 1950 the country remained closed to all but a few invited guests, retaining its medieval traditions and corrupt governance. When neighbouring India gained independence in 1947, a Congress Party was formed in Kathmandu. The powerless king became a symbol for freedom from the despotic Ranas. However, freeing the country from the shackles of the old guard meant great sacrifice. Many activists and freedom fighters were executed before King Tribhuvan finally ousted the Ranas in 1951.

After 1950, when Tibet fell under new masters, Khampa freedom fighters moved into the isolated valleys north of the Himalaya and established bases. However, when Nepalese monarch King Birendra announced the 'Zone of Peace' initiative, they left the country. Some refugees and ex-fighters settled in the upper reaches of the Budhi Gandaki at Samdo on the Manaslu Circuit trek.

A fledgling democratic coalition government was installed and the country was opened to foreign visitors. In May 1953 Mount Everest was finally conquered from the Nepalese side after so many failed expeditions from its Tibetan faces. King Tribhuvan died in 1955 and his son Mahendra assumed power. Becoming dissatisfied with political paralysis, King Mahendra ended the short experiment with democracy in 1960. He introduced a partyless governance, called the *panchayat* system, based on local councils of five (*panch*) elders, with a tiered system of representatives up to the central parliament. Following the death of Mahendra in 1972, King Birendra inherited the throne. His official coronation did not take place until an auspicious date in the spring of 1975.

The *panchayat* system was retained following the 1980 referendum. After 1985, rapid urban expansion changed the nature of the Kathmandu Valley. The traditional rural lifestyle began to disappear under a wave of construction as the population grew astonishingly. In April 1990 full-scale rioting and demonstrations broke out, forcing the king to allow full democracy. Parliamentary democracy flourished with King Birendra as a ceremonial monarch and the country prospered. Unfortunately corruption and political ineptitude grew, and in the late nineties a grass-roots Maoist rebellion developed.

Many people had genuine sympathy with the need for greater social equality, but violent demands for a leftist dictatorship naturally met with resistance. In June 2001, after a tragic shooting spree, King Birendra and almost his entire family were wiped out by his son, Crown Prince Dipendra. Although not directly attributed to the Maoist uprising, the event changed the situation dramatically. King Birendra's brother Gyanendra became king, but in October 2002 he dissolved parliament and appointed his own government until elections could be held. The Maoist rebellion continued, with intimidation and coercion rife in the countryside. Following huge demonstrations on the streets of Kathmandu in 2006, King Gyanendra relinquished power.

The Maoist leaders entered mainstream politics after winning a majority of votes in the subsequent election. However, almost ever since then, the governments have been paralysed, with a political stalemate derailing much development. A constitutional election was held in November 2013, with the Maoist vote significantly reduced. A new constitution was promulgated in September 2015 but it remains to be seen where the country's ruling elite will take it.

Political and economic instability have resulted in an increasing number of young Nepalese seeking work outside the country, particularly in the Arabian Gulf and Malaysia. Along with their remittances, tourism also remains an important source of income, and tourists are still given a warm welcome across the country.

Religion and festivals

> Holy places never had any beginning. They have been holy from the time they were discovered...
> ***The Land of Snows*, Giuseppe Tucci**

Life across Nepal is still significantly influenced by religious and traditional beliefs. Everywhere, from a hilltop monastery to the back-alleys of Kathmandu, people follow cultural traditions through daily rituals and frequent festivals. Hinduism, Buddhism and Shamanism are encountered on a trek around Manaslu, with a few isolated pockets of Bon, the ancient faith of Tibet.

Hinduism

Hinduism is the main faith of Nepal and until recently the country was a Hindu kingdom. Many Hindu ideals have come from the ancient Indian Sanskrit texts, the four Vedas. In essence, the ideas of Hinduism are based on the notion that everything in the universe is connected. This means that one's deeds in this life will have a bearing on the next. One's own bad actions might be the cause of misfortunes. Natural disasters are seen as the vengeance of the gods. Although hundreds of Hindu gods exist, they are in essence one, being worshipped in many different aspects. Evidence of Hinduism in the Manaslu region is sparse; there are very few notable temples.

The three main Hindu gods are Brahma, the god of creation; Shiva, the god of destruction; and Vishnu, the god of preservation. They appear in many forms, both male and female. Brahma is rarely visible. Shiva has special powers of regeneration and many forms, such as Mahadev, or the dancing Nataraj. Shiva is Pashupati – the Lord of Beasts – and Bhairab in his most destructive form. Shiva's wife is Parvati; she also has many aspects, including Kali and Durga.

> **The legend of Ganesh**
> Shiva and Parvati have an elephant-headed son called Ganesh. It is said that Ganesh was born when Shiva was away trekking. When Shiva returned he saw the child and assumed that Parvati had been unfaithful. In a furious rage, he chopped off Ganesh's head and threw it away. Once Shiva had taken a shower and relaxed, Parvati explained the matter. In great remorse, Shiva vowed to give Ganesh a new head from the first living being that passed; it was an elephant.

The third god, Vishnu, worshipped in Nepal as Narayan, is the preserver of all life. Vishnu has ten other aspects. The eighth aspect/avatar is the popular blue god Krishna, who plays a flute and chases after the cowgirls. Other notable avatars are Rama and Buddha. Other Hindu deities include Lakshmi, the goddess of wealth, and the humorous Ganesh, who is worshipped for good fortune. Hanuman is the monkey god. Machhendranath is the curious rain deity, the compassionate one with two forms, white (Seto) and red (Rato).

Hindu Festivals

Nepal has an extraordinary number of festivals. Any excuse is valid for a good celebration and most are also celebrated in the lower reaches of the Manaslu area. In autumn, the Dasain and Tihar festivals are in full flow. The goddess Kali and Durga are feted during Dasain, and the terrifying white Bhairab is displayed in Kathmandu Durbar Square. Blood sacrifices are the most noticeable aspect of these celebrations. Tihar is a more light-hearted affair, with crows, dogs, cows and brothers showered with flowers and devotion before a night of fairy lights and candles.

During spring is Shiva Ratri, the night of Shiva, most fervently commemorated at the Pashupatinath temple in Kathmandu. Holi is another Hindu spring festival celebrated across the country. The main manifestation of this festival is the throwing of coloured dyes at passers-by; tourists and trekkers included. Normally in March the tall wooden chariot housing the white Seto Machhendranath idol – the rain god – is dragged with much merriment through old Kathmandu. Sometimes the power lines are pulled down, adding to the load shedding difficulties, and the top storeys of the old brick houses of Asan are almost obliterated. In May, during a similar festival, the red Rato Machhendranath is hauled around Patan and back out to Bungamati.

Buddhism

Buddhists are found in the Kathmandu Valley and in the northern regions of the country. Buddhist monasteries and culture are encountered on the Manaslu Circuit beyond Jagat and around the trail until Tal in the Marsyangdi valley. The whole region of Tsum is also Buddhist. The famous Tibetan poet and sage, Milarepa, spent some time in meditation in the Tsum region.

Buddhism could be considered as a philosophy for living, with adherents seeking to find peace of mind and a cessation of worldly suffering. Nirvana, perfect peace, is achieved through successive lives by good actions and thoughts. (For details of the Sakyamuni, earthly Buddha, see brief history.)

Buddhism has two main branches – Hinayana and Mahayana. The latter path is followed in Nepal and Tibet, where it has evolved into a more esoteric philosophy called the Vajrayana (Diamond) path. It blends ancient Tibetan Bon ideas with a phenomenon known as Tantra, meaning 'to open the mind'. Tantric themes suggest that all people can become a Buddha and find enlightenment from within. Buddhist artistry and iconography is startling and is found in monasteries across the high Himalaya.

The following Buddhist sects are found across the Manaslu region:

The **Nyingma-pa** is the oldest Red Hat sect. It was founded in the eighth century AD by Guru Rinpoche. Today adherents of the Nyingma-pa sect are found across the high Himalaya of Nepal, in Tibet, Spiti and Ladakh.

The **Kadam-pa** school was developed by Atisha, a Buddhist scholar from northern India, following his studies at Toling gompa in the Guge region of Western Tibet. Followers are expected to find enlightenment after careful reflection and study of the texts.

The **Kagyu-pa** is attributed to the Indian mystic translator Marpa (1012–1097), a disciple of Atisha. Followers need to concentrate their meditations on spiritual matters and inner mental themes, and listen to the wisdom of their teachers. The Kagyu-pa sect split into a number of sub-groups, such as the Drigung-pa, Druk-pa, Taglung-pa and the Karma-pa.

The **Kangin** (Karnying-pa) is a unique blend of the old sects Nyingma-pa and Kagyu-pa found in the Tsum Valley. Another obscure sect is the Ngak-pa, practiced at Rachen Gompa.

The **Sakya-pa** began under Konchok Gyalpo from the Sakya Gompa in Tibet in the 11th century. Its adherents study existing Buddhist scriptures. The Sakya-pa school initiated the creation of the Tangyur and Kangyur – two great Tibetan Buddhist bibles.

The **Gelug-pa** is the Yellow Hat sect of the Dalai Lama, initiated by the 14th-century reformer, Tsong Khapa. He returned the Buddhist practices to a more purist format, removing the liberal themes of Tantra and putting more emphasis on morality and discipline. It is not found in the Manaslu and Tsum regions.

Buddhist Festivals

Losar, the Tibetan New Year, occurs just before the spring in the cold season of January/February. It is primarily celebrated at Boudhanath and also across the northern mountains. Celebrations involve Tibetan drama and colourful masked Cham dances that commemorate the victory of Buddhism over Bon. Many Buddhist festivals related to Tibetan traditions take place in the mountains during the summer monsoon. The Tsumba festival is enjoyed in the Tsum Valley; the dances and traditions are very colourful. Similar festivities take place in the higher reaches of the Budhi Gandaki valley. Every three years a masked dance festival takes place in Samagaon: November 2018, 2021...

Other Tibetan festivals celebrated across the northern Himalaya are: **Saka Lhuka** held in the first month of the Tibetan calendar, performed for an auspicious harvest. **Fagnyi** is a week-long festival of song and dance during the seventh Tibetan month.

Bon or Bonpo

The Bon religion was the earlier faith of Tibet; they also seek the eternal truth and reality of life. The Bon worship natural phenomena, like the heavens and mountain spirits, as well as the spirits of natural powers, such as thunder. The chief icon of the Bon is Tonpa Shenrap Miwoche. Pockets of Bon worship are scattered across the Manaslu and Tsum regions. The Tibetan government-in-exile recognised the ancient Bon as a Tibetan sect in 1977. It is rare for active Bon traditions to be observed, but those interested can visit the Triten Norbutse monastery near Swayambhunath in Kathmandu.

Shamanism

With its roots in the mists of time, Shamanism is a difficult religious theme to observe. Much is only apparent through observation of strange tokens such as bones, feathers and fetish-style trinkets. Shamans have their own rituals and even medical treatments. These are often performed by jhankris/oracles, who communicate with the ancestors through trance-induced rituals. Shamans worship natural phenomena, much like the early Bon. Such practices seem very primitive to outsiders, but rely on ancient wisdom.

Other religions with a limited following are Islam, Christianity and Sikhism, not generally found in the Manaslu region.

Cultural aspects

Ethnic diversity

According to the latest estimate, the population of Nepal is around 33 million. (In 1974 there were just 8 million.) At least 26 major ethnic groups are encountered across the whole country. Most of the people in the southern zones can be broadly classified as Hindus, while those from the northern Himalayan valleys are Buddhists. However, there is no clear traditional divide in either the middle hills or the Kathmandu Valley, especially since the insurgency.

The **Newaris** are the traditional inhabitants of the Kathmandu Valley; they are a mix of Hindus and Buddhists. Along the plains of the Terai are the **Tharu**, whose ancestry might be linked to Rajasthan in India. Other Terai people, also related to Indian Hindu clans, are collectively known as the Madhesi.

Throughout the central regions of Nepal, including the Manaslu region, the people are mainly **Magars, Chhetris, Gurungs** and **Brahmins**. The Brahmins are the higher caste priestly group, who traditionally paint their houses blue. Chhetris are defined as a warrior caste. Smaller subgroups, such as **Kaamis** and **Ghale**, inhabit the Budhi Gandaki valley. Gurungs and Magars are found in scattered settlements along the Budhi Gandaki, but are more concentrated to the west of Himalchuli, around Gorkha, along the Marsyangdi valley and towards Pokhara. Gurung men are particularly noted for their service to the Gurkhas.

As you climb beyond Jagat and Philim, the people belong to the **Tibeto-Burmese** ethnic groups, with wide faces and Tibetan characteristics. **Tamangs** are found, as well as locally named groups such as the **Lho** and **Tsumba**. People of Tibetan stock are found all along the border regions – in the villages and settlements of Lho, Sho, Shyala, Samagaon and Samdo. Samdo became one of the first refugee encampments for exiled Tibetans after 1959. In the more isolated region of Tsum, traditions are fiercely guarded. The Tsumba (Rhu-Pa) people wear typical Tibetan-style dress, but in addition they have unusual flat hats rather like pancakes, worn especially during the Tsumba festival.

Basic customs

Despite contact with the outside world since 1950, Nepal remains a conservative country, especially in the remoter hilly districts. A few basic customs should be observed by visitors. In houses the cooking area, the hearth and fire should be treated with respect, so do not throw litter there. Never touch a Nepali on the head. Pointing the soles of your feet at your hosts, or stepping over their feet, should be avoided. Eat with your right hand if no utensils are supplied.

Non-believers are rarely allowed into the inner sanctuaries of Hindu temples anywhere in the country; remember that leather apparel, belts and shoes are certainly not permitted inside.

When visiting Buddhist gompas, guests should remove trekking hats and boots before entry. Small donations are appreciated and trekkers should ask permission before taking photographs inside. On the trail, keep to the left of mani walls and chortens and circle them in a clockwise direction. The prolific array of mani walls, mani stones and prayer wheels display the mantra Om Mani Padme Hum – Hail to the Jewel in the Lotus. Many in the Manaslu/Tsum region display pictures of Buddha or Milarepa.

The Tsum Valley has had a 'violence-free' creed for over 90 years. No animals are slaughtered in the valley; in fact they are actively protected and great pains are taken to avoid the accidental killing of insects or animals.

Begging

The rest of the world often views Nepal as a permanent begging-bowl case. Perhaps it is this attitude that encourages the general malaise of development in the country. Foreign governments, the UN and large donors continue to provide funds, but fail to account for such funding and ignore corruption within the system. Inevitably Nepalese view all foreigners as rich, whether it's their governments or themselves. Ordinarily no one will mind giving to those obviously in need, but over the long term local people need to be helped to help themselves. Begging is not confined to the poverty-stricken lower classes; the higher echelons have the same attitude. Endemic in Nepal, begging is clearly putting a brake on development and local initiative. However, the 'make do and mend' culture shows a level of ingenuity that has almost disappeared in the throwaway societies of the developed world. Given the opportunity, Nepal will flourish and prosper.

Helping the people

The big donor organisations and charities are naturally attracted to Nepal, probably due to its welcoming people, many of whom are exceedingly industrious. Sadly the impact of these multi-national donations is rarely felt by the majority of the people. This means there is plenty of opportunity for guests to contribute to smaller initiatives. Often such projects like improving village water supplies or bringing local electrification can really make a difference. Some of these localised projects are listed below.

Asha Nepal is a human rights organisation working towards the social and economic empowerment of women and children affected by sex trafficking. Asha is the Nepali word for hope. Asha Nepal is fighting for women's social status to be raised, to help victims break free from this vicious, violent circle. (www.asha-nepal.org)

Autism Care Nepal There was very little knowledge of this condition in Nepal when their son was diagnosed with autism, so two Nepali doctors founded this organisation to raise awareness and help others in the same situation. (www.autismnepal.org)

Beni Handicrafts products are made by women forced to move from the hills to the city, providing them with training, employment and income for their families. Beni and her team collect sweet wrappers, inner tubes and other waste from city streets and mountain trails. The rubbish is then made into attractive and functional products. View and buy them at the Northfield Café in Thamel. (www.benihandcrafts.com)

Steps Foundation Nepal is a charity supported by profits from Beni Handicrafts. It works on the step-by-step principle that through education for all and increasing awareness of hygiene, the health and well-being of families will be improved. (www.stepsfoundationnepal.org)

Community Action Nepal co-founded by mountaineer Doug Scott, seeks to improve the infrastructure of villages in the hills by building schools, health posts, clean water projects and developing cottage industries. (www.canepal.org.uk)

International Porter Protection Group (IPPG) began in 1997 after a number of porters suffered unfortunate accidents. It seeks to raise awareness of the conditions and plight of frequently exploited porters. They focus on the shelter, medical care and provision of clothing for often-overlooked porters across Nepal. (www.ippg.net and www.portersprogress.org)

Kathmandu Environmental Education Project (KEEP) was established in 1992 to 'provide education on safe and ecologically sustainable trekking methods to preserve Nepal's fragile eco-systems'. They give important information to trekkers, help harness tourism for development, run environmental discussions and manage a porters' clothing bank. They also help to improve the skills of tourism professionals and run volunteer programmes as well as running wilderness first aid training. They are found down a back lane in Thamel. (www.keepnepal.org)

Light Education Development supplies solar lights, medical supplies and school materials to the Manaslu region. (www.lighteducationdevelopment.org)

Mountain People has the motto of 'Helping mountain people to help themselves'. Its operation centre is in the Hotel Moonlight in Paknajol, near Thamel, Kathmandu. It is a small, independent, non-profit, non-political, non-religious and cross-cultural organisation with a lot of energy and drive. They help with schools, porter welfare, women's projects and bridge building. (www.mountain-people.org)

Destruction or development

There is no doubt that the fragile environment of the Himalaya needs the attention of local environmentalists and the good management of resources. However, much as we, as visitors, may wish to see the land untainted, we do not have to spend our lives shivering beside a smoky fire. Inevitably, if there is no viable reason for the youth to linger in the high Himalayan regions, the culture will be diluted.

Tourism is one obvious way in which the culture and livelihoods of the upland people can be sustained in the long term. The main trekking trails have already had almost sixty years of tourism and the effects have been generally positive. The difficulty is finding the right balance, by improving local living conditions without destroying that which every visitor wants to experience here. It's not a unique problem, as anyone who has visited the popular Nepalese trails or anywhere else that attracts many visitors – even Chamonix or Machu Picchu – will have observed. As visitors we have our own views, but ultimately it is for the local people and the various tourism concerns to decide on the future of their region.

Practicalities

Time and calendar

Nepal is 5hrs 45mins ahead of GMT. Nepal follows two calendars; the Gregorian calendar used by most of the world, and a lunar-solar Bikram Sambat (BS) calendar, which is approximately 56 years and 8 months ahead of the Gregorian dates. (i.e. 2016–17 corresponds to 2073–74 BS). The Bikram Sambat year begins in mid-April and was introduced by the Ranas in the mid-1800s. This calendar means that Nepal is ahead of the rest of the world, which it might be in terms of coping with adversity!

Getting to Nepal

Flights to Nepal

Air Arabia and **Fly Dubai** from The Gulf; **Air India** via Delhi, Kolkata (Calcutta) and Varanasi; **ArkeFly** a seasonal charter service from Europe; **Bangladesh Biman** for budget travellers with time to kill via Dhaka; **various Chinese airlines** link Kathmandu with Lhasa, Chengdu, Kunming and Guangzhou (Canton); **Dragon Air** from Hong Kong; **Druk Air** from Paro, Bhutan, to Kathmandu and on to Delhi; **Etihad Airways** via Abu Dhabi from Europe; **Indigo** a budget Indian carrier; **Jet Airways** (India) has a through-service from London to Nepal via Delhi; **Korean Airlines** from the Far East; **Nepal Airlines** flies from Delhi, Bombay, Dubai and Hong Kong – for those with bags of time; **Oman Air** via Muscat; **Silk Air** from Singapore; **SpiceJet** a low-cost Indian carrier; **Thai Airways** via Bangkok, from Europe and Australia/New Zealand; **Qatar Airways** via Doha from Europe; **Turkish Airlines** via Istanbul, plus **Virgin, BA** and other airlines to Delhi, then one of the Indian carriers to Kathmandu.

This information is subject to change.

Overland routes to Nepal

Nepal has open land borders with India and Tibet/China. Land borders into Nepal from India are through Sonauli/Belahiya near Bhairahawa;

Raxaul/Birgunj; Nepalganj; Mahendranagar; and Kakarvitta. The Sonauli/Belahiya border north of 'lovely old' Gorakhpur is the most-used entry point from India. Buses connect Bhairahawa to Kathmandu and Pokhara. A long journey by local transport links Nepal to Delhi in the west, through Mahendranagar/Banbasa. Those travelling between Kathmandu and Darjeeling or Sikkim can cross the eastern border at Kakarvitta. Kathmandu is linked also to Lhasa in Tibet by the Arniko/Friendship Highway through the border at Kodari/Zhangmu. The road is tarred from Zhangmu to Lhasa but poor on the Nepalese side north of Barhabise. The 3–4 day journey (not to Barhabise but to Lhasa) will blow your mind. It climbs over a number of spectacular 5000m passes through Nyalam, Shigatse and Gyangtse to Tibet's once-forbidden capital, Lhasa.

Travel within Nepal

Although most trekkers to the Manaslu area will travel from Kathmandu to Arughat or Gorkha by road, many will spend time in Pokhara after the trek. Travelling between Kathmandu and Pokhara (200km) by bus is quite straightforward these days, since the road has been improved almost all the way.

The usual journey time is 6–8hrs, but traffic can get heavy in the afternoon if you are heading back to Kathmandu. Currently the most luxurious bus is the Greenline service: US$25 including a great lunch halfway at the Riverside Springs Resort. Other slightly less deluxe (but generally reliable) tourist buses depart around 7am from Kantipath near Thamel. More unreliable, and definitely not comfortable, are the 'local' buses, which are even cheaper and leave from the Gongabu bus depot, northwest of the city. These are only recommended for those wishing to rub shoulders intimately with the locals. Ironically the taxi fare to the bus station is normally more than the bus ticket, so there is little to recommend this option. The local buses often stop in Mugling, an infamous eating place which, in days gone by, served dishes of 'hepatitis and rice'.

Visa information

Nepali visa

All foreign nationals except Indians require a visa. Currently visas are available from embassies and land borders, as well as at Tribhuvan International Airport on arrival in Kathmandu (check for any changes before arrival). Entering or exiting the country at the remoter crossing points and from Tibet may be subject to change, so always check the latest requirements in all cases.

Applying in your own country will cost more. Remember to apply well ahead of travel, in case there are any holidays at the embassy due to festival periods in Nepal. Obtaining a visa on arrival is normally the easiest option, but check in case of any new restrictions. The maximum length of stay in Nepal is five months in one calendar year, although the fifth month is not always possible.

Tourist visas are available for 15, 30 or 90 days, at a fee of $25, $40 and $100 (payment in cash) respectively. Extensions in Kathmandu are obtained at the Immigration Department at a cost of $US30 (the minimum fee) or for a daily charge of $US2 per day. All visas are currently multiple-entry, making visits to places like Bhutan, Tibet or India much easier than before. Check www.nepalimmigration.gov.np for up-to-date fees. For comprehensive embassy listings see: www.mofa.gov.np

Indian visa

Allow at least one week if you intend to get your Indian visa in Kathmandu. It may be cheaper to do this in Nepal than in Europe. Do check this before travel; change is likely at any time! www.indianembassy.org.np Applications need to be made online in most cases. www.indianembassy.org.np

Tibet/China entry

For those planning a trip to Tibet/China from Nepal after a trek, it's currently of no use to obtain a Chinese visa in advance. The Chinese visa will simply be cancelled at the Kathmandu embassy, because travel to Tibet from Nepal currently requires special arrangements. It is necessary to prearrange the visa for Tibet in Nepal through a Nepalese agent. Allow a few days in Kathmandu to complete the application well ahead of your arrival in Nepal if prearranging by email. Visas for travel across Tibet are normally issued on paper for the duration of the stated itinerary. Budget (not that cheap) tours are offered by Kathmandu travel agents for independent travellers, thus making that fabulous trip a possibility. The Chinese authorities frequently close the Tibetan border at short notice.

Money matters

The currency is the Nepalese Rupee (Rs). Notes come in the following denominations: Rs5, 10, 20, 50, 100, 500 and 1000, and coins: Rs1, 2 and 5.

Approximate exchange rates (2016)	
	Rs
£	155
€	115
US$	103
CHF	104

In Kathmandu and Pokhara, ATMs are now common. Moneychangers are very quick to change cash but travellers cheques are no longer accepted in Nepal. It's a waste of time to head for a bank these days, as most rarely exchange money and if they do are generally exceedingly slow. Currently there are no banks on the trails. In the hills, you may find a self-appointed moneychanger offering poor rates for cash. Take more cash rupees than you think you will need, and then a bit more.

Language

The main language is Nepali, but many people also speak some English. It is taught in schools across the country and is understood to varying extents by all staff involved in tourism. The main ethnic groups also each have their own language, including Sherpa, Newari and so on. Everyone understands '*Namaste*' – hands held together, with a smile.

Internet and phone
A full range of internet-based services are available in Kathmandu and Pokhara. Around Manaslu there are virtually none. The international dialling code is +977.

Mobile phones have completely changed the nature of 'getting away from it all' on holiday anywhere these days and in Nepal it is the same. It's no big deal these days to call anywhere across the globe from Everest Base Camp and even high up the peak! When some disgruntled trekkers can call their travel agent at home to complain about the lack of hot water in their lodge in Philim, perhaps things might have gone a bit too far!

Nepal never really got past the first hurdle in developing landlines and thus avoided that vast investment. For a few brief years landline phones did have great novelty value, with roughly one phone booth every four days' trekking distance. Nowadays people in the smallest village or trailside shack are busy keeping in touch with family down the valley. Monks seem very enamoured of phones, to keep in touch with the middle way perhaps! However, there are some corners of Nepal, including the Tsum Valley, where mobile coverage is absent or erratic. Tsum Valley does, however, have a system of landline phones that work via satellite, so some advanced technology has reached this far-flung corner of the Himalaya! The Larkya La pass has neither, so try not to break a leg!

Postage
You'll need to trek into the old city to find the Central Post Office. To send a letter or postcard it's normally better to use your hotel or a bookshop. To send home heavy souvenirs, check out the packing agents in Thamel.

Electricity
Electricity in Nepal is 220volts/50cycles, with most sockets having two pins of varying distances apart. Electrification of the countryside is progressing well, but power cuts (load shedding) in cities are extremely common, especially in Kathmandu during the dry seasons. It can be quite a shock to experience such long power cuts in Kathmandu, but

in the rural areas the situation is much better. In recent years electric schemes have been installed across some villages in the Manaslu and Tsum regions. The power generated is enough to provide adequate lighting and a little extra in some places for TV. Surprisingly, every village in the Tsum Valley has electricity. However, at present several of the power plants on the Manaslu Circuit are not functioning. In fact only solar battery power is available above Philim at the moment, since a couple of hydro stations are awaiting repairs. Charging camera batteries is thus a slightly unknown prospect – be sure to bring more spare batteries than you expect to use.

National Holidays

Sometimes there seem to be more official and unofficial holidays than there are normal days. As luck would have it, the busy trekking season in the autumn coincides with the biggest festival period. Enjoy the colourful festivities, but allow more time to get your permits.

1 January	New Year
February/March	Tibetan New Year Tibet
14 April	Nepali New Year
23 April	Democracy Day
1 May	Labour Day
28 May	Republic Day

Plus many other religious festivals.
For comprehensive listings, see
www.qppstudio.net/publicholidays2016/nepal.htm.

Trek planning

Trekking Permits and TIMS

TIMS permits are necessary for most treks in Nepal, but strangely not Manaslu and the Tsum Valley. Do check www.timsnepal.com for the latest information.

Restricted area permits for Manaslu and Tsum

Across the northern zones of Nepal, in particular close to the Tibetan border, there are still some 'restricted areas'. The Manaslu Circuit and Tsum Valley fall into this category. Permits are available from the main immigration office. Both areas require you to take a guide. All the places to be visited should be mentioned in the application. Permits are issued for one week plus the number of days requested per person. Currently one week will cost US$70 (Sept – Nov) or US$50 (all other periods). In addition each day is charged at US$10 (US$7) per person per day. Two weeks is the absolute minimum timeframe for Manaslu, while three weeks could include a brief visit to the Tsum region. Note that the permit area for Manaslu commences at Jagat. There is a fee of US$35 for up to eight days to enter the Tsum area from Lokpa, to be paid in Kathmandu. Time spent in Tsum does not require the $10 daily Manaslu fee to be paid in addition. For example, a 21-day circuit of Manaslu with one week spent in Tsum will cost $140 +$35 = $175. Check for the latest information at www.nepalimmigration.gov.np

Manaslu and Annapurna Conservation Area Permits

Visitors to the Manaslu and Annapurna region are also required to pay for entry to the conservation areas that encompass the mountains. The trek passes through two conservation areas, so expect a hefty fee. Currently the fee is Rs2000 for Manaslu and Rs2000 for Annapurna, per person.

Important Note
The **single entry** to the conservation areas of Manaslu and Annapurna does mean just one entry. This means that if you leave one part of the conservation area hoping to re-enter in another, you will be refused re-entry. This rule affects trekkers to Annapurna, where roads mean it's possible to shortcut some trails, but as yet it is not of concern to Manaslu hikers.

Manaslu and Annapurna Conservation Areas
The Manaslu Conservation Area Project was founded in 1998, following the establishment of ACAP in 1986. The aims are to regulate activities within the designated areas and to promote conservation. In association with local community development, the projects seek to develop ecological ways of improving the environment. Prior to the formation of these conservation areas, there was fairly uncontrolled deforestation, since local people relied on the timber for cooking and heating. Kerosene dumps were established and trekking groups were forbidden to use wood for cooking. The scheme sought to improve hygiene levels by establishing small health posts and safe drinking water depots. Bridges and basic infrastructure have been improved and new schools have opened. The preservation of the local culture has been another important contribution; evidence of this is seen through the restoration of key cultural monuments, such as the once-decaying monasteries. Apparently approximately 2000 permits were issued for the Manaslu area in 2011, 3700 in 2012 and 4439 in 2013.

Associated Organisations
NTNC (National Trust for Nature Conservation)
www.ntnc.org.np; www.forestrynepal.org
TAAN (Trekking Agents' Association of Nepal)
www.taan.org.np
See also www.welcomenepal.com and www.tourism.gov.np

Choosing the season

A trek to Manaslu and Tsum is best undertaken in either autumn or spring. The autumn period is usually the most stable period and thus will be the busiest time on the trails. Normally early October heralded the beginning of the season after the monsoon rains abated, but in recent years the weather has sometimes been more unsettled. Unseasonal rain and heavy cloud has intervened, causing the much awaited and colourful harvests to be delayed. However, after mid-October the weather is usually better, with clearer skies and magical views. The ripened rice-terraced hillsides are ablaze with fabulous colours from gold to brilliant greens of all shades. November is generally the clearest month, with crisp and sparkling days. December is much colder at higher altitude, but trails are quieter. Just occasionally the stable conditions of autumn are disrupted when a storm blows in, bringing rain with heavy snow in the mountains.

Trekking throughout the winter is perfectly possible lower down, but heading to Manaslu and Tsum during late December/January and early February will mean encountering more cloud, snow and bitterly cold temperatures and is not recommended. Many inhabitants descend to the warmer foothills for winter, so lodges may be closed. Crossing the Larkya La on the Manaslu Circuit in winter is also a matter of chance and not recommended; heavy snow makes this dangerous if not impossible, with a risk of avalanche even before the pass and a very steep, slippery descent. (The Dharamsala/Larkya Phedi lodge has a nominal closing date of 15 December.)

The spring season, late February to early May, is the other popular trekking season. The weather is generally stable, but clouds often cover the mountains by mid-morning. The lower valleys (below 2500m) are sultry and hot. Haze will unfortunately mean those photographers who want their mountains crisp and clear might feel frustrated. However, keen botanists are sure to be delighted and satisfied with the prolific array of rhododendrons and magnolia. Heading into the high country, wind tends to be more of a feature, particularly closer to the Tibetan plateau.

For most, trekking at the height of the summer, July and August, is not really recommended, with mountain vistas a rare luxury. Monsoon cloud, rain and snow can be expected at any time from mid-June to mid-September. Incessant rain in the lower hills causes dangerous landslides, road and trail damage. Blood-sucking leeches are a plague. The one positive advantage about a visit to Tsum in the monsoon is that the valley is green and experiences its most active time, especially for the farmers, who cultivate buckwheat, mustard, barley and potatoes. It is also one of the best times to enjoy the rich cultural heritage of the region, with festivals and colourful events.

Maps

There are an amazing and varied number of maps available in Kathmandu. The quality has improved dramatically in recent years, with excellent colour maps showing all the aspects and features that any casual trekker to Nepal might wish for. Place names on maps are often spelt differently from those seen on lodge signs and so on. Most of the maps are produced by Himalayan Map House & Nepa Maps (www.himalayan-maphouse.com), who have a bookshop in Freak Street and opposite KC's restaurant in Thamel: the Map Centre. In Thamel there are a number of other map stockists, who also sell books on all aspects of the Himalaya.

A selection of titles is listed below:

Lower Manaslu	1:125,000
Manaslu and Tsum Valley	1:125,000
Ganesh Himal	1:100,000
The Ruby Trek, Ganesh Himal	1:100,000
Annapurna Base Camp	1:50,000
Around Annapurna	1:100,000
Around Annapurna	1:125,000
Nar-Phu Area (adjacent trek)	1:60,000
Mustang to Annapurna	1:165,000

In the UK, Stanfords in Long Acre, London is one of the best places to search for maps of Nepal and the Himalaya. (www.stanfords.co.uk)

Photography

The Himalaya and anywhere in Nepal are a photographer's Shangri-La. The variety of the subject matter is mind-boggling. The mountains in all their aspects, the colourful people, the architecture and antiquities, bustling markets and every conceivable subject all offer wonderful opportunities. For much of the season the clarity of the mountain light is often brilliant. Keep all your photographic equipment in plastic bags, away from the unavoidable dust. Batteries do not like the subzero nights and need a warm up in the mornings just as much as the trekkers!

You may need to sleep with your camera/battery when temperatures drop at night; keep the camera tucked up close to your body inside a jacket to warm it up before use. Bring cleaning equipment. Be sure to buy all your film beforehand if you haven't gone digital, as it's virtually unavailable in Nepal now. There are some opportunities to recharge batteries on the trails, but power supplies can be erratic, so pack extra batteries and memory cards.

Avoid taking photographs of any military-looking subjects, such as check posts, some bridges, communication towers and border crossings. You are strongly urged to ask permission of people before taking photographs, especially in the remote areas, where they still believe it will upset their spirits or ancestors. Yaks love having their photos taken, but not from a point blank range, when they will surely be frisky and aggressive – watch those horns! If you manage to capture a snow leopard on digital, you'll probably be able to pay for your trek.

Budgeting

For full-service group trekkers there will be few extras other than drinks on the trails, souvenirs, staff tips and meals out in Kathmandu. Independent trekkers need to calculate with much more care. They will need to plan for porters (if required), accommodation and food, as well as the above extras. Allow at least Rs2500/US$25 per day per person for your own on-trip expenses. Add another US$25–30 per day for a guide, $20–25 for a porter-guide and $10–20 for a porter. Be sure to confirm in advance that these wages **do also include** his or her expenses en route. Don't forget to have insurance for local staff. Take a lot more cash than you have calculated, as there are no regular places to change money. If you should need a pony, that will cost an additional Rs14,000 (US$160) for 1 or 2 days. Expect prices to rise by up to 10 per cent or so a year in future.

> **Costs on trek**
> The higher you go, the higher the bills for food and accommodation. The authors spent roughly Rs2000–2500 (room with half board for two) below Deng and theoretically after Dharapani (except that we ate more after Dharapani!). We spent Rs2200–3000 around Manaslu from Deng to Dharapani, including within the Tsum Valley. A couple of actual menus are included in the relevant sections.

Tipping

Since the 1960s when trekking in Nepal was developed, there has been a tradition for groups and independent visitors to tip their crews at the end of a trek. It's no great hardship to budget for this and it is a very rare affair when anyone is dissatisfied with the service. As a rule and through tradition, the head cook should get a little more than the porters, 'sherpas' and kitchen crews. The sirdar and leader/guide would expect a little more again. Allow around 15% per cent of the wages or around one day's wage for each week on trek. Trekkers may also wish to donate some of their clothing and equipment to the crew.

Style of trekking

As much as anything, the itinerary you choose and the destination will dictate the style of trek undertaken. The Manaslu and Tsum area is currently in transition, from only camping to teahouse/lodge treks. This change will accelerate rapidly over the next couple of years, as more trekkers explore this remote region. However, for the time being the residents are wary of investing money in lodges with no guarantee of a financial return. Some, but not all, of them expressed the feeling that tourists are going to come anyway, so why do they need to do anything to improve facilities? There is little variety of food and mattresses are thin, while toilets are miles away down the garden path and showers come only when it rains. Trekkers will find facilities rough and ready compared with the Annapurna Circuit, whose lodges have long welcomed trekkers with good food and hot showers.

Most trekking trails traditionally connected the villages and very little of Nepal is true wilderness. The trails of Manaslu and Tsum are generally less populated. However, the lower stages can be quite busy with local porters, people off to markets, children engaging visitors, wary dogs, banana-snatching monkeys, mad cows and 'mad' trekkers as well as mules, yaks and even yetis. Beware the 'yak yak yak' attack! The following section outlines the trekking style options.

Independent trekking

Those fit and able to carry their own equipment often choose this style of trek. It is a very popular option on the main trails of Annapurna, Everest and Langtang. It is currently not possible on the Manaslu Circuit or Tsum Valley, since a trekking company registered in Kathmandu has to organise the permits and a guide is a minimum requirement. Although adding to the cost of the trek, having to take a guide/porter guide is probably a wise rule so far. Parts of the route are exposed, rough and deserted for long periods. The pass has no emergency facilities and any accident up there could have very serious consequences. The guide can act as a translator with the locals, few of whom speak much English.

Going independently does allow for perhaps greater interaction and a more intimate rapport with the inhabitants. It is also a cheaper way to trek in Nepal and ensures that your cash goes straight to the local people. Those who have already been to Nepal or other developing countries will have the added advantage of knowing roughly what to expect. It remains to be seen whether independent trekking will be allowed on the Manaslu Circuit/Tsum Valley when lodges and backup structures have improved.

Independently organised trips

Those trekkers who have a dislike for organised trips will find this an appealing option. It offers a good deal of freedom and flexibility. The trek can be tailored to the needs of the person, couple or small group of friends. Many trekkers hire a local porter/guide through a reputable agency, paying all their living expenses as well as the wage.

This approach can be applied to the Manaslu and Tsum Valley so long as the trek is organised by a trekking agency that is authorised by the government to deliver the necessary permits. It doesn't make a lot of sense to hire only a guide, since the extra cost of a porter is not a significant amount on top of all the permission and conservation fees. That said, it's perfectly permissible to take a guide only and carry all your own gear. Make sure that the guide, porters and any staff are insured and adequately clothed for the high pass. Make sure also that the agency will cover any additional porter insurance if you find your bag too heavy and hire an extra porter along the way.

Although not so relevant for Manaslu trekkers, be aware that hiring porters off the street and hotel areas is not necessarily a good idea these days, unless it comes through reliable recommendations. Be sure to read the sections in this guide on altitude and mountain safety. The points may seem obvious, but every year people are evacuated from or die in these mountains. During our research, on the day from Samagaon to Samdo, half the trekkers we saw were actually returning from the pass for various reasons – ten hikers in all.

Organising a trip through an agent in your home country or Nepal for a couple or a small group is not necessarily more expensive than a big company group trek. Naturally, booking the trek directly with a Kathmandu-based company is cheaper. However, unless you are familiar with the agency or have a recommendation, there may be snags. The main one is that you will not be covered by any foreign company liability if things do go wrong. At the very least make sure your insurance covers a helicopter evacuation and is not limited by absurd altitude limits such as 'not above 1500m.' There is a good selection of excellent local trekking agents in Kathmandu who have years of experience in dealing with overseas trekkers approaching them directly. Sometimes getting an answer to your enquiry quickly does not happen because of the fickle nature of power cuts experienced in Kathmandu these days – just keep on asking. Choosing to arrange the trip with a Kathmandu agent means you can finalise the trip and pay the operators directly, but remember that if an internal flight is involved – from Pokhara after the trek, for example – then the agent might ask for some advance payment.

An independent trekker's day

Independent trekkers have the option of a luxurious lie-in, making all those group members envious. Invariably though you will be up, up and away at the same time as the early birds, catching the dawn chorus, with the first rays glinting on that fabulous peak outside. Lodgers might have to be patient over breakfast if a large group has chosen the same hostelry, although this is pretty unlikely at present, since most commercial groups in the Manaslu region are currently camping. After breakfast the day is much the same for all, except that you can dictate your own pace, itinerary and lunch spots. There are a few downsides to the independent format, of course. That backpack always seems to get heavier throughout the day, especially on all those dastardly steep hills. That's why taking a porter makes such an appealing difference on Manaslu – a hard and demanding trek. Living off the lodges generally means a simple diet of chapattis and noodles; currently food and accommodation on the Manaslu trip are not of the standard enjoyed on the Annapurnas, as you will find when you descend to the comparative warmth and luxury of Bimthang.

Fully supported group treks

For many years this was a popular option (until guidebook writers came up with notes on the main trails!). For those with limited time, this option provides maximum security and the least amount of hassle getting permits, for example, in Kathmandu. The tour operators can smooth over the local difficulties and sort out internal flights, which can pose a snag in high season for individuals (although none are involved in the Manaslu area unless you want a private helicopter!). The agent will arrange the trekking permits in advance as well as sort out comfortable private transport to the trek roadhead. All day-to-day logistics such as accommodation, food and carriage of baggage will be arranged. Most trips are fully inclusive, with few added extras. Clients can admire the scenery in as much comfort as is possible in a high mountain environment. Group treks utilise both lodge accommodation and tents, because in some places there is occasionally insufficient lodge space in high season.

There are a few disadvantages to commercial group trekking. Larger groups with the support of a Nepali crew can have more of an impact on the environment. Sometimes clients have to wait at a lodge or campground for the porters to arrive. The major disadvantage of an organised trek is that there is a loss of flexibility concerning the itinerary and any other issues. Of course there is always the risk that your fellow trekkers are on a different planet – although this is extremely rare. Perhaps the biggest snag of a group trek is the unnecessary danger posed at altitude by 'peer pressure' within the group. No one wants to be 'tail-end Charlie' or the first to admit to a headache or nauseas. At its worst, this pressure can overrule common sense, with some members ignoring symptoms of altitude sickness in the unacknowledged race to compete. **Do not fall into this lethal trap**.

A typical group trekker's day

Fully supported hikers can expect a mug of steaming hot tea and a bowl of almost boiling water to be thrust through a tent flap or lodge doorway at dawn, around 6am. This is the wake-up call, to 'get up now and pack your bags'. During breakfast, the porter loads will be organised and home sweet home – the tents – will be dismantled. Lodge trekkers can luxuriate in a warm dining area. Poor old campers will be served breakfast outside and must gobble down their fried eggs before they freeze to the plates. But they can, of course, watch the sunrise over the peaks beyond their porridge!

No sooner is breakfast over and the loads packed, then it's on with the trekking – be sure to use the loo tent before it collapses or the lodge toilets before heading out! Normally the longer walks during the day are before lunch, to luxuriate in the cool, refreshing air and the clarity of the mountain views. Generally the pre-lunch hikes last 3–4hrs, including the odd tea stop along the way where possible. Lodge-based groups take lunch 'fooding' en route. Campers can slouch along until the kitchen boys come racing ahead to prepare lunch, and most important, before the cook arrives. Lunch for campers could be pancakes, bread or chips, tinned meat, fruit and other tasty goodies – probably a wider selection than available to the lodgers. Some you win, some you lose!

Most of the afternoon walks are around 3hrs, with some less and some more depending on the terrain. Campers have no need to outperform the kitchen boys, or they'll have to wait for afternoon tea and biscuits, served on arrival at the night's halt. This is the time to read, check the itinerary notes – oops, rest or explore the locality. A three-course dinner of delightful goodies is served piping hot a little after sunset. For campers their day is done, except for crawling into that tight, uncooperative sleeping bag. Those in lodges can utilise the light, enjoying a beer at lower altitudes or risk a tipple of the local brews – although this is not recommended at the beginning of any hard trek due to the dubious quality control of the liquor. It's wise to avoid alcohol of any description before any high pass or high terrain, since it adversely affects acclimatisation.

Guides and porters

Group trekkers will be lead by an English-speaking Nepalese leader/guide who normally knows the routes. Not so many have been to recently opened Tsum, of course. The Nepalese crew are led by the sirdar. He can also act as leader/guide in a small group. His job is to organise all the porters, cooks and accompanying 'sherpas.' The cook naturally is in the spotlight and will have several kitchen boys to do the donkey work. The kitchen boys carry all the cooking gear and race ahead of the trekkers to prepare lunch, afternoon tea and dinner. Other crew are the sherpas, which in this context refers to the job of guiding the group on the trail. They put up the dining tent and tents for the campers. The porters for a large group might number 30–40. In that case there will also be a *naiki* – a head porter, who takes some of the responsibilities from the sirdar, organising and distributing the loads. The naiki has a hard job deciding who carries the tricky loads, like the eggs or the kerosene, and watching for that 'wily old fox', who unloads his heavy items on to another porter.

As mentioned before but reiterated here, independent trekkers hiring a crew or a porter locally or from Kathmandu should ensure that insurance is obtained to cover any misadventure involving the guide/porters. They should also ensure that suitable high-altitude clothing is provided for all guides/porters. Check out KEEP in Thamel for guidance on the correct actions when hiring porters or guides privately.

When booking a commercially organised trek, be sure to check if all the food and meals are included in the price. Some overseas companies count food as an option to be paid locally. Not including food appears to give the company a competitive edge in terms of the basic price of the trek. Do check this aspect of the 'fully inclusive' arrangement.

Porter welfare

Being a porter is a hard and often dangerous way to make a living in the hill country of Nepal. Every year a few porters are killed through accidents on the trails of Nepal, and occasionally some of them are in the employ of foreign trekkers. Fortunately today there is much more awareness of the conditions once endured by porters. Exploitation has always been found in most societies, but in Nepal the theoretically outlawed caste system, which still pervades the roots of its culture, ensures the situation is very complex. However, visitors can avoid such attitudes. Following the Maoist insurgency, general wage levels for porters and many other often poorly treated people throughout society have risen dramatically – perhaps the one rare benefit of that long reign of violence!

The International Porter Protection Group and Tourism Concern have both made an impact on porter welfare, All trekking agencies in Nepal are now required to provide adequate insurance and clothing for all their staff.

ABC Porter guidelines for all trekkers:

A. Always ensure that your porters have adequate clothing and equipment for the level of trek you are undertaking: footwear, hat, gloves, warm clothing and sleeping bags or blankets as necessary.

B. Be prepared with extra medicines for your porters, and don't abandon them if they are sick; carry funds for such a situation.

C. Choose a local or foreign trekking company who implement the ethical practices outlined above and keep an eye on the reality on the ground.

Accommodation

With increasing numbers of trekkers, one might expect healthy competition to result in an improvement in accommodation facilities. However, the peculiar rules set up by village development committees mean that all lodges/homestays within a village have to charge the same for food and rooms, whatever the quality. And once you have settled in a lodge, you will be expected to eat all your meals there or risk causing trouble for your guide if you decide to move to a different lodge.

Lodges

The style and condition of accommodation on trek will depend on the sort of trip chosen and the destination. Lodges en route around the Manaslu Circuit are relatively basic, with small but adequate twin-bedded rooms. Beds tend to be fairly hard, and the dividing walls hardly provide a private boudoir – expect a lot of communal interaction. Mattresses are getting thicker each year, but on Manaslu's less frequented highways, carrying a Thermorest is a good idea for some places (and for some homestays). In the Tsum Valley, even more off-the-beaten-track, only a couple of lodges and a few modest homestays have been opened so far. Mu and Rachen gompas also have a few adequate twin rooms for trekkers. Tibetan carpets look beautiful and soft, but just wait till you rest your weary bones on them for the night! Expect changes soon as the number of trekkers increases.

Camping

Some trekkers to Manaslu and Tsum do camp, mainly when in large groups. Group camping trekkers can expect quite a degree of comfort in often wild, remote regions. On a traditional camping trek, large two-man tents are used and a mess tent is provided to act as a dining room and porter shelter when necessary. In addition, dining tables, chairs, toilet tents and mattresses come as standard. A wide variety of food is provided and cooked by the crews.

Homestay

Homestay is a new but essentially old concept, where trekkers overnight in local people's houses. Normally a separate room will be set aside for the guests. Most homestays are basic, with outside toilets and primitive washing facilities – much as the first trekkers found. As more local hydro plants come on stream in many rural areas, the lack of comfort may not be such an issue as it used to be. Mattresses may be thin or even thinner! Meals are provided by the household, using available wholesome local produce. Don't expect much other than nourishing dal bhat (lentils and rice), pasta and potatoes for dinner, or local buckwheat tsampa in Tsum, but you could be surprised! Eating too many buckwheat chapattis and pancakes may cramp your style and make it hard to get moving.

Washing

Normally you can ask for a bucket of hot water if there are no proper showers at a lodge, but of course you'll have to pay for it. Where hot showers exist, they are generally provided by solar systems. Any other shower option is likely to be utilising scarce resources (wood or kerosene), meaning a conflict with conservation. Camping group trekkers receive a bowl of hot water during the mornings before breakfast, and often now on arrival at camp as well.

Nightlife in Tsum

One evening just after dark I needed to go... to the toilet up the garden path, gleaming white porcelain but no door. I inched my way down the steep wooden staircase, trod precariously alongside the water channel and finally into the back garden, where two spaced-out eyes stared at me. I stared back. Was it a wild dog? A yeti? The eyes seemed too far apart. Nothing moved. Silence. But when you've got to go, you've got to go! It was not until the following morning that I discovered the owner of those two fluorescent flashes – a baby calf!

How can we be out of soap? Judging by appearances, we have not been contaminated by soap for weeks.
***Stones of Silence*, George Schaller**

Toilets

It's a certain bet that the subject of toilets is being discussed at any time, almost anywhere on trek across Nepal. Around Manaslu, most are outside, invariably up or down (or both) small, steep steps. A trekker's worst nightmare must be that of dropping their moneybelt down the hole, so be extra vigilant. Along the trails, toilet paper should be burnt and waste buried where possible. Campers will be privileged with a special toilet tent with appropriate hole – they're better than nothing! Even before you hit the Annapurna trail, on the other side of the Larkya La there are loos that look modern, with a few lodges even offering 'Flash Toilets'.

Food

On the Manaslu trails in the past, a liking for dal bhat would have been a great advantage for live-off-the-land independent trekkers. Now they have a wide choice of potatoes and pasta too, but tomato sauce normally means ketchup only. Fruit and vegetables exist only in your dreams. Those on fully inclusive group or independently organised treks with full services will enjoy filling breakfasts, including porridge/cereal, bread/toast with eggs, plus hot drinks. Lunch is a favourite meal, especially the real chips. Other items are likely to be tinned meat/fish, noodles or cooked bread and something sweet to round off. At night campers are provided with three-course dinners: soup, noodles/pasta/rice/potatoes plus a dessert of tinned fruit (dream on, independents... you might just find a tin of fruit left behind by an expedition when you reach Samagaon!) and so on. Plentiful amounts of hot water/drinks are available at all meal times to ensure dehydration is avoided, especially the higher you trek. As a rule, the food stocks dwindle the further you get from Kathmandu, as the fresh products are consumed. However, by now anything tastes good!

> **'Fried chaps'**
> The Nepalis' use of the English language is one of the most endearing features of the country. You'll see this on signboards advertising the lodges' 'faxsilities', such as inside 'to lets', 'toilet free rooms' and, on enticing teahouse menus, 'fried chaps', 'apple panick', 'banana crape' and the like. Flash toilets invariably mean toilets flushed by water (or ice blocks), and it is a notorious fact that toilets and Nepal are not cuddly bedfellows.

Kathmandu now has a good variety of supermarkets, but don't anticipate many treats elsewhere. New city malls are the latest trend in Kathmandu, with imported food items suitable for trekkers. Be sure to stock up on goodies – chocolate or power bars and any other cravings that need to be satisfied en route. There's not much on offer in the small shops unless you like chewing tobacco and rough cigarettes!

Trekking around Manaslu, and especially in Tsum, living in the teahouses, the food can get rather monotonous. It's worthwhile taking other food items if you have a porter or two. Muesli is a good standby for any time of day – even with water. Instant potato, soups or noodles and tinned fish are easily prepared as an emergency dinner at a high camp. Ensure that indestructible rubbish is carried out, or use the places set aside for disposal.

What to take

Some of the equipment listed below will involve a considerable expense when purchased at home. Some commercial trekking companies do now provide basic gear – sleeping bags, mattresses etc – but others do not. A few trekking gear shops in Kathmandu offer equipment for hire quite cheaply. Buying new gear is also good value, with excellent locally made items like sleeping bags and down jackets – Mingma at the Everest Equipment shop (near the Kathmandu Guest House) has such items. We have been buying boots in Kathmandu for a number of years and most have proved quite durable. Boots can cost as little as US$20, although the last pair cost Rs4000 (US$50) and were strong enough to withstand the rigours and rocks of the route around Manaslu.

The motto for mountain and wilderness trekkers and visitors around the world is:

"Leave only footprints and take only photographs"

Lipstick
Add a touch of glamour and protect your lips at the same time! For many years I have simply used colourless lip protector sticks, but returned from Dolpo with a horribly cracked lower lip despite frequent use. So this time I decided to try a standard coloured moisturising lipstick... and it worked!

> **The following list is a guideline only:**
>
> | | |
> |---|---|
> | Kitbag | Trainers or sandals |
> | Sleeping bag and sheet liner | Fleece and woollen hat |
> | Toilet rolls and many plastic bags | Sun hat |
> | Torch (flashlight) | Gloves and scarf/buff |
> | Sunglasses | Waterproof jacket |
> | Washing kit | Overtrousers |
> | Wetwipes, large and small | Warm sweater |
> | Toothbrush & toothpaste | Down jacket |
> | Sun cream & lip cream | Down trousers – optional |
> | Water bottle | Penknife and tin opener |
> | Trousers or cotton skirts | Padlock for lodge rooms |
> | Shirts, T-shirts or blouses | Ear plugs |
> | Underwear | Camera & batteries |
> | Boots and various socks | Adaptor for electric plugs |

Staying healthy

The main problem concerning health issues in Nepal are generally related to food, water, hygiene, the remoteness of the trekking regions, and the high altitude. Outside the main urban centres it cannot be emphasised enough that there are virtually no adequate medical facilities anywhere other than tiny often barely functioning health posts. The nearest serviceable hospitals for the Manaslu region are literally in Kathmandu and Pokhara. Hardly any health posts exist around Manaslu and Tsum above Philim. The rural health posts and clinics provide only the most basic treatments; however, helicopter evacuations are possible from almost all parts of the mountain regions. You must have proof of medical evacuation insurance or payment before a helicopter will take off. (Helicopter quotes range from US$1600 up to a whopping US$10,000 but anything above US$2000 per hour might include a 'booking fee' – so beware!). In general fewer bugs survive at high altitude, making the high zones of Nepal marginally more healthy than the humid lowland destinations – a small comfort at least. Personal hygiene and what you eat really does matter. Unfortunately some local levels of hygiene still leave a lot to be desired by most standards.

> **Do your best to keep healthy:**
> Wash/clean hands regularly
> Never drink untreated tap water
> Avoid salads
> Peel fruits
> Brush teeth in bottled/cleaned water

Water sterilisation

Many difficulties on trek concern the lack of clean running water. Just keeping hands clean can significantly reduce the ailments transmitted through dirty water. The lodges on the trails are slowly becoming more aware of hygiene these days, especially on the part that joins the Annapurna Circuit. Group trekkers are at a distinct advantage, being regularly supplied with plentiful boiled water and hot drinks. Independent trekkers will need to be more vigilant as a rule. Antibacterial gel for hands and large baby wipes for other parts are extremely useful! Bring plastic bags for storing used items and carry out rubbish.

Water boils at a lower temperature at high altitude, so add sterilising tablets to the water as an added precaution. Iodine or chlorine tablets, or Micropur, can be used. Bottled drinking water can also be bought in Kathmandu and Pokhara. Along the trails, when available it gets very expensive, especially the higher you go. Plastic water bottles have littered trails in the past but these days most are being carried out of the mountains by trekkers and crews. For independent hikers, the best option for safer water is to request boiled water from the lodges.

Vaccinations

At present no vaccinations are legally required on entry to Nepal, but always check before travel in case of any recent changes. Your GP can advise you about the latest advice regarding vaccinations. Be sure to allow plenty of time for the series of vaccinations – they cannot all be given at the same time and some require a number of weeks between. Keep a record of all the vaccinations, even though it's not a legal requirement.

The following are normally recommended by health professionals, but there could be others added at any time.

BCG tuberculosis Vaccination is often recommended by GPs.
Cholera Although not required by law or particularly effective, it might be recommended if an outbreak has occurred.
Hepatitis This nasty disease has various forms; hepatitis A is the main risk for travellers. New vaccines are being improved for all strains of hepatitis.
Meningitis/Japanese encephalitis Outbreaks do occur in rural parts of Nepal, often in the lower country. The risk is minimal and expensive vaccines are available. Clinics in Kathmandu can give vaccinations for a much lower negotiable fee than payable at home; the CIWEC clinic is highly recommended.
Rabies The disease is found across Nepal, but the vaccination is normally only suggested for those spending extended periods in the rural areas away from the cities. The vaccination is expensive and the procedure lengthy. Seek advice at least six months before the planned trip. The main thing for casual visitors is to keep a sharp lookout for suspiciously acting dogs and 'dog patrols'. Although not necessarily a risk for rabies, the guard dogs of herders in the high uplands can be rather intimidating and occasionally menacing if the owners are not present. A few monasteries have guard dogs, so beware!
Tetanus/polio Recommended.
Typhoid/paratyphoid Vaccinations are strongly recommended, as there are possible risks.
Yellow fever Vaccination will give cover for 10 years. It is only required in Nepal if coming from an infected area.

Other nasty bugs

Giardia is a wretched bug to watch out for, since there is no preventative treatment apart from careful eating and drinking. Infected drinking water is the main culprit. Giardia lives happily in its host until sent packing by a course of Flagyl (Metronidazole), Secnidazole or Tinidazole (Tiniba in Nepal). Sulphurous foul-smelling gases, cramp and sometimes diarrhoea are the main symptoms, but let's not dwell on those.

Dengue fever outbreaks are sometimes reported in Nepal, but the risk is generally fairly low. Try to avoid mosquito bites, since there is no treatment other than rest.

Malaria

Fortunately malaria is not found in most of Nepal, being confined at the moment to parts of the southern lowlands bordering India. However, those trekkers travelling overland to India, or relaxing in Chitwan National Park or anywhere in the Terai, will be exposed to malaria. Using insect repellent at and after dusk and wearing suitable clothing will give some protection against bites. The three main drugs used in Nepal are Mefloquine (Lariam), Doxycycline and Malarone (Atovaquone/Proguanil). For some users, Lariam can have very nasty side effects, so it is wise to test it out before travel. Some travellers may be recommended to take Proguanil daily and Chloroquine weekly, if going to a high-risk area. Doxycycline can be bought in Kathmandu if you need supplies. Do not ignore the risks of malaria.

See also http://ciwec-clinic.com/articles/malaria_advice.php and www.masta-travel-health.com.

Common ailments on trek

The most common problems on trek are colds, blocked sinuses, headaches and stomach disorders. Common remedies (available from the chemist) for headaches, blocked noses, sore throats, coughs and sneezes should be easily accessible in any medical kit. The dry air often causes irritations. Take a good supply of decongestants and painkillers for headaches on any high altitude trek. It is necessary to drink more liquids in high dry regions.

If the dreaded stomach bug appears, the use of Imodium, Loperamide or Lomotil is initially recommended if symptoms are not serious. These drugs will make a road journey much more comfortable. The antibiotic drugs Norfloxacin and Ciprofloxacin can be used in more debilitating cases, and are available from pharmacies in Kathmandu. Dioralyte will help rehydration in cases of fluid loss due to stomach upsets. Stemetil can be used for those prone to travel sickness.

It may seem obvious, but don't ignore the power of the sun at high altitude, despite low temperatures; wear a suitable hat and cover; use sun cream on exposed parts of the body.

Dental care

A visit to your dentist for a check-up before the trip is advised (unless you wish to rely on the 'tooth temple god' near Tahity Square in Kathmandu for treatment). Competent dentists do exist in Kathmandu, but you are unlikely to meet any serving time in the hills. If the 'tooth god' has failed you, try Healthy Smiles in Lazimpat in Kathmandu – it has the latest high tech gadgetry.

First aid kit
The following list is only given as a suggestion:

Pocket First Aid and Wilderness Medicine Dr Jim Duff and Dr Peter Gormly (Cicerone)	Eyewash
	Insect repellent
	Knee bandage
Antibacterial hand gel	Safety pins
Antibiotics (general course)	Scissors
Antihistamine cream	Sterile gloves
Antiseptic cream	Sun cream
Aspirin/paracetamol	Thermometer
Blister prevention	Water sterilising tablets
Dioralyte rehydration sachets	Wet wipes
Dressings	

Plus:
Cold and sinus remedies
Personal medications
Stomach upset remedies and Tinidazole
Drugs for altitude sickness: Diamox, coca tablets, ginkgo biloba

---

If this lot fails to sort you out, there are always self-proclaimed ascetics on the trail, shamans with local remedies as well as Ayurvedic Indian and Tibetan medical cures!

Clinics

Consult one of the specialist clinics or their websites listed below for the latest medical advice for travellers. Your doctor should also be consulted.

CIWEC Clinic Lainchaur, near the British Embassy in Kathmandu, www.ciwec-clinic.com
International Society of Travel Medicine www.istm.org
Hospital for Tropical Diseases Travel Clinic www.thehtd.org
MASTA (Medical Advisory Service for Travellers Abroad) www.masta-travel-health.com.

Altitude sickness & precautions

All mountain walking presents hazards, but in the Manaslu region the biggest danger comes from the dehydrating high altitude, severe cold and bitter winds. Be careful on the rough and rocky trails; bear in mind that the next hospital is hundreds of miles away. The real problems of altitude sickness occur at heights above 3000m (10,000ft), especially if you climb quickly. In general, altitude problems in the region are encountered from above Sho (2880m) or Lho (3180m) on the Manaslu Circuit until Bimthang (3590m), and in the regions of Tsum above Chhokang Paro (3030m) and Rachen (3240m).

Serious altitude problems occur in the highest mountain regions of northern Nepal. Kathmandu is at 1317m and presents no problems. To combat the problems of altitude, it is important to learn about its effects before you start hiking along the trails. The most common symptoms of altitude are headaches, nausea, tiredness, lack of appetite and disorientation. It is often difficult to sleep and breathing becomes erratic (Cheyne-Stokes breathing). The heart might thump a bit disconcertingly at times. Be very careful not to overexert on arrival at any destination; symptoms often only begin to appear after an hour or more. Having some of these does not mean abandoning the trek, but watch out for any changes as altitude is gained. Mild symptoms, perhaps just a slight headache, are acceptable so long as they do not get worse or persist all day and night.

It is vital to walk very slowly at altitude, especially when climbing any hill. If in doubt, be sure to admit any problems and don't be pressured by your fellow trekkers. Altitude sickness does kill. If you are having any serious effects before a high pass, it might require another intermediate night or at worst an immediate return downhill. Minor effects of altitude above 5000m are felt by most – nausea and extreme lethargy – but symptoms will improve on the descent. Continuing to ascend with any persistent symptoms can lead to the serious risk of Pulmonary and Cerebral Oedema or even death. Deaths occur each year in the Himalaya and Nepal, despite all the warnings. Complications from altitude sickness can strike very quickly.

Remember: descending is the only safe cure, whatever the time of day or night.

As an aid before the trek, some start a course of Diamox (Acetazolamide), a diuretic which thins the blood, making you urinate more – which is generally considered good at altitude. It can have the disturbing side effect of pins and needles in the fingers. Another option is to try homeopathic coca, a version of the substance used by natives of Peru and Bolivia. Coca is available as homeopathic tablets that some trekkers (including the authors) swear by. Others swear by ginkgo biloba tablets, which appear to work for unfathomable reasons. It is suggested that these can be taken twice a day for five days before arrival and one tablet a day during the trek. However there are some side effects when taken with some prescription drugs and other substances so check with your GP.

Gamow bag and oxygen cylinders

A Gamow bag is a large plastic bag used to temporarily relieve the effects of high altitude. The ill person with serious altitude problems can be cocooned under higher air pressure for a limited period to mimic a lower altitude. Oxygen cylinders are not generally required, nor likely to be available on, the Manaslu Circuit or lower treks – it's better to proceed slowly and avoid the problems.

Mountain safety

It's not just the altitude that trekkers need to watch out for; all mountain walking presents hazards. In Nepal, apart from the high altitude, severe cold and bitter winds are another menace to guard against. Just after sun up, be sure to keep well wrapped up and during any day always carry enough warm clothing. This is particularly important to group trekkers, who will not have access to their portered baggage – having only their daysack. In the deep gorges the sunlight disappears early in the afternoon (sometimes as early as 2.30pm) and temperatures plummet. Breathing through a scarf at high altitudes can help to retain fluids, and will help protect against dust and icy winds. The Larkya La pass, as emphasised already, is notorious for its deathly cold winds.

Unnoticed dehydration is easily overlooked; you may not necessarily feel like drinking – remember that tea and coffee are both diuretics, so keep vital fluids up. Electrolyte powders can be added to clean water if lethargy arises (apart from when going up steep trails, when a little tiredness can easily be explained!). Noting the colour of your urine is one good way to be aware of dehydration. Too yellow means you are not drinking enough. Always concentrate and take care on the trails – the nearest hospital is just a distant dream. At high altitudes you may not be thinking as clearly as normal. Leaping carelessly across streams, boulders or log bridges is an easy way to fall foul of snags.

Remember too that evacuation by helicopter is not guaranteed: you might be too high, there could be bad weather or there might easily be no serviceable helicopter in Kathmandu. Porters with cut-out baskets on their backs do occasionally carry out trekkers in an emergency, as happened when we crossed the Larkya Pass. To avoid this rollercoaster ride, it's best not to fall over! As mentioned above, unruly dogs in Nepal are a less obvious menace. Normally these dogs are docile and easily controlled. However, during a night-time visit to the toilet, watch out! Ideally, don't plan on going out at night at all, but improvise some sort of suitable receptacle. Find a large-necked plastic container and make sure the lid seal is good! Of course there is no need to be put off by all the above advice; just take care and enjoy the trek!

Weather

No man or woman yet, including trekkers and climbers, has tamed the weather. However, today there are some high-tech sages who can predict, with surprising accuracy, the weather patterns to come. Perhaps the gods were on our side when we arrived in Samagaon and found a French expedition who had just had a forecast from our good friend Yan in Chamonix. The grey clouds and snow would vanish and several days of 'le grand beau' would follow. And so it was for our crossing of the Larkya La.

> **The Sorcerer of the Clouds**
>
> Who is this modern-day high-tech, 'Sorcerer of the Clouds'? What can he do to weave his magical spell over the Himalaya? The mountaineer has one aim – to get to the top. However, skill alone cannot guarantee success; modern equipment, better protection against the biting cold, better food, oxygen and all manner of tools can enhance the chances of reaching the summit. Their destiny is also controlled by the clouds – well, the gods at least. Early climbers on Everest in the 1920s argued incessantly about the ethics of using of oxygen. Was it sporting? A new aid to the mountaineer is that of the 'router'. They are meteorologists, invariably of great dedication and skill, using real time, space age satellite imagery and superb communications to advise climbers about the prevailing weather conditions anywhere in the world. Incredibly accurate predictions and detailed information about wind speed and direction, cloud conditions and imminent changes in the weather can be obtained. Today 'The Sorcerer of the Clouds' can wave his wand to aid both safety and the chances of success on the peak, yet it is still ultimately the gods who cast the final spell. Yan Giezendanner is one such sorcerer who has 'climbed' the Himalaya through this meteorological technology without setting foot on any slope: he has done this from his wheelchair in Chamonix. A French book, Editions Guérin, Le Routeur des Cimes, tells his extraordinary story. It has been translated into English by Siân as The Sorcerer of the Clouds (Pilgrims).

Security

Once upon a time, as the fairytale goes, there was virtually no crime in Nepal, but those days have long gone. However, it is still an amazingly safe country for foreigners to visit. It is unlikely that anyone would encounter any danger in Kathmandu, even well into the night (though night owls might want to avoid grungy dogs in the early hours). Embassies and the tourist departments do not recommend trekking completely alone. You are strongly encouraged to register your trip at your embassy or online. Isolated incidents and attacks have occurred in the hills, and tent theft close to main towns has increased. Take the usual, sensible precautions that you would observe almost anywhere these days.

Kathmandu – gateway to the Himalaya

Kathmandu (1317m) is the normal gateway to the Manaslu and Tsum region. Trekkers should spend a few days exploring the magical parts of the city. It's a friendly, welcoming place, despite some obvious distractions. The longer you stay, the more of a home away from home it becomes. There is a wide range of excellent hotels and guesthouses to suit all tastes and an astonishing array of eateries and restaurants. Despite the obvious modernisation, the city and the whole valley still have some enchanting places to discover.

The Kathmandu Valley probably has the greatest concentration of temples, shrines, monasteries and idols of anywhere across the globe. Kathmandu is the trading crossroads of the Himalaya between India and China, through Tibet. The city is a great melting pot of migrating peoples. The religious mix of Hinduism, Buddhism, Tantra, Vajrayana, Tibetan Buddhism, Bon and Shamanism is intoxicating. Legends, folktales and myths influence every Nepalese ritual and festival, as well as everyday actions. Idols once outnumbered people, but that is not quite the case today, although they do still outnumber tourists.

No visit to Nepal would be complete without a thorough exploration of the **Durbar (palace) squares** of the three great cities, Kathmandu, Patan and Bhaktapur. In Kathmandu, be sure to investigate the Jochen

> **A day in Kathmandu**
> As a misty dawn stirs over the valley's stupas and temples, the dog patrols fall silent. A chaotic cacophony erupts; pedestrians lose the battle with bicycles, cycle rickshaws, motorbikes, taxis and minibuses in the vibrant, colourful streets and alleys. Yet in quiet corners, little has changed; a few holy cows linger beside a grotesque, gargantuan gargoyle or a serene, stony-faced idol. Hidden in the intricate maze of the old cities, potters spin their wheels by hand; antique sewing machines spin their cotton threads. Buddhists spin their prayer wheels. The rumour mill is in full swing; Bob Dylan or Cat Stevens are in the low-roofed, dingy café around the corner. People offer devotions to the golden Ganesh idol near the old 'pie and pig' alley of the 1970s, behind the Kasthamandap temple. Trekkers scurry about trying to find the current location of the immigration department. Others seek out the cheapest sewing shop, getting a T-shirt embroidered with their latest trekking route, or 'Yak Yak Yak'! And the dog patrols lie dormant, gaining strength for another night of barking...

Tole alley once known as **Freak Street**. It's still there, bearing a faded resemblance to its glorious past. Those 'idle' hippies were the eccentric pioneers of Nepal's tourist industry. The bustling byways of **Asan**, Kathmandu's old market streets, are a kaleidoscope of colour and confusion. Brass pots, fabrics, metal and woodwork crafts and everyday items almost block the narrow lanes. In Asan area is the **Jan Bahal**, a fairyland of glittering temples and devotional artwork. The enigmatic Seto (White) Machhendranath idol with the strangest mesmerising eyes resides here, surrounded by goldleaf. **Itum Bahal** is a typical Newari courtyard housing complex, hidden in a maze of dark mysterious alleyways close to Durbar Square; finding it is quite a mystery as well. **Sano (Little) Swayambhunath** and the temple of **Nara Devi** lie north of Durbar Square. To the south, down a small street from the Kasthamandap temple, are a number of tiered temples, like **Jaisi Dewal** and other shrines or stupas set in quiet courtyards – bahals.

Patan, across the river, is a city of artisans and quaint, quiet lanes. The Durbar Square here is perhaps the most exotic of the three such squares of the valley and the number of impressive temples and palaces merely adds to this dimension. Deep in the old quarter are the **Kwa Bahal** (Golden Temple) and the temple of Rato (Red) Machhendranath, plus many other exquisite temples and shrines.

Bhaktapur, 11km east of Kathmandu, is the least modernised city of the valley, although a new multi-lane highway makes the journey there less of a Himalayan expedition today. Its **Durbar Square** is intriguing, with some impressive restoration after various earthquakes destroyed the once vast complex. Be sure not to miss the other squares. **Nyatapola Square** displays a five-tiered temple and topsy-turvy temple cafe. **Dattatreya Square**, some distance to the east, magnificently illustrates the fabulous artistry and skill of the Malla-era builders. The whole scene is of overwhelming grandeur, with intricately carved wooden windows and fine brick structures. In the quiet medieval streets of Bhaktapur, time stands still – it is a living relic of a forgotten era.

On a hill to the west of Kathmandu is **Swayambhunath** (the Monkey Temple), a picturesque Buddhist stupa surrounded by shrines and temples. It's quite a climb up, but the views are stunning – it's a good workout for the trek to come. The great stupa of **Boudhanath**, with its all-seeing eyes and peaceful atmosphere, is east of Kathmandu. Pilgrims, monks, Tibetans and tourists circle the base in a clockwise direction, turning the prayer wheels, breathing the sweet aroma of juniper incense and enjoying the relaxing atmosphere.

Close to Boudhanath is the great Hindu temple complex of **Pashupatinath** beside the holy Bagmati River. Non-Hindu foreigners cannot enter the main shrine, where stands the great golden bull of Nandi – Shiva's vehicle. Across the river in a forested monkey-infested area, sadhus congregate and show a few surprising tricks. Along the riverbanks is a more sobering sight, where Hindus are cremated before passage into the next life.

'There's a green-eyed yellow idol to the north of Kathmandu' (so says the famous poem), but today only an image of Vishnu covered in snakes and reclining in a pool can be found – at **Budhanilkanta**.

Further afield in the valley to the south of Patan are **Bungamati** (with a quaint square hosting the Red Machhendranath temple) and **Kokhana** (with old brick houses and the Shekali Mai temple). Southwest of Patan are **Pharping** (Buddhist monasteries and Guru Rinpoche cave), **Shesh Narayan** (a temple devoted to Vishnu) and **Dakshinkali** (where pilgrims offer live sacrifices to the bloodthirsty goddess Kali).

If you are a visitor with plenty of time, why not seek out other enchanting places: **Changu Narayan, Kirtipur, Vajra Yogini** near Sankhu, the boar-headed Vajra Varahi temple garden of **Chapagaon**, quirky Bishankhu Narayan and the mountain viewpoints of **Nagarkot** and **Kakani**. A few kilometres to the east along the road to Tibet are **Dhulikhel, Panauti** and **Banepa**, with some little-visited temples and shrines.

Accommodation

The main Kathmandu tourist enclave for hotels and restaurants is Thamel, where hundreds of hotels to suit all pockets vie for trade. Our new home, the Hotel Moonlight, is in Paknajol near Thamel; Pilgrims Hotel is nearby through a small alleyway. The famous Kathmandu Guest House, originally the backpackers' favourite, was damaged during the earthquake and is now being rebuilt as a more upmarket establishment. Other options include Hotel Northfield, Marsyangdi, Mandap, Manang, Potala Guest House, Utse, Vaisali, Norbu Lingka and Courtyard. For a taste of Tibet, try the Hotel Tibet in Lazimpat; nearby the Hotel Ambassador is being rebuilt. For greater luxury, lodge at the Hotel Malla on the edge of Thamel. En route to Swayambhunath is the atmospheric traditional-style Hotel Vajra. The Hotel Shankar (a former Rana palace) and the palatial Yak and Yeti or Annapurna hotels suit more well-heeled guests. Around Boudhanath there are many hotels to suit all budgets. The atmospheric, heritage-style boutique hotel of Dwarika's is near the airport and restored Ram Mandir temple.

Eating out

For returning trekkers, Kathmandu and Pokhara are a paradise of over-indulgence. Choose your food very carefully before your trek – there is nothing worse than bumping along Nepal's 'main roads' with an upset stomach, except lurching along a 'side road' with an urgent need!! Even in the better restaurants, avoid salads and unpeeled fruit as a precaution. The following are a few of the popular eating places in Kathmandu (exclusion does not imply any criticism): Northfield Café, La Bella Café & Aqua Bar, Gusto Italiano, Green Organic Café, KC's, Pilgrims 24, Rum Doodle, Helena's, Yin Yang and Third Eye (both sadly closed at the time of writing, reopening date unknown), Dechenling Garden, Kathmandu Guest House, Pumpernickel, Bamboo Club, New Orleans, Nargila's, Gaia, OR2K, Himalayan Java Café, La Dolce Vita, Roadhouse Café, Delima Garden, Electric Pagoda, Utse, Le Bistro, Fire and Ice, Kilroy's and The Factory. A reasonable meal will cost from Rs400 to Rs800 per person for a main dish, pizza, steak, curry and so on.

Tourist office/TIMS/MCAP/ACAP
This office is located in Bhrikuti Mandap, near Ratna Park bus station! MCAP/ACAP permits and TIMS are issued here.

Pokhara – after the trek

Pokhara (900m) has boomed over the years into a sprawling but still pleasant town of a considerable size. It was once a sleepy village surrounded by rice fields and some very dense jungle. Lakeside is the main tourist area, where hotels, restaurants and shops are found. There are not many historic sites in Pokhara, but it does have an old bazaar street and the Pokhara Mountain Museum. High above the placid Pewa Lake is the Peace Pagoda. Tibetan refugee camps are located around the town and to the southeast is the narrow ravine of Devi's Falls. Of course it's easy just to eat, sleep and muck about in a boat on the lake after a hard trek. Sarangkot is a spectacular vantage point, to watch the sunrise or sunset on the Annapurna ranges, untainted, brooding and standing sentinel over the valley.

Accommodation
Pokhara has hotels and guest houses to suit all budgets. The expensive Fishtail Lodge is a good place for afternoon tea on the lawn. In Lakeside is the comfortable Hotel Asia, the beautifully designed Heritage Hotel, along with many old favourites such as Snowlands (once a thatched

farmhouse), Oju Guest House (a comfortable budget guest house with fresh French bread and croissants baked every morning), Peace Eye, Hungry Eye, Meera, Trek O' Tel and hundreds more. Down a back lane opposite the Fishtail is the Comfort Inn, with good parking for those driving overland in their own vehicle (still just about possible).

Eating out
Pokhara lakeside has places to satisfy every cuisine and taste of returning trekkers, tourists and idle, ageing hippies. There are some great new places, too many to name.

Tourist office
This office is located in Damside area of Pokhara. Permits and TIMS are normally issued here.

Bandipur

Up in the hills just south of the road from Kathmandu to Pokhara is the small traditional hilltop village of Bandipur. With great mountain views, fresh air and many beautifully restored old buildings and temples, this historic village is fast becoming a popular getaway and stopover. See www.rural-heritage.com for more information and photos.

Using this guide on the trails

The following trekking route descriptions (and road routes) indicate approximate distances, timings and altitudes. Maps of the trekking routes sometimes show different figures, so it is has been necessary in places to give a 'guestimate' for altitudes. The trekking marches described mostly correlate to day-to-day itineraries, but not at every stage. The itineraries shown in the appendix summary section reflect the most popular routes and durations. With time and energy, it's perfectly possible to combine the treks described. The suggested trek itinerary appendix also gives a rough grade of difficulty. MCAP has been responsible for a few signs, with rough estimates of timings, but they may not be seen at regular intervals.

Much debate between trekkers centres on the accuracy of daily trekking times in guidebooks. This edition will no doubt raise the same issues. What is average for one trekker is desperately hard or astonishingly easy for another. The times shown are an attempt to give the average time for the walk, with extra time added to cover a few photo stops, pausing to tie up a bootlace, and for those quick visits into the vegetation. A trek in the Himalaya is supposed to be an enriching experience and a holiday. A trek is not, for most hikers, a competition to see who can climb the Larkya La pass faster than a yak herder. Most existing teahouses and lodges on the route have been named, but there will no doubt be others by the time this book is published. There is little to choose between most of them – it is often determined by where you happen to be by late afternoon and which place catches your attention.

New 'roads'

As a rule, the effect of a new road in Nepal is rather negative, with the creation of noise, pollution, dust clouds and chaos for pedestrians. Inevitably the destruction of the once-pristine environment is noticed quickly. Most of the 'new roads' are little more than farm tracks, meaning rough rides, dust or mud, delays due to avalanches, floods and bridge washouts. The journey time is never set in stone. Bear this in mind when planning your itinerary, anywhere, including the Manaslu area.

Trekkers who visited Nepal some time ago lament the coming of roads, but from a Nepalese point of view this is progress. There is no more humping of ridiculously heavy loads along narrow, exposed, slippery trails or crossing precarious log bridges, not to mention the leeches. Generally local people are in favour of new access dirt roads, since they do significantly reduce prices of food goods (sugar Rs200/kg down to Rs80). It is the same on the Manaslu approaches, where roads are pushing northwards.

As temporary visitors it's hard to disagree with local dwellers, who have to pay those high prices for goods. The main downside of the new country roads is that some lodges and people who earn money from passing trekkers are going to lose their most valued asset – those passing trekkers. The trekker today has to take the treks as they are now. Nepal is there to change you, and not for you to change it. Experience so far suggests that very few hikers are put off by the quiet, almost traffic-free, jeep roads close to trails – just look at the Annapurnas, where the numbers of trekkers has increased.

You would hardly think there is any need to define a road in so many ways, but in Nepal nothing ever quite conforms to the norms.

Sealed road: A tarmac highway – but expect potholes and even broken-up sections.
Jeep track: Any side road used by jeeps and tractors.
Wide trail: A regular trail, often one that the mule caravans have used for centuries which may end up being a dirt road.
Trail, path: As expected, away from the road

Of course roads and trails will change – surprisingly fast, in contrast to the recent high speed of destruction and slow pace of reconstruction in Kathmandu. Please make allowance for these changes when criticising this guide – *Dhanyabad*!

Pre-trek checklist

Don't trek alone: hire a guide.
Don't set off without your MCAP and ACAP entry permit, and restricted area permit(s).
Register your journey with your embassy (if trekking independently).
Make sure there is adequate insurance for yourself and your staff.
Carry a photocopy of your passport details page.
Carry a first aid kit and medications.
Be forewarned about the dangers of altitude and act accordingly.
Treat porters properly.
Register with the check posts.
Respect the culture, the environment and local sensibilities.
Dress appropriately.
Watch your step!

Manaslu Trail Race (manaslutrailrace.org)
by Lily Dyu

Devised by Richard Bull, a British trail runner living in Kathmandu, the Manaslu Mountain Trail was launched in 2012. It takes place each November, attracting global participants, ranging from elite endurance athletes to marathon runners with a goal to 'just get round'. Richard set up trailrunningnepal.org to bring more people to come to run in Nepal and to support Nepal's talented trail running athletes. The first two events were won by Nepali runners in astonishing times, the fastest being 18hrs 42mins by Phudorjee Lamasherpa in 2013.

With rocky and often technical trails, huge climbs and descents, and the challenges of altitude, this is a demanding event. Supported by a fantastic Nepali team, baggage and supplies are moved by mules and staff between trekking lodges while the runners complete the day's leg, carrying spare warm clothing and food. Usually ranging from 20–40km, the race stages also include a 'sky race' of almost a vertical kilometre (900m), climbing from Samagaon up to Manaslu Base Camp and back.

With the motto 'Run for light', the Manaslu Mountain Trail also works to improve access to reliable lighting in the valley. Partnering with the charity LED, during the event solar lights are carried and distributed to selected villages. These, as well as donations to local hydro-electric schemes, are funded from a portion of the race profits. (www.lighteducationdevelopment.org)

The race includes a lot of cultural interaction with the villages along the route, and a highlight of the event is an overnight stay at the monastery of Hinang Gompa. The team organises a fun run for all the children of Samagaon school during the two days staying there, and there are visits to village homes and the monastery in Samdo.

Taking part in the 2013 race, this was my first stage race and the toughest thing I have ever done. And yet it was also the adventure of a lifetime, giving me a different perspective and enriching my life in so many ways. I will have lifelong memories of the beautiful scenery, fascinating villages and culture and, most of all, the wonderful people I met; the runners, Nepali crew and villagers whose lives we briefly passed through. While I was running around Manaslu, the 'ornamental heap of riches' cast a spell on me that will draw me back to Nepal for many more adventures on her sky-high trails.

THE TREKKING ROUTES

Manaslu Circuit

Introduction

The Manaslu trekking route might be one of the closest mountain adventures to Kathmandu, but it could hardly be further from the frenetic pace of life in the valley. It's a kaleidoscope of colours, vegetation, landscapes and climates. The sensational mountain vistas and unworldly landscapes will be etched into the memory forever.

Make no mistake; trekking around Manaslu is hard and relentless. During our trek in the cold of late November, at least 40% of the trekkers we met turned back from Larkya Phedi or Samdo for a variety of reasons – altitude, bad health, extreme tiredness and a short, isolated spell of bad weather. Perhaps in the warmer seasons the dropout rate would be less – let's think so. That said, the joys of the trek far outweigh the hardships.

Planning

Following the basic route around Manaslu, for there are few alternative routes, is what most trekkers plan. Side trips are mentioned in the appropriate sections. At present it is wise to take some additional food supplies and all those regular goodies that anyone craves on a long trek. Normally the basic circuit can be done in two weeks, which allows for a few extra days for side trips and acclimatisation. Everyone should spend two nights in and around both Samagaon and Samdo. In addition, all will need to overnight at Larkya Phedi/Dharamsala, even though it's currently not the most convivial of stops. Some may need a second night at Phedi to be in tiptop condition for the pass.

No one should rush this pass; the views are so fantastic that they should not be squandered because of feeling rough. It is almost impossible for these speechless scribes to find the words – this is some of the most outstanding mountain scenery anywhere in the Himalaya, for its grandeur and awesome treasures. Despite the stunning dramas through the gorge of the Budhi Gandaki, to be honest the Manaslu trek really saves up most of its finest jewels for the days from Lho to Bimthang and on to Kharche/Surki Khola. Everyone should set aside lots of chocolate bars and energy bars for the crossing of the Larkya pass, since there will be no sustenance from 4am to perhaps 6 or 7pm.

The biggest headache, apart from the pass perhaps, is the status of the Larkya Phedi lodge. In the 2011 season it was closed erratically and even shut down for a while by MCAP as being an illegal structure – even though a lease was given by the authorities to a management duo. The politics of opening up Manaslu have become as befuddled as the central authorities in Kathmandu. In the latter part of November it's possible that the Larkya Phedi lodge could be closed, so anyone contemplating the late season should ascertain if it is still open (not that much can be done if it is closed suddenly, as happened to us). Theoretically it is supposed to remain open until 15 December or thereabouts. However, should the worst happen, there are three options apart from a forced retreat down to Arughat – yuk!

It's usually possible to bivouac in the grotty dung-laden porters' shed at Larkya Phedi. People in Samdo can help you and provide extra food and mattresses for the night's bivouac, plus a porter to carry all the extra equipment needed – pots and fuel etc. Otherwise it's possible to hire ponies to enable you to do the whole run from Samdo to Bimthang in one hit. Be aware, though, that the ponies may not be able to reach the summit of the pass, owing to ice in late season. On the way there are also several streams to cross, which become iced over in winter, so again you'll be out of the saddle. And you will have to walk all the way down to Bimthang on your own two feet! Some of the very fittest and well acclimatised can do it on Shanks's pony (walking) in one day, but it's rare for most trekkers to be able to achieve this. It can prove very dangerous if altitude problems creep up fast after hours of ascent. No one can ever be sure of not suddenly coming down with altitude sickness, such is the speed and indiscriminate way in which it can strike. Anyone contemplating making the crossing on foot in one long day should spend a day or two more in and around Samdo, sitting high above the village on its plentiful ridge tops.

Itinerary and routes

First opened as a complete circular route in 1992, the Manaslu Circuit remains a relatively undiscovered classic trek that is bound to be 'discovered' soon. In some ways it is very similar to the Annapurna Circuit, a trek that remains very popular despite some road building. However, the higher trails around Manaslu are far more rough and rocky, involve significantly more demanding climbs and descents, and are often quite exposed. The pass of Larkya La is lower than the Thorong La, but the tricky trail is slow to negotiate in the upper areas. The length of time spent above 5000m is longer, and there is no organised backup other than your own crew and possibly the odd pony. Any accident or altitude problem could rapidly become a major incident. The pass is also notoriously windy and thus extremely cold, especially towards the end of the autumn season – though clear skies are the main bonus of this period. Currently taking a guide is mandatory and this is a good thing in these wild, untamed hinterlands.

Just about all along the way above Philim the health posts are closed, invisible or nonexistent. That important ingredient of all treks (apart from the toilets) is the 'lodgings and foodings'. In this regard, food quality, food choice, its availability and general facilities are far more primitive than their counterparts on the Annapurna Circuit. Many villages still do not have electricity. In general the villages above Philim are quite small, often little more than a few houses. Ghap, for example, comprises just a couple of houses, a lodge and immense 'ghaps' between farmsteads. Sho, Lho, Samagaon, Samdo and later Tilje are the only true villages. From Bimthang onwards, 'lodgings and foodings' are far superior to those currently 'enjoyed' between Arughat and the Larkya La.

Most people do the trek in an anti-clockwise direction, saving the best (or worst) – the Larkya La pass – for last. In fact this direction gives a slow, fitness-enhancing build-up and the pass is less steep on the eastern side. It's just a short hop down from Bimthang, below the Larkya La, to the main trail of the Annapurna Circuit, where deluxe lodge trekking is to be savoured after the privations of the high country. If you are a gregarious trekker wanting to meet everyone doing the trek, then going clockwise is possible but dangerous, owing to the altitude gain from Bimthang to the Larkya La pass (unless completely self-sufficient with tent and cooking gear). That said, we did meet two supermen who had done just that.

A comprehensive summary of routes and itinerary options for the Manaslu trek is given in the appendix. The trek can be started from Gorkha or Arughat. Real fanatics can actually begin in Gorkha, head to Arughat on the old trail and complete the whole loop around Himalchuli, Ngadi Chuli and Manaslu by following paths from Bhulbhule along the east side of the Marsyangdi and climbing back up to Gorkha for the grand finale. Of course the newest adventure option is the week-long (or more) detour into the Tsum Valley – a truly worthwhile add-on, and it saves you the trouble of repeating much of the lower Budhi Gandaki on a future occasion. Doing all of Manaslu and Tsum as a lodge-based option will, for the time being, be quite a long, hard and tiring choice. Bereft of comforts and good food at present, things will probably improve quickly over the coming seasons, as more, better lodges are completed.

Manaslu Circuit Trek Summary

Start	**Arughat** (608m) or **Gorkha** (1060m)
Finish	**Dharapani** (1963m), **Tal** (1700m), Bhulbhule (840m) or **Besisahar** (760m)
Distance	approx. 140–220km (76–140 miles)
Time	14–18 days
Max. altitude	**Larkya La** (5160m/16,925ft)
Trekking style	Lodges or camping
Transport	Bus, jeep, private car or pony

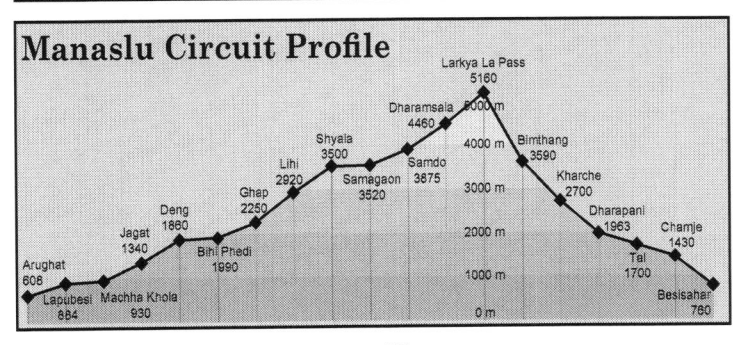

Manaslu Circuit Profile

Larkya La Pass 5160
Dharamsala 4460
Shyala 3500
Lihi 2920
Ghap 2250
Samagaon 3520
Samdo 3875
Bimthang 3590
Kharche 2700
Deng 1860
Jagat 1340
Bihi Phedi 1990
Dharapani 1963
Chamje 1430
Arughat 608
Lapubesi 684
Machha Khola 930
Tal 1700
Besisahar 760

Kathmandu – Arughat via Dhading

This route offers the shortest approach to Arughat, but the dirt road after Dhading is extremely rough and thus very uncomfortable – it will shake your skeleton, rattle your bones and make you roll all over the road.

From Kathmandu the sealed road follows the busy Prithvi Highway almost as far as Malekhu Bazaar, then crosses the fast-flowing Trisuli River, a popular river for rafters. It takes about 2½–3hrs to reach this junction from the capital, although the distance is only about 70km. From here a well-engineered, single-lane sealed road climbs into the foothills. After 18km it crosses the river before reaching the western area of Dhading in another 11km. From Kathmandu the rich rice-growing bowl of Dhading (99km) is 3–4hrs drive, depending on transport – private or public.

The track for Arughat leaves the sealed road on the left just before Dhading to begin a steep and slow climb to the Gola Bhanjyang pass. The rice fields are left far below and idyllic-looking, picturesque farmhouses set in fields of millet higher up are the new companions on the ascent. Gradually the cool, willowy sal forests are replaced by chir pine jungle. The road passes through Jyamire and Ghola Bhanjyang (km122 from Kathmandu), where panoramic views of Manaslu and Ganesh Himal entice, raising the anticipation of days to come. After crossing the wide valley and bridge of the Ankhu Khola, the dreadfully rough and often narrow road climbs to Salyantar. The road from Salyantar to Arughat has been improved and is much wider these days.

The route goes left at Salyantar and briefly south before turning northwards along the Budhi Gandaki (Budhi means old woman). The Budhi Gandaki (traditionally also called the Buri Gandaki in western guidebooks), is the trekkers' highway to Manaslu, as it snakes its way northwards into tantalising gorges and canyons. From the bus depot (and camp area), Arughat is just a 10mins walk across the river.

If you want a jeep to Soti the next day, you need to arrange it in Arughat, because they do not normally pick up trekkers en route; they are already bursting at the seams.

Alternative: Kathmandu – Arughat via Benighat

A new route is now open from Benighat, further west of the Dhading turnoff. A new bridge has been built over the Trisuli River and the dirt road, although poor so far, heads along the valley of the Budhi Gandaki, thereby avoiding the passes of the Dhading option. Timewise there is little difference, that is until improvements to this new valley route have been completed.

Alternative: Kathmandu – Arughat via Gorkha

Following this once-traditional approach to the Manaslu Circuit can add a couple of extra walking days to the itinerary. A good road leads from Kathmandu to Abu Khaireni on the road to Pokhara. It's about 125km from Kathmandu to this turnoff. From Abu Khaireni the road twists and turns on many hairpins up to the central Nepal town of Gorkha (1060m). Gorkha has a reasonable selection of hotels, so it's worth stopping overnight here; buses arrive in the early afternoon as a rule. This leaves enough time to visit the famed Durbar palace. Gorkha has rapidly expanded from a two-horse country bazaar into a sizeable town with hotels, guesthouses, bus syndicate wheeler-dealers and wily horse traders.

The narrow Budhi Gandaki canyon

Gorkha Durbar Palace

Within the famous fortress and royal palace above Gorkha bazaar is the Dhuni Pari palace, the birthplace of Prithvi Narayan Shah, the most famous of the Shah kings, who unified Nepal in 1768. The first Gorkha kingdom was established by King Drabya Shah in 1560. Subsequent rulers established the Shah kingdom centred on Gorkha on a more permanent footing between 1604 and 1641. The palace seen today was constructed on the strategically important hilltop under Ram Shah during this period. Apparently there are about 1700 steps leading up to the complex, but it's likely that most will lose count on the steep and tiring ascent. The palace is built in Newari style, with typical wooden windows and carvings set into beautifully executed brickwork. The foundations are substantial, with stones to support it on the hillside. Trees have grown up around it, blending this fine building with the finest nature and the finest views. The section to the west is called the Kalika Mandir, used only by kings and priests. The eastern part apparently contains a sacred flame, but this too is out-of-bounds for most heathens, like tourists. This eternal flame, so it is said, has been burning since the unification of Nepal. (A slight flicker is being experienced these days, as Nepal seems less unified.)

Gorkha – Arughat (3hrs jeep or 2 days)
Gorkha – Taple – Khanchowk – Arughat

The trail for Arughat climbs to the palace and then descends less steeply around the hillsides. A dirt road now heads this way, so expect some jeeps and dust to boot. The jeep road goes to Arughat, but it can be prone to wet weather problems and landslips. If you plan to walk all the way, allow a day and a half. A superb camping place can be found just down on the north side of the palace. The views here are stunning at dawn and sunset, with Baudha and Himalchuli almost within touching distance.

From Gorkha the route heads to Ahale, a prosperous settlement with shops and basic lodges. Most of the route (by foot or jeep) is gently down. The next village is Taple, a beautifully tidy and flower-bedecked spread-out settlement of some note. Its school has a large catchment area and is one of the better institutions of its kind. Some way down the hillside is Khanchowk (930m), a major crossroads. From here a trail heads north to Dharche Danda and the Rupina La (4720m). After Khanchowk the route descends briefly before climbing to the saddle of Koyapani (900m). It takes about 5–6hrs to reach this place on foot. From here the route descends almost all the way to the low altitudes of the hot Budhi Gandaki gorge and the bazaar town of Arughat. To the north of the Mukti Khola the new dirt road snakes its way into the Budhi Gandaki valley. Lodgings en route are reported to be basic.

Arughat

For centuries Arughat has been a trading crossroads. Before the Kathmandu–Pokhara road was built, it was the main thoroughfare between the two towns. Today its new lease of life comes from being the new roadhead (approximately 6–8hrs from the capital) for Manaslu and the Tsum Valley. The Budhi Gandaki slices Arughat into east and west bank settlements, linked by a well-worn suspension bridge. A new road bridge can be seen upstream to the north. The western part of town sits high above the river on a fragile, sheer-sided bluff. This area has a fine Newari-style temple and a courtyard complex with Buddhist prayer wheels on the southern side. Hidden in the main street is a small Ganesh shrine, helping to keep the town prosperous. From the west bank another dirt road runs to Gorkha, the district headquarters. Journey times to Gorkha are quoted to be 3hrs (or 1½–2 days' walk, see below).

Currently the best hostelry in town is the pleasant Hotel Manaslu. If coming from the eastern bus depot, turn right after crossing the suspension bridge and go steeply uphill into the main area. The hotel is found on the right after a short dog-leg north of town. The garden area of the hotel has a new block of rooms with super-soft mattresses, so don't end up on the straw ones of the old wing – unless you're anxious to experience the 2cm mattresses that await ahead. Arughat offers the road traveller the alternative Third Steps Hotel, but you'll need to ask where it is located. Arughat was quite badly damaged in the spring earthquakes of 2015. However, much has already been renovated.

Arughat – Soti Bazaar (2hrs by jeep)
Arughat – Mangaltar – Arkhet – Kokhetar – Soti Khola

The trek starts at Arughat Bazaar (608m), heading north upstream along the Budhi Gandaki river. At this altitude the hot semi-tropical valley floor supports rich agriculture, with mangoes and fruits in abundance. The distant Himalayan peaks adjacent to Ganesh Himal beckon with a fleeting glimpse.

The jeep track climbs gently through the terraced rice paddies to **Mangaltar**, with its typical houses, neatly coloured by red earth and with comfortable patios at ground level. Shanti village is well known for sugar cane production. The next settlement at **Arkhet** is the second main bazaar of the region en route north, about 45mins along the rough, bumpy dirt track from Arughat. Brahmin, Chhetri, Newar, Gurung and Kaamis are the major inhabitants. Arkhet has two basic lodges.

The dirt route passes below some slender waterfalls and makes one major climb around a rocky bluff en route to Soti. Even this far south you may encounter mule caravans. If you decide to walk part or all of this section, you will find plenty of life in these warm, sundrenched lowlands. En route local teahouses offer *dudh chiyaa* (a wholesome, milky sweet tea), tasty *samosas*, chowmein, beans, *roti* breads and *tarkari* (vegetables). Shady rest stops (*chautara*) for travellers, built under the pipal trees, provide porters with resting places and a chance for the children to meet the strangers.

By jeep, Soti (700m) is reached in about 1¾–2hrs from Arughat – quite long enough to 'enjoy' the delights of the new road. Soti Bazaar is noted for its crystal clear waters and natural pools. The waters are also used to generate local hydro-electric power. Currently the lodges of Soti are: ABC Lodge, Manaslu Lodge, Satkar Guest House, Sanyhaat and one other 'No Name'. Since there is, as yet, no road bridge over the Soti Khola, trekkers can finally tighten up their bootlaces and begin walking.

Soti – Machha Khola (6–8hrs)
Soti – Liding – Lapubesi – Khanibesi – Machha Khola

The trails today are some of the most exposed in the Himalaya. If the idea of walking a tightrope hundreds of feet above a raging torrent scares you, do the Annapurna Circuit instead!

The trekking begins by crossing the Soti Khola, starring a spectacular waterfall to cheer the soul. It's a gentle introductory walk, as the route follows what will become the new dirt road beyond Soti. In 30mins is a small settlement and a former camping site with a lodge. The path climbs a little through woods to another settlement, Kursanibari, also referred to as **Liding** (750m) now. Across the Budhi Gandaki on the towering hillside are views reminiscent of the Annapurna Circuit between Bahundanda and Syange; quaint farmhouses and steep terracing soar to the skyline above the raging river. If you took the jeep today, Liding makes a good first lunch spot, since it is only about a 1hr walk. There is a beautiful waterfall to photograph while you wait for the chapattis to be rolled out. A sign here indicates that it is 1hr 35min to Lapubesi – but it might take longer (2hrs for us).

As if to put you in your place, the trail descends immediately for almost 30mins down through *sal* forest to a landslide area. The *sal* tree has very shiny leaves, but it is the refreshing shade from the sometimes oppressive and unpleasant heat that really makes an impression. High above is an overhanging rocky outcrop called Hawa Danda, meaning 'windy hill', which catches the invigorating breeze.

Ahead are three substantially steep climbs up and down over the high bluffs that dog the west bank of the Budhi Gandaki along here. It's a reminder of why the Manaslu trek is that bit harder than the Annapurna Circuit, for the Budhi Gandaki gorge is cut much more deeply though the Himalaya than the Marsyangdi. Years ago these bluffs posed serious challenges to the trails, often being negotiated on logs sticking out precariously from the cliffs.

The circumvention of the first bluff is particularly exposed; great care should be taken when it's wet and slippery. The path is very narrow and is literally carved out of the solid cliff face, being only about 1m wide. The dripping cloud forest that is interspersed with exposed cliffs all the way to Lapubesi ensures that much of the trail remains damp, wet and slippery. To the east is the high valley of the Richet Khola and a bridging point for the high terraces to the east. Beware of any mule caravans along here! Wait on the **inside** of the trail until it is clear to move on. Apparently there is a fleeting glimpse of Shringi Himal, but with unseasonal showers, we were not graced by the gods to see it. High above to the east is the trail that offers a window on to the little-visited southern ridges of Ganesh Himal, described later.

The first houses of Lapubesi hide the fact that the main area is another 20mins further ahead. **Lapubesi** (884m), also noted on maps as Labubesi, is a substantial settlement and there is a sign here for Khanibesi 1hr. Gurung and Ghale people populate the village, which has a good campsites, lodgings and foodings, a rare health post and drinking water. Water buffaloes are reared here for their rich milk and local shops often sell yogurt, milk and curd. Currently it has three lodges, 'No Name' lodge, Manaslu and Laliguras. From here some respite is had, as the trail undulates for a while, but soon there are more ups. Across the river there is a huge landslide area, reminding one of the impermanence of these fragile lower hills. The dark and forbidding cliffs of Dharche Danda lie high above on the left. Ahead the Budhi Gandaki is wider, with gravel banks and a more meandering, apparently benign nature.

Just here is a sign: the summer trail is ahead while the winter trail is down to the right – the best way onward. Khanibesi is quite a scattered place and the route continues to **Nauli Khola** over a long suspension bridge. Near Nauli Khola there is a prominent rocky outcrop, where people pray to both the river below and the hill above, honouring them as local deities for a safe passage. Ahead are frequent areas of avalanche debris and tumbledown hillsides. Soon there is a super many-stranded waterfall, one of many that characterise the steep-sided gorge. There is a new hydro plant here.

Once more the path is unable to continue straight ahead, owing to the incessant need to climb over yet another steep bluff that drops abruptly to the valley floor. The roar of the Budhi Gandaki drowns out all the birdsong. Encouragingly, some level river flats are ahead, allowing trekkers to amble blissfully along the sandy beaches. Eventually the trail passes beside three isolated chortens together, heralding the arrival in **Machha Khola** (869m).

Machha Khola, meaning 'Fish River', is a rapidly expanding village of two parts – lower and upper. Here flagging (or not) trekkers can find the Everest Lodge, hidden away in the upper area, while in the lower part are the Hotel Chum Valley, New Manaslu and, opposite the Hotel Chum Valley, another hotel, which has some attached loos for added delights!

Alternative trail following the earthquakes

The trail to Machha Khola requires more up and down efforts following the earthquakes, so it will be tougher and longer in time. There are many landslides on the east bank of the Budhi Gandaki here. Although not currently necessary because of landslides, there is a higher trail between Soti and Machha Khola. It might be necessary to go this way if further landslips occur. Unfortunately the route involves a massive 800–900m ascent and descent. The path goes from a little beyond Soti up and up to Amala, then via Lapu, Kanigaon and along the ridge via Lapsibot before dropping to Machha Khola.

Machha Khola – Jagat (6–8hrs)
Machha Khola – Khorlabesi – Tatopani – Dovan – Yaruphant (Bagar) – Jagat

It will be quite another long day with considerable exposure. At the end of the day, Jagat is a welcoming village, so don't despair if your legs are dragging... Watch for animal life along the banks – you may catch a glimpse of the bird-catching stoat.

Stage 1: Soti – Jagat

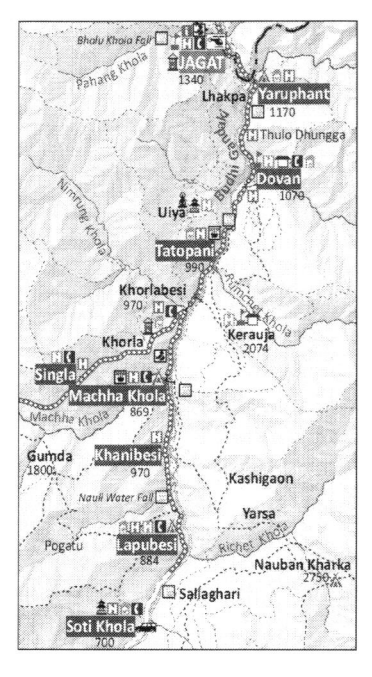

There are two routes out from the upper and lower areas of Machha Khola. Generally it's possible to follow the winter riverbed route with those trademark ups and downs to concentrate the mind. Wild marijuana plants are found along much of the trail before Khorlabesi and beyond. Nepal, of course, was famed for its marijuana in the 1970s, when hippies chose the back alleys of Kathmandu Durbar Square to indulge their lethargic habits. Again there are summer and winter route options en route.

The first part of **Khorlabesi** (970m) is reached in about 1hr. Lodges here are: the Bagaincha Mustangki, the Mustang and a simple Guest House of No Name. Note the coffee trees on the right of the Bagaincha Mustangki, where the enterprising owner has imported the plants from the eastern hills of Ilam so that passing trekkers may enjoy the finest brews. Ask at the house here for Mr Kasiram. In the main part of the village ahead are the Shangri La Home & Camp, the 'No Name' homestay and Manaslu Valley Lodge. There is a sign here for Tatopani 1hr.

The trail heads into a narrow ravine where the Budhi Gandaki is squeezed into a raging bad temper, calmed perhaps only by the lush vegetation that clings to the steep-sided cliffs at the water's edge. Banana trees are still found in these warm, humid areas. To the east is the narrow ravine of the Rumchet Khola. More foaming rapids give testament to the river's pains as it seeks a way south. Smoke-blackened overhanging cliffs en route indicate where traders, porters, mule caravans and local people used to overnight before lodges developed. Just beyond a landslip, where the path is scary

– don't think too much about it – the trail rounds the bluff to reach **Tatopani** (meaning hot water). Here three spouts gush forth their hot nectar, with a strong sulphurous odour much in evidence. Adjacent to the spouts, a small shrine bedecked with poinsettias hosts a nondescript wooden idol. Tatopani has a new lodge to accommodate those needing a night's rest here. A sign provided by NTNC/MCAP states that Dovan (Dobhan) is 1hr ahead.

A side trail at Tatopani to Kerauja links to the Ganesh Himal/Great Himalaya Trail route, passing the settlements of Thingle and Hulchuk. Our trail keeps close to the riverbank heading northwards. About 15mins from Tatopani, cross to the east bank to avoid a tremendous cliff, draped with waterfalls, that blocks the passage ahead. With the smell of marijuana in the air, the trail forges a tiresome but short climb around the spur to the fields of **Dovan** (1070m). Dovan means riverside and thus hundreds of such places are found across Nepal; this one is about 3–4hrs from Machha Khola. Dovan has surprisingly few new lodges. The main one so far is the recently enlarged Himalaya Hotel & Lodge. The village has a primary school facing the once well-used campsite. The Dovan Khola originates from the southern glaciers of Ganesh IV (Pabil).

After Doban catastrophic damage can be seen. The forest has been destroyed and there is a tremendous landslide about an hour up the trail. A new route is being used here. The stupendous cliffs opposite eventually culminate in the upper buttresses of Baudha peak (6672m), which is seen to great effect from Gorkha. Meanwhile the Budhi Gandaki is still cascading steeply down as a thundering cataract, spilling over huge boulders and generally making her presence known. The area around here has been proposed for an ambitious hydroelectric project, but it will take some daring engineering to tame the old girl's waters.

Further along, watch for a few red-berried peppermint trees – a rare encounter. According to Sange, our guide, such peppermint is apparently found in the Everest region near Lukla by those who know what to look for. Once more the trail is cut from the cliffs, but a sign to cheer one up appears: Yaruphant – a mere 1½hrs ahead. The trail here is lined with stinging nettles, so beware: the slightest touch may result in two days of painful tingling. As if that's not enough to make you move fast, there is a demanding climb soon to **Thulo Dhunga**, meaning 'big rock.' And so it is!

Fortunately drinks are on hand at the Manaslu Santo lodge near the 'big rock', 1hr or so from Dovan. Looking ahead, there is a high conical-shaped hill and to the west the Budhi Gandaki is falling more steeply between huge boulders and almost choking cliffs. This step-like fall of the river is very reminiscent of the Marsyangdi on the Annapurna Circuit trek, as it too suddenly leaps down a 'staircase' of drops near Tal. Between Thulo Dhunga and Yaruphant more massive debris has annihilated the old trail. Makeshift bridging points between large boulders have been installed. The Budhi Gandaki is squeezed here and the boulders are almost across the riverbed. It is all a very scary affair to date. Improvements are being made quickly so it is expected to be much better for coming seasons.

Occasional views of the boiling cauldrons and tempestuous rages of the silvery Budhi Gandaki far below are glimpsed. The roaring of the river blocks out the cicadas, who up to now have been a constant companion through the forests. About 1hr from the big rock the top is in sight and the thunderous cacophony dies away.

Up here the meandering Budhi Gandaki is observed flowing serenely beside the settlement at **Yaruphant** (1170m), also commonly known as Bagar. The village is located below a new and menacing-looking landslide.

There is an eye-catching waterfall high above Yaruphant. Sellers offer refreshments to quench your thirst and allay your appetite. Generally in low-water season the Yaru Khola is crossed on a log bridge, although a higher route offers a modern suspension bridge. Shortly after the flats there is a precarious ladder up a cliff, roughly 5m in height, to be negotiated. It can be avoided by taking the higher trail out of Bagar. Impressive views abound in the hemmed-in canyon, with near-perpendicular rock walls soaring skywards. As is common in the afternoons, a stiff wind blows up the valley. The route forges on along a well-made path of large stone slabs before crossing to the west bank. After a short staircase, a sign is encountered indicating a 4hrs tramp to Uhiya on the left. Ignore this temptation.

The first houses, of **Jagat** (1340m), decorated by vivid red poinsettias, are roughly

3–4hrs from Dovan. Jagat is the entry check point of the Manaslu Conservation Area Project (MCAP). Jagat is a very old settlement with neat and clean streets; the trail is paved with massive flagstones. In the centre of the village is a mani wall – the first major sign of Tibetan Buddhist culture. Jagat boasts substantially made houses, teahouses, lodges, campsites, a telephone and the MCAP checkpoint. Jagat means Customs post, and that is what it used to be. Traders from both the Tsum Valley and the Manaslu area paid their taxes here. A sign suggests Salleri is a mere 1hr 20mins hike. Lodges, which have been improved, are the Budhi Gandaki Guest House, the Manaslu Shanti & Camping and the Rubinala Lodge (named after the famous Rupina La pass). The hydro plant has been enlarged.

Jagat – Philim (3hrs)
Jagat – Salleri – Sirdibas – Ghatte Khola – Philim

The normal itinerary for this section would continue to Deng. Here it is broken into two stages, since there are no options for accommodation beyond Chisopani until Deng, a long stretch, and some will be branching east for the Tsum Valley.

The trail after Jagat descends to the Dudh Pokhari Khola. The waterfall is used to generate the local power supply. Again there are high and low water trails here. Cross the rocky bluff shortly after Jagat to a viewpoint of Salleri and its fields of rice and millet. **Salleri** (1353m) is a little over 30mins from Jagat, with a chorten and clean, picture-postcard houses. Cows munch happily on scrubby vegetation. Poinsettias here act partially as fencing for the fields but also attractively decorate the wayside. Local people sit outdoors, weaving baskets and doing their laundry. In the autumn this village is very windy, so every house has protected areas to enjoy the warming sunlight. Trekkers might want to stop here forever, given the arduous trails beyond Deng! But so far there is no suitable lodge here.

The trail leaves Salleri to climb along the west side of the Budhi Gandaki, with glorious but distracting views north of the glittering summit of Shringi Himal and the fine fluting of Langju Himal to its east. Both peaks guard the hidden Tsum Valley. West of Shringi Himal are the Kutang and Nubri regions.

> ## Shringi Himal (Chamar)
> The highest peak of the snow-draped, rocky fortress of Shringi Himal (7187m) is also known as Chamar. Dominating the lower part of the Tsum Valley, it was first climbed in 1953 by a small expedition from New Zealand led by Athol Roberts. Looking at the mountain from the south, it looks a seriously formidable prospect. They chose a route up the northeast ridge from a base camp in the Syakpa Glacier valley north of Domje. Curiously, since then only three further attempts have been made and none have succeeded.

The trail soon descends gently to the village of **Sirdibas** (1420m). This long, spread-out Gurung village has about twenty households with ground floor barns facing the trail. As is common, the trail acts as the communal space for day-to-day living, drying of grain and clothes, and as a children's playground. The typical stone two-storey houses have sunny verandas and shingle roofs. A sign indicates that Ghatte Khola is only 10mins ahead, but first there is a short, sharp ascent just at the end of the village up to the left.

Ghatte (meaning mill) **Khola** is indeed graced with a couple of streams where watermills are grinding corn. By the chorten and mani wall is a sign to Philim – just 45mins up the way. Before this, however, it is necessary to scramble rather steeply up to access the swinging suspension bridge across the Budhi Gandaki. A local teahouse sells rakshi (local tipple), but this is unlikely to aid the trekker on the steep climb ahead! The suspension bridge here is probably the longest one over the Budhi Gandaki and it has superseded an earlier bridge that previously had two big towers on each side.

A steep climb follows, which even the marathon runners walked up (yes, there really is a race around Manaslu!), but in 30mins the large and prosperous-looking village of **Philim** (1570m) is reached. It's a shade less than 3hrs from Jagat to Philim for slower hikers. The Buddha Residential School in Philim is to the far left; this is supported by Japan. Lower Philim is a new settlement primarily focused on the business of trekking. It has a large MCAP conservation office and some new, modern-looking lodges, either already open or about to open. In this lower area, ever-improving lodges are the are the Maila Gest House, Hotel Philim & Lodge, the Royal Garden Guest House and the New Karki Hotel. Two of these can now boast of having cosy cottages and some en suite rooms for the lucky. The opening of the Tsum Valley has helped developments here.

The higher part of the settlement is much further up the hillside and the effort required to reach it is seemingly too much for passing hikers – that is, unless you have an afternoon to while away. There is sometimes a check post operating in Philim. Most of the locals speak three languages: Nepali, a local dialect and Tibetan. People here follow both the Hindu and Buddhist cultures. If you have time, the main village and local gompa at Phrakpa are worth a visit. Continuing on, it is easy to reach Chisopani on this stage; see route description below.

Note: Those heading to the Tsum Valley can reach Lokpa (7–8hrs) from Jagat in one day. The onward description is given in the Tsum Valley section.

Philim – Deng (4–5hrs)
Philim – Chisopani – Eklebhatti – Pewa – Deng

Ahead now the canyon is astonishingly sheer and narrow; dark shadows cling to the eerie western walls. In places the towering cliffs overhang, almost waiting to tumble into the torrid waters below of ice and fire (or should that be Fire and Ice – a well-known pizzeria in Thamel).

The trail out of lower Philim turns left near the Green & Purple lodge, where a sign says Eklebhatti 1hr. The path climbs much less steeply now to an isolated house with a bright blue roof (30mins). The village of Bhangsing is seen high across the valley but few are likely to be enticed over there. A trail from Bhangsing leads to Nyak village and the Rupina La pass.

Chisopani, meaning cold water, is less than 1hr from Philim and can be an intermediate stopover. It's ideal for those arriving here a bit late in the day and not wishing to push on to Deng or Lokpa, both of which would be a considerable distance to make before sunset.

Improved facilities at the two lodges of Chisopani also make it an attractive choice for the night.

Gushing cold water spouts from the hillside, but it's not very inviting for a wash. There is a place called Eklebhatti (meaning one house), which could be any number of single houses. It's probably a place just beyond Chisopani. What is certain is that Gum Pul is 1hr ahead according to the signboard (most have been quite accurate so far). About 2hrs from Philim is the junction that separates the trekkers bound for Tsum from those heading on to Manaslu. Only a sign

Stage 2: Jagat – Ghap

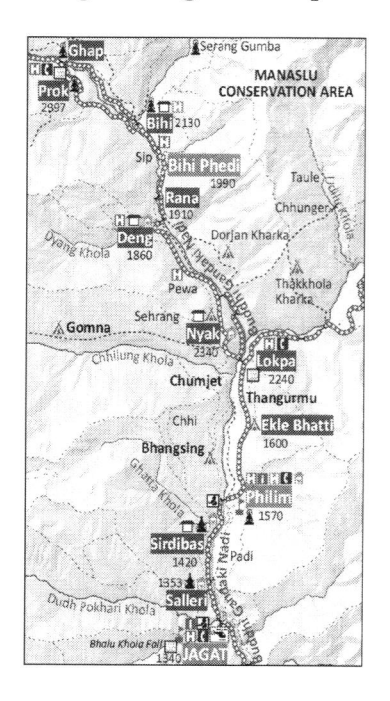

and information board exist here at present.

Heading for Deng, the loose trail drops to the bridge over the Budhi Gandaki and begins a steady climb along the west bank through woodlands and below cliffs. At a junction, a trail to Nyak goes left; today this steep, exposed route has been abandoned by trekkers. Pewa is roughly 1hr 20mins ahead, but it could take longer. There is a new lodge on the right with a few rooms that should be open. It might serve trekkers from the Tsum Valley leaving from Chumling, or others who want a shorter day from Philim. As the path rounds the corner, it enters a deep and sunlight-starved canyon, where the trail is forced to switch from bank to bank to avoid impossibly sheer cliffs. A ribbon of misty green, dense vegetation clings to life here.

After crossing to the northeast bank, there is a short but very steep ascent. Then a more restful contouring stage follows until the next bridge back to the southwest side. **Pewa** (or Bewa) now has two lodges, so that makes for more space in this pleasant stopover with the Manaslu and Rupina Hotel and Lodge, although which part is the lodge and which is the hotel is hard to discern! The trail continues to climb, albeit not too steeply, passing a strange cave-like indentation on the left, sculpted from the loose cliff. A short exposed section ensures that no one can doze off along here, mesmerised by the ever-becalming noise of the river and cicadas. Following another stiff uphill, Deng appears in sight – far ahead – well, not so far ahead as to be depressing.

Meandering high above the river, the path soon enough passes under the entrance kani, but it's still a short, sharp drop and climb into and out of a side-stream before the welcoming hostels of **Deng** (1860m) are reached. There are three and a half lodges in Deng, the blue Manaslu Trekkers Home with soft beds and soft corridors, the Shangri La Home a bit further on and the odd-looking shiny, tin-bedecked Baudha Himal Lodge – a mix of old and new that is sure to improve. The Thakali Lodge rounds off the choices. Deng has solar electricity for dining but no permanent supplies as yet.

Typical Menu at Deng (not all items available)

Cereals cornflakes	Rs150–200
Eggs normal	Rs130–180
Chapatti (2 pieces)	Rs170
Pancake	Rs160–200
Manaslu Bread (Tibetan bread)	Rs160–200
Pasta	Rs200–300
Dal bhat	Rs350–450
Fried veg	Rs180–220
Potato dishes	Rs180–300 (Rosti)
Pizza	Rs300–450
Momo	Rs250–350
Apple Fitter	Rs200
Black Tea	Rs50/130/250/350
Milk Tea	Rs60/160/300/430
Coffee	Rs60/160/300/430
Hot water	Rs40/120/230/300
Pepsi can	Rs100
Room	Rs200–300 per person
Camping group (whole)	Rs500–1000

Deng – Ghap (4–5hrs)
Deng – Bihi Phedi – Ghap

Although most trekkers will make Namrung for the night, some from the Tsum Valley might choose an easier day after the trials of Chumling to Lokpa, with a shorter day's walk to Ghap. Either way, if the morning coffee didn't wake you up, then the exposed trail from Deng barely 5mins from your cosy lodge down to the river surely will.

It is a rude awakening but takes no more than 20mins down to the bridge over the Budhi Gandaki. Now follows perhaps the most frustrating few hours, as the trail climbs and dives continuously all the way to Bihi Phedi. In fact, you never really know where and when you are in Bihi Phedi, since it has at least three separate clumps of houses (or house) along the hillside. But we get ahead of ourselves here – wishful thinking, of course.

From the bridge the trail climbs very steeply, zigzagging for 20mins up to Rana, a small village of separate farmhouses and fields clinging to the abrupt hillsides. At the various junctions the way (unusually) chooses the lower paths. Ahead the trail continues up or down, then passes what could become a new lodge. Chillies were drying on the roof, so we called it Chilly Lodge. After the next stubborn hillock the trail descends into a dank side canyon, where the stream is crossed on a wayward log bridge. Just down on a wet path is an active watermill, where villagers bring their grain to be ground. Soon after this, entering through a kani, one imagines the village of Bihi Phedi is near but all that greets is a solitary but well-made lodge – the Himali Guest House, where drinks are inviting. Is this Bihi Phedi?

Not far ahead is a small mani wall, where an intricately carved stone has images of Guru Rinpoche, Chenresig and Buddha, all in one showing. A not-so-noteworthy sign informs us that Ghap is still 3hrs more – oh no! The Manaslu Hotel & Lodge is another hostel along here, near a map board of the region. Is this Bihi Phedi? Nearby and down to the left is the trail and bridge to Prok, although it looks very dangerous as it assails the sheer cliff's slopes. (A better route heads up from just near Ghap.) Some way above here is Bihi village itself, off the main trail, but on the route to Serang Gompa. Bihi village apparently has a very iconic kani gate, but few will want to make the detour just for that. By all accounts Serang Gompa is quite a large complex of great reverence. It lies a considerable distance up the valley that is topped by the Dwijen Himal, west of Shringi Himal. See side trip below.

Our path crosses the Serang Khola and climbs on again. A new lodge is under construction here, then quiet farmsteads and fields characterise the route. The sheer cliff across the valley still seems to preclude any approach to Prok. Eventually there is a tantalising view westwards towards Ghap, but it remains hidden, as does the mighty Budhi Gandaki, almost forgotten now far below. Continuing on, the path soon comes to the Mountain View Restaurant/Baudha camp, but there is no mountain in view. It's a chilly place once the sun has gone, but was once a busy camping place for groups. The altitude given at this isolated former place of refuge here is 2380m. Looking back, only the lower ramparts of Ganesh can be seen – where have all the mountains gone?

Just beyond the camp is a chorten with some ancient paintings (up inside) and also a small mud building that houses a big prayer wheel. There are no inscriptions of Om Mani Padme Hum on the wheel, but the paintings around the walls are presentable. Just before Ghap the Budhi Gandaki's foaming fury is crossed once more.

Ghap central (est. 2250m) is home to the New Budhi Gandaki Guest House and a few fields. Fortunately the lodge is well run and clean, even if drinks are pricey. Also in Ghap, the new Kuthang Longha Stonebridge Peace Guest House, a nice wooden-looking lodge, is now open (kpeacehotel@gmail.com) with wifi (maybe!). Try saying its name after a long hard slop up the Budhi Gandaki! Upper Ghap is 10mins further on and that is barely more than the small Manaslu Camp area (and probably a lodge one day).

High above the tranquil meadows of Ghap is the monastery of Kwak, said to be virtually abandoned now. It is just visible with the naked eye. To visit **Prok** from Ghap central here you need to head west to the big rock adjacent to the rest of Ghap and take the trail left back uphill. (A couple of smaller paths shortcut the access to this trail on the left before the big rock). The trail is quite lonely and perhaps best not done alone. A welcoming chorten for Prok stands stark against the skyline.

Side Trip: Bihi – Ghap (2–3 days) via Serang Gompa
Bihi – Syarang – Serang Gompa

Unlike Bihi Phedi, which must remain an enigma rather than an entity, **Bihi** (2130m) is a 'proper' settlement with many small gompas situated on its hillside. Bi Gyahu is another village yet higher up. The most famous side trip from here is to visit Serang Gompa, one of the largest gompas in the Kutang valley, situated below Shringi Himal. We did not have time to visit Serang, Prok or the Kal Tal lake, but the following notes have been written from notes supplied by Sonam Lama and Lopsang Chhiring Lama.

The trail for Serang Gompa follows the eastern bank of the Serang River for about 3hrs before crossing to the west bank. A tough 500m climb ensues, to a small village known as **Syarang** (about 3hrs from the riverbed). This section of the trail is rocky, and characterised by many mani walls. This is because the famous Tibetan sage, Guru Rinpoche, is believed to have established this trail. Syarang village and the region of Kutang are famed for the skills of the local stone carvers and sculptors.

En route the Golpon Gompa is located on a small hillock with beautiful views. The trail from Syarang passes through a kani and then enters some forest as it climbs to over 2000m. **Serang Gompa** is just after a deep gorge; it is situated in the valley between two glaciers tumbling from Shringi Himal. There are a number of interesting kanis, chortens, finely-carved mani walls and a cave monastery. Two watermills owned by Serang Gompa are located another 3hrs walk away.

Serang Gompa

Serang is the most important and the largest gompa in Kutang. It is also known as 'Beyul Kyimulung', 'the hidden lands of happiness', established by Guru Rinpoche (Padma Sambhava). The cult of the 'hidden valleys' is found, where the faithful take refuge at times of strife and when warding off the enemies of the Dharma. Here they hope to find a land of peace and plenty, places that are usually located in isolated and inaccessible places throughout the Himalaya. Both Serang Gompa and the Kyimulung area have so far escaped the notice of the outside world, because they lie at some arduous distance from the main routes. Serang literally has two different meanings. 'Ser' for gold and 'dang' for fly, thus meaning a golden fly. It is also called 'Serthang', which translates as 'golden field.' The architecture of the complex is similar to other monasteries in the whole region, with its trademark tiered pagoda style. Small rooms for the monks surround the main temple, while the nuns' quarters are below. There is another temple close to the kitchen and the central building of the principal lama.

Serang Gompa – Ghap

The way back to the main trail is the same until 30mins before Syarang, where a different path leads to an ancient mule route.

This trail proceeds through oak forest and ascends to over 3000m, from where you can see Manaslu to the west. There is also a panoramic view of Prok and the Budhi Gandaki valley. Along the quiet trail you might encounter Himalayan Tahr and with luck, many different birds – Himalayan Griffons and Lammergeyers. More finely carved mani walls feature along this trail to the settlements of Kwak, Lau and Chhak. Four rocky hilltops joined together here are called the 'four sisters', waiting to welcome travellers. Chhak and Kwak villages, plus a spectacular waterfall named Taiul, are located on the hills of the four sisters. The route descends across the open but sometime precipitous hillside to a bridge over the Budhi Gandaki River to reach Ghap.

Side Trip: Prok & Kal Chhuman Lake
Ghap – Prok – Kal Tal Lake – Prok – Ghap

Prok (2397m) is a large village with more than 50 houses. It has a primary school, five gompas and a gorgeous waterfall along the Tarang Khola, about 20mins walk from Prok. Prok village is characterised by flat and gently sloping meadows and dense, little disturbed forests below the Rani (Lidanai) ridge. The towering ridges of Lapchun Himal are on view across the Budhi Gandaki. From Prok, the panorama includes Ganesh Himal to the east and Shringi Himal to the northeast. The access route from Ghap to Prok is described above.

Day hike: Kal Chhuman Lake/Kal Tal

Kal Chho (Lake), also known as Kal Chhuman Chho, is probably the largest lake in the eastern Manaslu area. This beautiful lake is situated at an altitude of 3574m east of Baudha and Himalchuli and is surrounded by birch forests. There is a gompa at the western end of the lake – the Kal Chokang monastery. A trail around the lake offers magnificent views of the mountains as well as showing the diverse flora and fauna. Since the altitude gain from Prok on this walk exceeds 1000m, it will take a full day to reach the lake, explore its shore and perhaps visit the monastery – if it's open. According to some trekkers who took this option, visitors are required to engage a local guide in Prok for the trip, since 'outsider guides' are not permitted to act as guides for their clients here.

Ghap – Lho (6–8hrs)
Ghap – Namrung – Banjam – Lihi – Sho – Lho

Today the way ascends through pleasant leafy forest on pine needle-cushioned dust rather than rocky trails. Forest stages are interspersed with a few demanding steep stone staircases. The Budhi Gandaki continues its thunderous descent, plunging through the chasms below. It's quite possible to reach Lho from Ghap in a longish day. Namrung has lodges and food. With the villages of Lihi and Sho en route, there is plenty of variety to savour. New lodges are expected to be finished in both villages soon, giving more choice of overnight stops in future.

Just 10mins from central Ghap is a large rock and a sign for Namrung 3hrs. Prok is up to the left as mentioned. It is a further 20mins to the Kyimlung Camp & 'Hotel'. The 'hidden lands of happiness' remain firmly hidden, for the time being at least. High above Ghap and the trail to Lihi are the jagged ridges and furrows of the Kutang Himal, draped by glistening dollops of ice. The sheer immensity of the sublime rock faces is hard to believe. The trail enters quite dense forest of blue pine, oak and rhododendron and, indeed, it stays within these woodlands all the way to Namrung, making a pleasant change.

Roughly 45mins–1hr walk from Ghap is an interesting natural stone bridge carved by the flow of the Budhi Gandaki. In a clearing nearby, where the river is funnelled into a narrow chasm, is a mani wall and small waterfall. A new, grand-looking lodge is being constructed in the clearing. The forest is a delight, with tall trees and wispy lichens. Some trees are well over 2m across in diameter. From another clearing there is a view east of Shringi Himal, glistening in the morning sun.

The trail passes beneath a large overhanging rock and crosses the Budhi Gandaki again. Despite the continuing charms of the forest, the relentlessly steep uphill path is less glamorous with some exposed sections. Quite a big change has occurred before Namrung, where a new landslide means a detour uphill – even more uphill, that is! The trail now descends into Namrung (2630m) just for fun (perhaps an added 100m+, so not so bad really). The village has small shops, new lodges, camping areas and a somewhat obscure security check point. Lodges here at the moment are: Thakali Guest House, Namrung Guest House and Manaslu Tibetan Camping. The new Nubri Four Seasons Resort (Four Seas-On Resort) will be open by now with an attached... museum! Round the corner down the hill and up again are the Thakali Hotel and a new 'No Name' Lodge. At the sign it says Banjam is 30mins, although we took 40mins – 'tail-end Charlie' yet again!

In Namrung the people are mostly of Tibetan origin, with a unique Sino-Tibetan dialect. The village houses, as a rule, are more closely knitted together with dry stone masonry. **Banjam**, though, is a spaced-out place of fields and flat areas. To the east, Ganesh Himal is beginning to lose its shyness and pops out from behind the ridge at last. Banjam sustained substantial damage unfortunately, but will surely bounce back soon, so look out for the Nubri Trekkers Inn. A sign indicates Lihi 1hr 15mins further on. Make the most of Banjam's flat path, for the next stage to Lihi is almost all steeply up. Only those eastern views of Ganesh provide any respite from the upwardly mobile track – if you are still mobile.

Lihi (2920m), Li or Ligaon is a beautiful village of houses, roofed with pine shingles. There is a small gompa, which is unlikely to be open, and a new lodge is going up nearby. The three-tiered chorten has some old paintings and the people are pleased to see a visitor, although it's quite a sleepy place. There is no view other than that of Ganesh to the east. However, close by is the well-hidden Hinang glacier valley, a spectacular sight for anyone with the time and energy to explore this long glen below Himalchuli. **Hinang monastery** can be visited by following a small trail heading into the forest, taking 2hrs to reach it along the bank of the Hinang River.

North of the main trail, the great 1500m vertical walls of Kutang Himal utterly dominate the valley. **Sho** village (2880m) really is just over 1hr from Lihi. Sho has some rustic (old!) houses and a small

Timeless occupations

> **Tong Monastery**
> This gompa is an elaborate place with chortens, a new-looking lhakhang adjacent to the old one and an array of prayer flags. To reach it from Sho, one needs to have patience, for, although it's not far as the crow flies, for lesser beings (un-winged and perhaps unhinged!) there is a rather huge descent to cross the Budhi Gandaki, followed by an equally daunting steep ascent to the gompa. The Budhi Gandaki gorge is so deep here that we are not even sure if there is a bridging point far below, so please check with local people about access to this apparition of a gompa across the valley. Nasa Gompa is even further up the hillside and it is very unlikely anyone will be found for the key.

gompa. It is quite spread-out and, after the ravine, is a big prayer wheel set in a mini gompa. There are some new paintings in here; arhats or learned men feature in some paintings. Milarepa is by the door with his hand to his ear.

In Sho a sign tells you it's about 1hr 20mins to Lho. Ahead now is 'upper Sho', with one lodge on the right side of the path. There are also a couple of gompas opposite Sho, on the north side of the valley across the river.

Approaching Ghap

Lho Ribang Monastery

To reach the monastery, take the trail to the left at the junction above the village. The 'shortcut' route is steep but short as it zigzags up the hill. Less than 30mins is needed to summit the Lho Gompa hill by its daunting east face. A large courtyard greets the visitor and normally many novice child monks are in residence. At the time of our visit 150 children were present; most were between 6–10 years old. The combined noise of these boisterous young students should surprise no one. There are three female teachers and students come from all over Nepal, including Dolpo, Manang and the East. Morning puja generally starts by 8.45am and involves the usual chanting and horn-blowing (much more pleasing to the ear than the horn-blowing trucks of Kathmandu!).

Inside the main chamber of the monastery are some impressive paintings – of particular note are the many wise sages wearing a multitude of hats. In one corner is the Rinpoche's retreat and in the other the altar. Books are set each side of the three main idols – Chenresig, Sakyamuni Buddha and Guru Rinpoche. Above the doorway is a fearsome blue Mahakala and on his left is a fanciful version of Palden Lhamo on her horse. To the right of the doorway, a gruesome-looking image of Yamantaka guards the gates to the after-life.

Behind the monastery is a small hill; an amazing view west towards Manaslu, Manaslu North and Naike Peak is gained from this loftier vantage point. Returning to Lho, the best way is to exit the monastery to the north through what will be its main entrance (near the stupa and gateway). This way down is mostly wide but quite steep to the western end of Lho, where it rejoins the main route to Shyala.

The trail now ascends and traverses to a false kani gateway. It then climbs on to another entry kani and eventually up to the main settlement of **Lho** (3180m). When the trademark summit cloud is banished from Manaslu, its twin peaks utterly dominate the beautiful village of Lho. There is also a stunning view to the northeast of the Sauli peak of the Kutang Himal, a great sheer-sided lump with a crowning icefield. Apart from Manaslu, dominating Lho is Ribang Gompa and some impressive chortens and mani walls. In the centre of Lho is a colourful new stupa, and there are a couple of good lodges. The large Tashidelek is well used to the needs of trekkers, since it has been looking after mountaineers for years. Another Tashi Delek Lodge and the Gurkha Manaslu Homestay are other options. Everyone should plan on a night's stop here to savour the sunset, the even more impressive sunrises and visit the monastery complex. In the mornings there is a great viewpoint; go up through the village to a junction. Go right to a chorten and further up near yet another chorten to the bank of prayer flags. This place gives an unobstructed view for great sunrise photos of Manaslu, Manaslu North and Naike Peak – they glow a fabulous orange/red as dawn breaks.

Stage 3: Ghap – Samdo

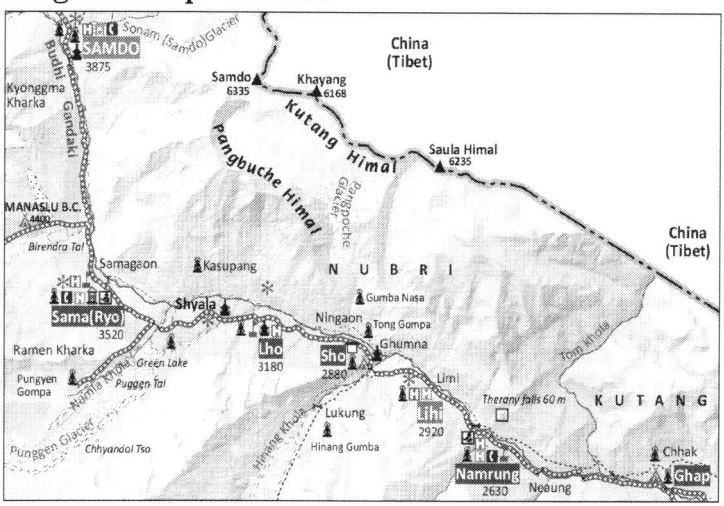

Lho – Samagaon (3–4hrs)
Lho – Shyala – Samagaon

Glacial rivers from the Punggen valley have carved out the intervening ravines between Lho, Shyala and halfway to Samagaon. In late autumn, red berry trees offer a splash of colour in contrast to the green and brown of the landscape.

Soon after leaving Lho, the trail drops steeply down and around before climbing back up above the braided streams to the west. There is a landslip area to negotiate and the river is crossed on several log bridges, so be careful in case they roll. It is not unusual to encounter yak trains here carrying timber, some of which used to end up in Tibet. The route passes a hydro plant, but power is a luxury that this area has yet to keep functioning. Much of the way is through trees and there is a fleeting view south towards the ridges of Ngadi Chuli (Peak 29). It is a brief, stiff climb up to round the spur. A vast new monastery complex is glimpsed through the trees – Hongsangbu Gompa. It is well worth the 10–15mins detour. The new buildings have a glorious view of Manaslu. Much of the work in all spheres was done by the well known Boudha Lama, Chokyi Nima.

Surprisingly, it can take up to 2hrs to reach **Shyala** (3500m) from Lho, but the walk is full of interest so it's no great ordeal. The houses of Shyala are well made, but there has been quite a lot of deforestation. There is a community campsite and two new lodges for the growing bands of trekkers. The original lodge is the improved Gurkha Manaslu Lodge, with a friendly lady who will feed you delicious pancakes. It is next to the large new school that will soon dominate the main street.

Shyala makes a good stopover, because the views of Ngadi Chuli to the southwest are outstanding. It's quite hard to determine the highest point of the Ngadi ridge as it stretches towards Manaslu (8163m). Another good idea is to stop in Shyala, then climb to Pungyen Gompa the next day en route to Samagaon, providing you don't have a heavy pack. It will save 30mins or so each way when compared to backtracking all the way from Samagaon.

> ## Ngadi Chuli
> Previously named Peak 29, Ngadi Chuli (7871m) is a formidable lump set between Himalchuli and Manaslu. The mountain has even been called Dungapurna (Dung-apurna!), but this name seems to infer a lowly status. Again it was the Japanese who set their sights on this peak, as they did with Manaslu. In 1970 a Japanese team of Hiroshi Watanabe and Lhakpa Tsering were last seen on the ascent of the mountain via the East Ridge. They disappeared, and it is not known whether or not they reached the summit and died on the way down. So as far as is known, it was first conquered by a Polish team in 1979, when Ryszard Gajewski and Maciej Pawlikowski reached the top via the West Ridge.

The trail climbs slightly from Shyala but soon drops down to an icy river that also originates from the glacier of Pungyen (Punggen). The route climbs back up to the next spur beside the raging icy torrent via a wooden bridge. The junction for the trip to Pungyen Monastery is about 45mins from Shyala on the left after this climb. From here it's mostly downhill to **Samagaon** (3520m). Samagaon (Sama) is sometimes known by the name Ryo. Ambling down now, the path passes the new school and soon drops into the large village. All around are the stone walls that the people of Samagaon have made to delineate their fields. After the entrance kani gate, which had to be rebuilt after the earthquakes, the path drops to a large enclosed area a bit like a last resting place for mani stones.

Inside the courtyard is a large prayer wheel enclosed within four beautifully painted walls, along with a series of statues including Guru Rinpoche and an unusual red deity, plus a typical large drum. There is also an imposing chorten with those mysterious eyes that always seem to be watching.

The houses in the main street have two storeys, with the ground floor given over to animals. The people live on the next level, taking advantage of the heat generated by the livestock. The chickens do not obey the rules, though, and can be seen fluttering up to the first floor in search of drying grains. Typical features are stone walls topped with layers of firewood. A beautiful stream runs through old Sama, where children 'lark' about and old women weave in the morning sun. One clump of houses of Sama dominates the rest, set on a small mound that appears to have once been a fortified area. The houses have neat shingle roofs; tin is not yet much in evidence.

The tourist enclave is to the west of the village. First up is the Tashi Delek Lodge and then a new 'No Name' Guest House near the public toilets that were always locked. The first public toilets on entry were also always locked – it would seem that no one in Sama ever needs to go! Opposite the friendly check post are the pleasant Samagaon Lodge and the Peace and Heaven. We are not sure if the 'Heaven' part related to the great view of Manaslu from the back or the toilet – also conveniently out of the back door on the same level as most of the rooms. The poshest place in town is the Hotel Manaslu with a heated dining room and new guest rooms having attached bathrooms: www.mountmanaslu.com

This is the real place of peace and heaven! It's well used to looking after mountaineering expeditions and has lots of tinned food supplies. (Ah... real heaven, fruit and meat instead of chapattis, rice, pasta and potatoes...)

Because of syndicates and committees in each village, menus and prices are fixed, so regardless of quality, you will pay the same for your noodles wherever you eat them, and the same for your mattress, however thick or thin. This 'closed shop' theme does not really have the desired effect of being fair to everyone. It simply means that there is no financial incentive to provide a better service or facility, because, as we frequently heard, 'the tourists will come anyway'. It could have the undesirable consequence that trekkers rush too fast to get to the better 'must stay in' lodge.

A temporary trade route

In November 2015 around a thousand yaks from the Nubri area were allowed to go to the Tibetan border at the Rui La (4998m) above Samdo for 10 days of intensive trading. The reason for this vast caravan of activity isn't sure. There was a blockade on the Indian border at the same time!

> **The Mani festival**
> This festival takes place every three years and lasts for several days during the late autumn or when the local lama decides it's an auspicious time. The opening day is marked by loud horn-blowing and the traditional masked or fancy-hatted dancers. These Cham dances are performed all over the Himalayan Buddhist region, from Bhutan to Ladakh; some commemorate the defeat of Buddhism over the Tibetan Bon faith. Mani festival, Cham masked dancing here, is similar to the Mani Rimdu festival of the Everest region, an event that is one of the most famous in Nepal.

Day trip: Pungyen Monastery (5hrs roundtrip)
Samagaon – Pungyen Gompa – Samagaon

The trip can be done as a roundtrip from Samagaon or with light backpacks en route between Shyala and Samagaon. The description below is from Samagaon. The trail beside the Pungyen (Punggen) glacier river is exposed and icy winds can make it a bitterly cold valley after mid-morning. There is absolutely no sustenance en route, so take food and water. The monastery may be closed.

It takes 30mins to return to the junction for the gompa en route towards Shyala. Head up right here – past the small chorten. The path, through juniper scrub and small pine trees, soon comes to a second small chorten. From here the climb is steep and often exposed. The trail is loose and narrow; climbing up is much easier than descending. The path climbs below a sheer cliff; later there are a couple of options but both meet higher up. About 35–45mins up are another chorten and some prayer flags, marking the end of the hardest part. Ahead is a gigantic wall of ice and rock – part of the Simnang Himal ridge that looks massive enough to be Himalchuli.

In fact, Himalchuli (7331m) and its accompanying vast icefields are hidden from view behind this great whaleback of a ridge

(Himalchuli will be obvious from higher up above Samdo). The vast ridge complex of Ngadi stretches into the valley westwards, although the true summit of Ngadi is also masked from here. Behind, however, is no such conundrum, for the Kutang Himal peak of Sauli Himal (6235m) is ever more impressive. Its great ice dollop and western glacier are superbly illuminated as they catch the morning sun. Further down the valley to the east is Shringi Himal, but it will be better photographed in the afternoon.

The trail reaches a small shed in 1hr or less from the main trail. After a small kharka there is a flagpole knoll to the left which offers a better view; it's just off the main trail. While you are off the trail, it's worth climbing for a few minutes to the top of the moraine to see the Punggen Tal – 'green lake' within the massive rubble banks and ice of the Punggen Glacier. The dead and dying glacier is an amazing sight and on a grand scale. It's best to return to the main trail from here, since the moraine top is cloaked with tangled juniper and bushes that make any forward progress messy.

The path continues to wind around to the west beside the moraine on poor meadow and up through boulders. Mostly the going is not steep, although one short section is rather demanding. Eventually the valley opens and the moraine is left behind and to the south. A collection of sheds offers some shelter or respite from the wind once on this flat valley floor. If Manaslu is not hiding behind its guardian top cloud, it must be an amazing sight from here. Sadly, we were not privileged to see this view. However, the vast ridges of Ngadi are enough to satisfy most mountain buffs, especially if the frequent avalanches are active. At this point the monastery cannot be seen, and it's a daunting prospect thinking the gompa is up yet another ridge, as most monasteries are in Nepal.

About 15mins from the sheds, across small icy streams, is the first sighting of the gompa. **Pungyen Gompa** is about 2–2½hrs from Samagaon. With a picturesque, photogenic chorten on the plain in front of it, the gompa sits serenely at the foot of a cliff while two small chapels cling to the lower slopes of the cliff behind. The monks are housed in a simple, small shed; the whole complex is quite strange in that it is nearly all set out on the open plain rather than on a hilltop. Through the misty glass of the locked main gompa, images of Guru Rinpoche and Chenresig can be discerned, but that is about all. Apparently the lama had gone to Samagaon for the festival on this occasion. In any case, few trekkers would come up here just to see the small monastery, since it is the fantastic scenery that really makes the day so enchanting.

Before leaving the flat valley area, there are a couple of small ponds to be seen close to the edge of the glacial moraine. The view from the crumbling edge is also quite astonishing, since the sheer size of the ice and rubble-strewn glacier is phenomenal. The return trip takes up to 2hrs, but beware of those exposed steep sections beside the Punggen Khola near the bottom of the descent. Although at some distance and partially hidden by trees, pause to take in the panoramic view of the Hongsanbu monastery complex near Shyala on the way down.

Samagaon – Samdo (4–5hrs)
Samagaon – Birendra Tal – Samdo

Before leaving the village, take time for a brief side trip to **Samagaon Monastery,** set on the hill west of the lodges. A short climb through the scrub takes you to the main courtyard. The views of Manaslu and its glacier are well worth the effort even if the gompa is locked.

The trail from Samagaon to Samdo crosses 'relatively flat' land, although at this elevation even the smallest hillock seems an effort. Heading north, the views of Manaslu behind get ever better. West of the main trail is the hidden **Birendra Tal**, a glacial lake where ice blocks tumble into the lake with thunderous displays. The lake can be accessed either directly from Samagaon or by diverting briefly from the Manaslu Base Camp trail. This path heads left from the main Samdo trail about 30mins north of Samagaon just before a field 'gateway'. Himalayan Tahr often frequent the lake area and the lower slopes that climb to the Manaslu Base Camp, a full day's excursion from Samagaon. Snow and ice often prevent casual trekkers from reaching the lower ramparts of Manaslu and the designated base camp area.

Manaslu (8163m)

The first attempt to climb Manaslu was by mountaineers from Japan, who sent out an initial reconnaissance party in the post-monsoon season of 1952. The following year an expedition set up base camp beyond Samagaon, but their attempts failed at about 7750m. In 1954, another Japanese team approached the peak, but they were met with hostility at Samagaon, when the villagers claimed that the gods had been angered by the climbers on the previous expedition. A huge avalanche had subsequently crashed down from the peak, destroying Pungyen Monastery and killing 18 people. Such was the ferocity of threats by the Samagaon villagers that the mountaineers were forced to retreat to Ganesh Himal. In 1956 on 09 May, Manaslu was climbed by another Japanese expedition under Yuko Maki, when Toshio Imanishi and Sirdar Gyaltsen Norbu Sherpa reached the summit. Since then Manaslu has continued to attract all manner of mountaineers and adventurers, even some who would ski down its vast snowfields. A Japanese team successfully climbed the peak next in 1971 via the northwest spur, followed by the first European (Austrian) team led by Wolfgang Nair. Kyoko Sato led the first successful Japanese women's expedition in 1974, but one climber died on the descent. Manaslu, though, is no slouch, with its bitter winds, dogged spindrift plumes and bitter, unpredictable weather.

The dangers of Manaslu are well documented, since it is one of the more menacing Himalayan peaks. Apparently there have to date been around 300 ascents of Manaslu and with 53 deaths it is recorded as the fourth most deadly 8000m summit after Annapurna, Nanga Parbat and K2.

Small clumps of alpine birch and rhododendron cast wispy shadows along the path for a while. The route soon crosses a wooden bridge, where the trail is marked by mani walls. Looking up the valley towards Samdo, the views of the eastern cliffs of Samdo Peak (6335m) (its Tibetan name is Pang Phuchi) are beautiful, serene and almost surreal. At ground level, the odd marmot scurries about, peeping from a cosy hole – cosier than many lodges. The trail continues to climb to a small rise, passing various forlorn-looking kharka shelters. Down the valley, Himalchuli appears more impressive by the minute.

After 3hrs or so, following the west bank of the Budhi Gandaki, the river is finally crossed. A stiff uphill climb ensues on to a nearly level plateau area. The last part of the climb is gentle, but the effects of the altitude here are kicking in as the entrance kani of **Samdo** (3875m) is reached. The village of Samdo was established during the 1950s Chinese move into Tibet. The people were originally from Ro, a Tibetan region close to the border. The sturdy houses of Samdo are made of dry stone walls and roofed by stone slabs. Juniper mesh has been used on the verandas for protection from the wind. The ground floors are used for yaks, dzos, dzopkios and horses, their hot breath keeping the inhabitants on the first floor warm. The local people spend their days working in the fields, collecting firewood and watching their yaks. watching their yaks.

Samdo now has four lodges, including the Yak Lodge, Tibet Lodge, Tashi Delek and the Chez Karsang run by a joint French-Tibetan partnership. Other facilities include telephone, internet and freshly-cut ice for those cocktails!

Also in Samdo, just above the lodge suburb, is the Samdo Mothers' Association, where a small shop sells handicrafts during the main season. The traditional 'pangden', for sale sometimes, is the colourful apron woven by the women and worn by married ladies. For information about the project, see www.samdoavenir.org

Side trips: Samdo hill and Border regions

Samdo Hill

For a less strenuous outing, the hillsides north and east of Samdo offer some pleasant exercise without burning up too much energy before the pass. The village of Samdo should be explored, of course, since it has lots of intriguing dark corners. It's almost worth making a phone call from the 'phone house', buried in the area below the monastery, just to see inside a typical house – a call to Kathmandu (affectionately known as Katters or K-town) is Rs10 per minute, but may be up to Rs30 for a foreign devil, so get your guide to make that call.

Heading east, a trail of sorts leaves the village from the northeast. The slopes are relatively easy if contouring and there is a chance of seeing snowcocks and other fowl darting between juniper patches. The barren and rugged Mayol Khola valley here leads eventually to the Lajyung La pass into Tibet. Pang Phuchi peak has a sheer-sided northern aspect and guards the whole valley with a sharp eye. Local people can usually be seen heading into the high meadows to graze their yaks, and perhaps in late May search for the yarsagumba treasures, so much desired by the Chinese.

Also above Samdo on this hillside are a couple of chortens that sit on the windy ridgeline. The trail up the spine of the ridge is steep, dangerous and loose underfoot, so it's better to contour back towards it from the less severe hillsides. The upper chorten is surrounded by thick juniper bushes and stands aloof. This ridgeline offers some great views towards the 'bottomside' of the Larkya La and of Larkya

What is Yarsagumba?

Until a violent incident over the collecting rights of the local villages occurred in the Nar-Phu valley a few years ago, the name yarsagumba hardly registered beyond the high villages of Nepal and in Tibet. Yarsagumba is one of the strangest plant/animal matters on the planet – it's only found in places almost off the planet – in the Himalaya at a height of around 4000m–4500m. Its worth is ever-increasing to US$60,000 per kilo, at the time of writing, more than the price of pure gold! The caterpillar lives underground and is infected with spores that seep through the ground and eventually kill it off; it metamorphoses into a dead entity with a sprouting, telltale pointed growth that barely protrudes above ground level. Harvesting of this strange object is normally during May and June, when whole villages become deserted as the local people forage in the high tundra for the treasures.

Himal. The staggering, tooth-like summit of the main Larkya peak, above razor-sharp cliffs, is clearly home to some evil demons. This lofty abode is an inviting place for those dastardly demons to lurk while waiting to prey on trekkers who haven't acclimatised.

For the first time on the whole trek there is an inspiring view of Himalchuli, with its sun-starved north faces. Continue up the hillside as far as desired, since the slope has no obvious cliffs en route, but be ever-careful in these remote areas.

Himalchuli (7893m)

Although Himalchuli looks spectacular from the Kathmandu Valley near Kirtipur on a clear day, its summit line is never properly seen on the approach march to Samagaon. The best views of Himalchuli are normally reserved for trekkers descending from Ngadi village to Besisahar on its southwestern flanks. The main peak of three is a touch under 8000m and the mountain has an amazingly complex system of ridges, peaks, snowfields and glaciers. The highest peak was first climbed by a Japanese team in 1960. Subsequently Himalchuli North submitted to a Korean team in 1985. It seems that Orientals have a strong connection with the three main summits of the Manaslu trek. Great views of Himalchuli can be had from Daman, on the old Hetauda–Kathmandu road, the Rajpath and also from Bandipur near Dumre.

Tibetan Border Area

Follow the trail from Samdo towards Larkya Bazaar and the Larkya La for 20mins and then head into the northern valley. The countryside is bleak and barren, but has that certain mystical charm that so inexplicably endears visitors to Tibetan landscapes. Chhenge Lake is on the east side of the valley further up, and continuing north it should be possible to get a view of Gyala Peak (5973m) and the glaciers that drape these northernmost mountains. We were not able to explore these areas because of the problems created by the unexpected closure of the Larkya Phedi/ Dharamsala lodge. Apparently some trade still continues with Tibet, but on a much lower scale than in the pre-1950s. The easterly Lajyang Pass is relatively low at 4998m.

Samdo – Larkya Phedi/Dharamsala (4–5hrs)
Samdo – Larkya Bazaar – Larkya Phedi/Dharamsala

Putting an accurate time on this walk is a fool's game, since trekkers have such a wide range of abilities at sea level let alone at this high altitude. It's not a time to larkyabout! The only way to attack this walk is not to attack it, but to plod slowly, methodically and without over-breathing (just a minute: some might say without hesitation, deviation or repetition – only a few might need to do some repetition).

Stage 4: Samdo – Bimthang

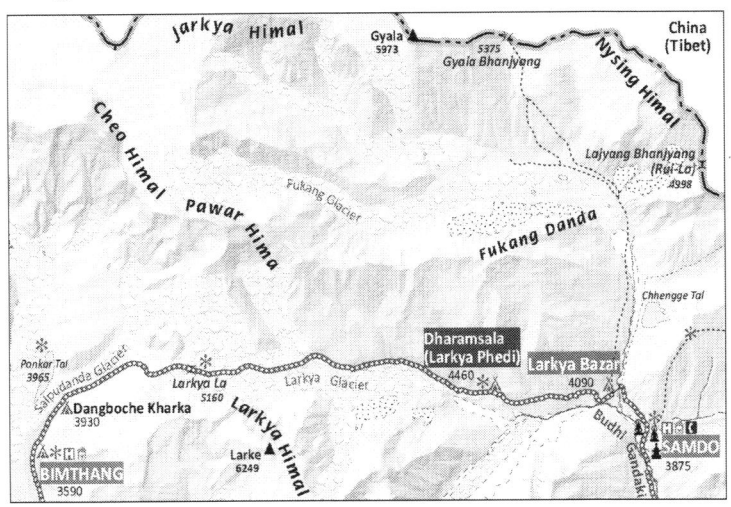

Leaving Samdo, the trail skirts the fields and drops to cross the Budhi Gandaki for the last time before heading west. The ancient settlement of **Larkya Bazaar** at the 'bottomside' of the pass was located here and used by traders. People from Tibet once exchanged salt, wool and meat here for rice, barley and wood before Tibet's status was changed.

A steep ascent ensues. It's a deceptive climb, which appears easier than it actually is. The path climbs in and out of small side-streams where ice may linger and the slopes are sometimes loose. These side stream ravines get bigger the further up you get. Before Larkya Phedi there are a couple of massive, sandstone ravines that make for some steep and 'jolly stiff' uphill sections – always try to walk at a pace where breathing is controlled and regular, since it aids acclimatisation if you don't get too puffed. The landscape is characterised by thorny berberis bushes and juniper; yaks, who never seem to breathe heavily, graze very close to the glaciers. Keeping your head down on this walk is inevitable, but be sure to gaze around; the mesmerising scenery will make you think you're hallucinating.

Pang Phuchi seems to be growing in stature and the great north wall of Naike looms. Looking to the south further up the trail, there are fabulous views of the Syacha Glacier as it tumbles from the knotted spires and rock faces of Manaslu North. This arctic vision captures the mood perfectly – it really is the home of the gods and demons here. As you get higher, the summit peak of Manaslu can be discerned high above the blue ice of the highest icefalls. Shortly after losing this view, the path reaches **Larkya Phedi** (4460m), which captures a different mood after sundown!

Larkya Phedi is also known as Dharamsala (meaning pilgrims' rest house). There are hundreds of places called Dharamsala across the Himalaya, so it's fitting that this one should be singled out as Larkya Phedi to distinguish it from all those lesser ones that are not so hard to reach. Phedi of course means 'bottomside' of a pass. Larkya Phedi has this vital but very basic lodge that is divided into 5–6 buildings including the bedrooms, kitchen, dining area and porters/yak dung shelter. In high season you may see and need to use the overflow tents – army style. Real group campers can find water and flattish spots – but not that flat.

The current lodge is adequate but in no way comfortable, with thin mattresses and icy nights. Food is basic and expensive, with only potatoes at the season's end, perhaps, if anything. Everyone needs to drink a lot of fluids at this altitude, which is also costly but essential. Enjoying the convivial atmosphere with fellow trekkers, all pumped up with anticipation of the joys to come, is the best aspect of the short night ahead.

The short night is one of the main pluses in this arctic tavern. Sleep is a luxury.

> ## The Pony Express
> It may not be the planned form of transport for crossing the Larkya La, but a pony can do wonders for those not so well acclimatised to the altitude. Currently a pony and pony man will cost Rs14,000, a fee that is fixed by the Samdo syndicate and whose members rotate in taking guests – just like a taxi rank at Delhi airport. It is a lot of money, but think about the added costs of retreating back down the Budhi Gandaki and all those ascents and descents to repeat. It is also quite risky for the pony men, since the track to the Larkya La is very rocky and ankle-twisting – especially if you have four ankles to twist. (Better to have four ankles of your own and no horse really, for this pass!). Normally the pony express trip is for two days, with the overnight at Larkya Phedi en route as for 'normal' trekkers.

With the Larkya Phedi lodge closed, we undertook this mammoth trip by pony. However, it was still necessary to cross all the icy streams on our own two feet and walk up several steep, exposed sections – so it's no picnic in the park. Close to the top of the pass the trail skirts an ice lake that ponies cannot cross. The rocky zone below the top cairn is also impassable for them; you will inevitably have to walk the last few hundred metres. Ponies will not descend to Bimthang either, as the track is too steep. En route the ponies seem to know the way without much input from the jockeys; just hold on near all those drops into the frozen lake. Jockeys need to lean forward on the uphill bits, and backwards on the small descents. If you have a heavy rucksack on, these manoeuvres can be quite 'exciting'. Ponies must normally be taken from Samdo, since Samagaon ponies are not allowed by the Samdo syndicate to take their business. If you do get one from Samagaon, expect to change mounts in Samdo!

Larkya Phedi – Bimthang (6–10hrs)
Larkya Phedi – Larkya La Pass (5160m) – Bimthang

The big day has arrived and its 3am at Dharamsala – or is it Larkya Phedi? No one has slept a wink and can't wait to arise from their slumbers – except the lodge staff perhaps. Breakfast passes unnoticed in the fog of high altitude waking – it's probably hardly worth eating, but 'needs must', for everyone should drink plenty and eat as much as is possible here.

On the Thorong La pass in the Annapurnas, trekkers are recommended to start just before dawn, but here things are different. It is desirable to start early in the morning for the pass because of the incessant icy wind that usually blows up by mid-morning. Most trekkers depart by 4–4.30am. Walk as slowly as possible, in order to conserve energy and to appreciate the day's attractive scenery later without stress. This is also particularly important for those who may find that they have not acclimatised so well, despite time in Samagaon and Samdo.

The approach to this pass is not geographically sympathetic to good acclimatisation. Elsewhere, it is easier to acclimatise properly by ascending in incremental steps involving only 300m of ascent per day – the recommended height gain – as in the Everest region. Here the steps are from Samdo (3875m) then Larkya Phedi (4460m) and then the pass 'topside' (5160m). This is why some may need, if not want, that extra night at the Larkya Phedi Motel.

The trail goes through the ablation valley on the north side of the Larkya glaciers, a particularly awesome and dread-locked region. However, despite this forbidding aspect, the mountains are sensational the whole way to Bimthang. The pass is notoriously cold and windy, so it will be vital to wear adequate clothing and wrap up with a scarf to breathe through, preventing some dehydration. Take all those essential snacks and loads of water in case it becomes a very long day. Remember your torch and spare batteries.

RISK: Remember altItude Sickness Kills:
descending is the only safe cure, day or night.

From Larkya Phedi the track climbs to a small meadow with a small stone shelter and on to the base of the whitish, rocky moraine. Working its way along the side of the moraine, the path is not so steep at this juncture. The unforgiving altitude, however, makes it seem hard. The barren hills to the north mock the gasping passing trekker, offering no hint of the gorgeous glaciers and peaks to come. Eventually the moraine bank is cleared and far below to the south is a vast icy lake (it could be turquoise in the early autumn season or in spring). The ill-defined glaciers and debris here drain the main Larkya Peak (6250m) and ahead is the amazing 'Eiger Sanctuary-like' but infinitely more extreme wall of Larkya Himal. Now to the north is the desolate-looking peak of Pawar Himal, an extension of the Cheo Himal wall. It has a curious red band that goes almost unnoticed by those who need to watch their footing constantly.

The trail ascends steadily for about 3hrs through the moraines. Smaller frozen lakes are encountered; watch out for possible sightings of bharal – blue sheep. As for the snow leopard, it may never be seen but the yeti might, as you hallucinate your way ever upwards. The chaotic jumble of massive boulders and rocks is astonishing – it's hard to work out which moraine belongs to which glacier. There is one rough stone shelter amongst this great mass of rubble. Eventually the trail climbs on a steeper trajectory towards the pass. The rock-fields are seemingly never-ending, with some false rocky ridgelines, then a small lake heralds the beginning of the end. The path makes a final lurch up to the summit cairn, with prayer flags being ripped apart (on most days) by icy winds that chill in an instant. Wrap up warm to avoid being freeze-dried!

For most it takes 4hrs or more to reach **Larkya La pass** (5160m) from Dharamsala. For those who still have any breath here, the views from the top will take it all away. To the east are Pang Phuchi and the Larkya Himal wall. To the west are the fantastic pyramid of Himlung Himal and the sheer ramparts of

Cheo Himal. Before the descent begins, there is a short, almost ludicrously exhausting, traverse to a second clump of flags and cairns. These too are being slashed by the frigid demons of the wind. As the descent begins in earnest, the views are sensational. A great arc of mountains appears – peaks that dominate the eastern side of the Nar-Phu valley of the Annapurnas.

From left to right are the tent-like pyramid of Kang Guru, draped by beautiful snowfields, then the little-known peak of Chombi. The great contorted icy knot of Nemjung is next and to its north are the enthralling faces of Himlung. Cheo Himal is on the Tibetan border northwards, but it is soon partially masked by a very sharp, black outcrop. A little way down the steep and unnerving icy slope, there is a shelf. To the southwest is the great whaleback ridge of Lamjung, with Annapurna II – the star performer – peaking up above the ridges.

Much of the trail can be slippery because of ice in early spring or late autumn, and after sporadic storms. Trekking poles are a real boon here. The trail cuts a steep route down the first moraine with a brief respite across a small icy stream, then the steep descent continues down another vast moraine. Care is needed here. On the way a beautiful view of Ponkar Lake appears. This high-altitude glacial lake, sometimes inhabited by hardy ducks, is a pleasant day hike for the next day. Three immense, chaotic, rubble-strewn glaciers meet just adjacent to Ponkar Lake, but that point is still a heck of a long way down. Up here you are still above 4500m and close to the domain of the dastardly demons – so tread warily. Don't lose your concentration dreaming about the balmy, golden beaches of Bali or the sumptuous chocolate cakes of Bavaria down here!

About 2hrs down, just off the steep moraine wall, is a small patch of grass where a picnic lunch might be in order even if it is 4pm – that dried-up frozen chapatti. The trail soon drops through juniper bushes into the territory of Himalayan crows, ravens and snowcocks (and people). The going is much less steep, following the base of another moraine alongside the Salphudanda Glacier. The glaciers here are a jumble of rock, ice and weedy vegetation, with pools and lakes dotted about.

About 30–40mins down this pleasant slope the path dives off to the left, zigzagging downwards more steeply. Fortunately the slope soon eases and follows the base of the Ponkar Glacier, which has now merged with the Salphudanda Glacier. Bimthang can finally be seen clearly not far ahead (or its lights can, if it's already getting dark). The trail is still surprisingly rocky but eventually the settlement is reached. **Bimthang** (3590m), literally means 'plain of sand'.

Historically these meadows were popular with traders from Samdo, who used to come here for the salt and to keep their animals in the winter. Bimthang has excellent new lodges plus good camping sites. In the morning the views are sensational, with Himlung and Cheo Himal northwards and the snowy ramparts of Manaslu, with its constant companion, Phungi Himal (6538m), seemingly blocking the way to the south. The lodges of Bimthang are delightful, with 10cm-thick mattresses and superb food. This is another world and a 'great leap forward' in luxury on this side of the pass. There are four lodges to choose from: Ganga Manaslu Lodge, Hotel Ponkar Mountain, Tibet Hotel and one other new one. Bimthang old city consists of a few stone houses.

Day hike: Bimthang – Ponkar Lake
Bimthang – Ponkar Lake – Bimthang

This side trip to the Ponkar ice lake just north of Bimthang requires care and attention, owing to the rough nature of the terrain. It essentially crosses the moraine and lower reaches of the Salphudanda Glacier. It is a short distance to hike, but it's tiring because of the altitude and the constantly moving rubble of the glacier. The three great glaciers below the cirque of peaks are the Salphudanda, Ponkar and the Kechakyu Khola Glaciers. Views from just above the lake are said to feature all those notables of the previous exhausting day – Cheo, Himlung, Nemjung, Manaslu and Lamjung. Most trekkers are content to have a leisurely day after the privations of the pass; this day trip is most definitely not one of those!

Bimthang – Kharche/Surki (3–4hrs)
Bimthang – Hampuk – Yak Kharka – Kharche/Surki

Even the early morning crowing of the roosters and the chirping of birds may not be enough to wake you up after a good night's slumber following the exertions of the pass. Some spend a morning relaxing in Bimthang, but if clouds rise up by noon you could miss some unexpected, exceptionally stunning mountain views. Before leaving Bimthang, climb the small ridge south of village for a view of the picturesque blue/green lake below the moraine.

The trail heads south from Bimthang down beside the moraine for about 30mins to a holey bridge. It then climbs over another small moraine to the main bridge over the fledgling Dudh Khola River, as it emerges from the long-distant snouts of those three glaciers. From the top of the moraine, across the bridge, there is a sensational view of the enticing and encircling peaks, Larkya Himal, Manaslu North, the great chunky mass of Manaslu and sky-piercing Phungi, as well as Nemjung, with a sharp spire on its southern flank, Himlung and Cheo. The sheer rocky cliffs of Manaslu and Phungi are clad in quite dense forest of cedar, blue pine, oak, birch and rhododendron trees. The unique feature of this high altitude forest is its age – said to be more than 1000 years old.

One of the most beautiful stretches of forest – of rhododendron, spruce, oak, cedar, juniper and birch – on the whole trek graces the morning descent. Some of the trees are around 2m in diameter. The forest boasts a diversity of flora from orchids to strawberries, while humming birds and colourful butterflies dart from tree to tree. The general stillness of the forest is enticing and very calming after the tribulations of the pass.

From open glades in the beautiful forest, dappled by willowy sunlight, more amazing peaks are spied. A vast glittering cirque of fluted walls and icy summits appears – part of the long ridge that runs from Manaslu to Larkya Peak. One peak is shimmering with vast, broken ice fields and glaciers; apparently its name is a mystery to mapmakers. (At 6416m it sits – soaring above the Dobhan glacier.) Locals call Larkya Peak the guardian of Manaslu, but which dreaded demon needs guarding the most? Underfoot, soft spongy pine needles carpet the path, replacing those punishing hard, rocky apparitions called trails, close to the abode of the gods. If paradise exists on earth, just for a brief few moments, it surely is here in this wispy, wind-in-the-willows forest on this morning after the harshness of hell's gate – the Larkya La.

The trail climbs high above the Dudh Khola River with more panoramic views; a landslip area requires another short climb up and over. The artistically sculptured snow fluting on the great cirque above is some of the most impressive anywhere in Nepal. High above to the west are the great buttresses of Kang Guru, the peak once more hidden from view, as it is from almost every angle on every route. The trail descends further near to the bank of the Dudh Khola, where red rocks are commonly seen. Ahead is yet another Yak Kharka, literally meaning pasture with shelter for the yak herders. There are many places called Yak Kharka in Nepal. This 'Yak Yak Yak' Kharka is between 2–3hrs from Bimthang, depending on how long you are mesmerised by the views. The pleasant teashop at **Yak Kharka** has been improved into a good lodge.

Masses of dead trees clog the river bank, suggesting there have been many floods in the valley of the Dudh Khola (or Deadwood Khola perhaps). The trail continues down, sometimes gently, sometimes stiffly, to a long landslip zone and then the isolated houses of **Kharche/Surki** (2700m) are seen down the valley. The Suti or Surki Khola is crossed on a fine bridge into Surki, where the Saat Kanya Hotel is set to greet you. It's a comfortable option with great mattresses. A few minutes further up into the meadows is the resort-like Himalayan Cottage Hotel. Both are quite charming.

Kharche/Surki – Dharapani (4–5hrs)
Gho – Tilje – Thonje – Dharapani

Dawn in Surki brings more views, but soon the forest trail hems in the walkers. Throughout the morning, the view ahead opens down the length of the valley, all the way to Dharapani, where the busy Annapurna Circuit trail is joined.

Stage 5: Bimthang – Tal

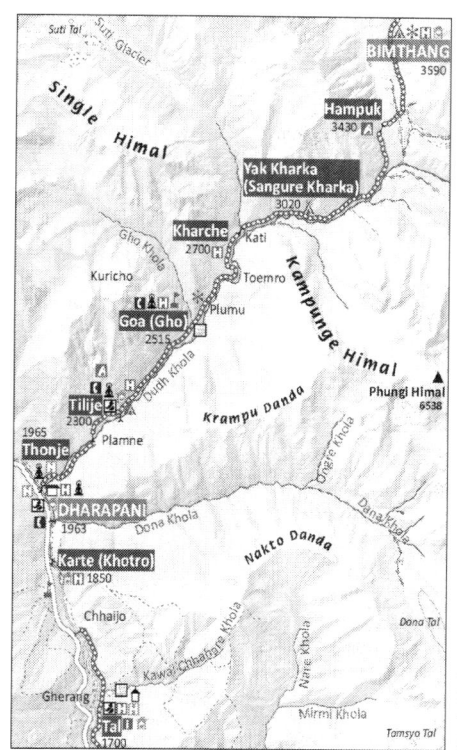

A sign marks Bimthang behind, but for most, it's not the arctic pleasures that anyone craves now, but the warming air of the lower Marsyangdi Of course some may already be heartbroken and missing the Larkya Phedi lodge! It's an easy stroll down to the houses and fields of Gho village.

Gho, Gao or Gowa (2515m) has four very well-designed lodges. One is the Hilltop, an elegant place with four attached rooms and four not (toilet-free!). Gho has a phenomenal number of ponies and horses. The hydro station is just before a suspension bridge on the right. The power-house also supplies nearby Tilje. After the bridge and lower down is the large and functioning Hotel Manaslu.

The route continues down with a few ups, mostly through fields, but also through some dense forest where bamboo is in evidence. Tilje (or Tilije) is less than an hour's march below Gho. **Tilje** (2300m) has a very mixed ethnic population of Ghale,

Within 15mins of cruising along the river bank the trail begins a very steep but mercifully short climb to a spur that almost blocks in the Dudh Khola, below to the left. The path drops and the eastern jagged and often snow-covered ridge of Lamjung can be seen clearly. Tilje can just be discerned down the valley, which is surprisingly straight from here southwards.

Gurung, Chhetri and Tibetan people. People here often speak two languages as well as Nepali. The picturesque traditional architecture of Tilje is also mixed, with buildings constructed in wood and stone. The stone pavement is extensively used by the locals for drying grains as well as for drying children, who must always find water to play with and pretend to splash foreign intruders. foreign intruders. Tilje now boasts six lodges, including Tibetan Hotel with Mountain Top, Hotel Choyu – it's a long way from Cho Oyu! The Apple Garden Guest House is a super spot for a drink. And what's this on the sign... Organic vegetables, hot showers, comfortable beds... Are you still hallucinating? Tilje has a small monastery near the Apple Garden. The main idol is Chenresig. Tilje is less than 3hrs from Kharche.

The route crosses the river, passes wheat fields and reaches the large school, where the children should be studying instead of splashing the trekker – we don't mind really, do we! Almost immediately after the school, the path becomes a dirt 'road'. No need to worry about traffic on this road yet, though, as it is not yet joined up to Dharapani. A few landslips might cause road builders some headaches, and a lot of blasting or bulldozing is still required, but the wide track makes for easy walking. In less than 45mins Dharapani is in clear vision but there is, in the already nostalgic tradition of the Manaslu trek, one more steep up (and one more steep down after the suspension bridge) to battle with. The mobile phone calls and text messages are coming thick and fast for our guide Sange, and we are not yet at Dharapani.

'How is your health? How is the weather? How are your ancient trekkers? How was the Larkya Phedi lodge; was it open? Who's the Prime Minister now?' Modernity!!!

The path drops into **Thonje**, a small village with an attractive monastery. At the junction go left, under the kani by the stupa and across the Marsyangdi up 80-odd stone steps into **Dharapani** (1950m) to join the main Annapurna Circuit trail. A new lodge is located close to the Marsyangdi River by the bridge just before Dharapani. A jeep is spied at the check post. The dirt motor road now continues to Manang.

Our Manaslu trek is sadly ending soon. It is quite feasible to reach Tal from Dharapani on this day, since it's only another 2hrs walk down the Marsyangdi valley, especially if following the near-empty jeep dirt/rock road.

Dharapani – Chamje (3½–4hrs)
Dharapani – Kharte – Tal – Sattale – Chamje

From Dharapani, trekkers have the option to continue on the Annapurna Circuit. This adds another 7 days or more to Jomsom (for a flight or bus to Pokhara); trekking on to Tatopani and up to Ghorepani takes another 6–7 days more. Most trekkers completing the Manaslu Circuit follow the Marsyangdi River down to Besisahar. Although the dirt road has been opened south from Dharapani, it's a much better option to follow the old trail to Tal and Chamje (the road journey is very scary high above Tal).

Leaving Dharapani, there are stunning views of the Dona Khola falls. From Kharte one can continue on the quiet new road or along the trails down to **Tal** (1700m). Beware of high winds if using the sometimes narrow trail to Tal from Kharte; one trekker was recently blown off the path.

The village is located on the sandy banks of the Marsyangdi River, with some superb bathing pools. Tal is hemmed in by sublimely sheer cliffs with the sky virtually shut out all day except at lunchtime, when trekkers can luxuriate in the warmth and enjoy the speciality of the village – pumpkin and bean curry (especially good at the Peaceland Guesthouse, who grow their own organic vegetables behind the hotel) – a real taste of paradise. Tibetan refugees settled here and run many of the lodges. The prayer flags, mani wall and chortens of Tal indicate it to be the last Buddhist village on the trek; from here on the people are nearly all Hindu. Before leaving, have a look at the little monastery. The Nyingma-pa monastery has images of those iconic triplets: Guru Rinpoche with Chenresig and Sakyamuni.

From Tal the trail drops steeply beside the Marsyangdi, which also plunges dramatically at this point right between the Annapurna and Manaslu massifs. The 'road' on the west bank looks horrendous, with sections blasted from sheer 800m cliffs – anyone fancy a rollercoaster ride in a jeep? However, it does make some sense for trekkers to walk the road from Tal to Chamje, since it is truly a mind-blowing option for views. It is also an exceptional example of Nepali engineering at its best – this road was completed and opened with breathtaking speed! It takes 2hrs or so to walk to Chamje.

Stage 6: Tal - Bhulbhule

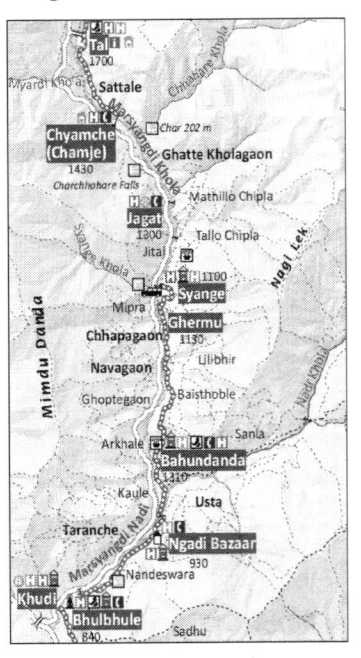

The 'road' can be accessed from either the foot bridge at Tal and the steep path, or by using the new road over the Bailey bridge and a less steep zigzag or two.

If following the old trail, drop from Tal beside the raging cataracts of the rapidly descending Marsyangdi. Lower down is Sattale, a small place inhabited by Gurung and Magar – the main village is higher up among the terraced hills. Take care on the trail down, then cross the main river and climb up to **Chamje** (1430m). Chamje (also called Chamche) is a small village with well-managed lodges. Ask someone at the hotel to phone the jeep operators for you to see if space is available on the next arrival in Chamje. Jeeps take around 3hrs from here to reach Besisahar, while trekking via Bahundanda will take a couple of days.

Chamje – Besisahar (2–3 days)
Chamje – Jagat – Syange – Ghermu – Bahundanda – Ngadi Bazaar – Bhulbhule – Besisahar

For many people the rather scary prospect of riding a jeep on these freshly blasted rocky roads is worse than riding a pony. Fortunately the classic trail is still in use and goes via Bahundanda and Bhulbhule for 'real' trekkers. The route keeps on the dirt road from Chamje through Jagat to Syange but then crosses to the east bank and climbs up through millet fields to Germuphant and Kanigaon. Ahead is a climb to Bahundanda – the hill of the Brahmins. The descent to Ngadi is easy and soon after the trail descends pleasantly to Bhulbhule. Most will take the bus to Besisahar. The Mount Kailash Hotel is comfortable, although others will be equally keen to take your business.

Should anyone be intent on completing the full circuit, then read on below:

Bhulbhule – Gorkha (2 days plus)
Bhulbhule – Simalchaur – Tarkughat – Luitel Bhanjyang – Gorkha

Perhaps the days of doing the full Manaslu Circuit from Gorkha and back are over, since jeep roads have somewhat diminished some sections. For the record, the following notes outline what was formerly the favourite option.

From Bhulbhule the trail climbed around the bluff overlooking Khudi through **Simalchaur**. The route followed the often-sweltering Marsyangdi through the villages of **Bhanjokhet**, opposite Besisahar and **Phalesangu**, near the new hydro dam lake. In springtime the valley was no place to linger. The route continued southeast to **Tarkughat** and then finally some minor respite from the humid lowlands was enjoyed with the crossing of the **Luitel Bhanjyang** after **Tadi Pokhari**. The final stage climbed (of course!) from the depths of the Dorandi Khola to **Gorkha**. Allow up to four days for this extension.

And with that we can conclude our trek around Manaslu.

Tsum Valley

Introduction

The Tsum area can be divided into three distinct zones. The lower, entry region is wild, forested and steep-sided, as one would expect of a lost world. The main populated zone of Upper Tsum is generally flattish, with a gentle upward slope going north. The valley here is quite wide, but is hemmed in by amazingly sheer-sided cliffs. Most of the villages are found in this fertile zone, where potatoes, buckwheat, winter wheat and barley are grown, along with mustard. The fields are separated by dry stone walls for protection against the wind. Walnut and apple trees prosper in the climate of the valley. Higher up beyond Nile and Chhule is the Tibetan region, where the landscape is dry, arid and reminiscent of the Tibetan plateau, with barren hillsides and soaring, strangely eroded mountainsides.

Planning

> Just as a white summer cloud, in harmony with heaven and earth freely floats in the blue sky from horizon to horizon following the breath of the atmosphere – in the same way the pilgrim (trekker) abandons himself to the breath of the greater life after, that leads him beyond the furthest horizon to an aim which is already present within him, though yet hidden from sight.
> **Lama Anagarika Govinda, The Way of the White Clouds**

There are two ways to plan this trek. Both require a guide or porter/guide, and taking an extra porter is advisable. Don't expect your staff to carry as much as normal, because of the nature of some sections of the trail. Carry emergency food supplies that do not require cooking, so that you can have a picnic lunch anytime, anywhere. The most comfortable way to trek is with a fully supported camping crew. This allows more flexibility, with altitude, accommodation and food issues eliminated, but it does cost more. A few local Nepalese agencies and a limited selection of western trekking companies can organise this style of trek. It is perfectly feasible to arrange this trek as a lodge trek, and it doesn't cost much more than 'lodging treks' on the main trails of the Annapurnas, once permits are arranged. Whichever way you do it, be sure to ask whether your crew members have been there before.

Bring heaps of your favourite treats, plus loads of chocolate/power bars/glucose tablets for energy. Some might want to indulge by bringing their own tea or coffee, peanut butter, marmite/vegemite and muesli bars. There is no food anywhere between the night stops of Lower Tsum or above Mu Gompa. Food in the lodges is simple but adequate for a week or so, particularly if supplemented with your own reserves and favourite goodies. Medical posts – what are they?! There is currently electricity everywhere on the trek, but bring extra camera batteries. You can extend the life of your batteries by warming them inside your clothing.

Itinerary and routes

The region is still remote and very exciting. Some trails above Lokpa and before Chhokang Paro are especially challenging, with some stages narrow, exposed and loose underfoot. There are, of course, sections of path that are a pure delight – through cool pines, across dry meadows dotted with sweet-smelling juniper and beneath the sublime cliffs of the Himalayan peaks. Surprisingly perhaps, the trekking in Upper Tsum, beyond Chhokang Paro, is pleasantly easy. That said, it is imperative to obtain proper insurance for both yourself and your crew. This is no place to have an accident, so care and concentration on the way are vital. Helicopter rescues don't come easily or cheaply.

Most villages now have a homestay option or a lodge of varying standards. Although the general altitude of Upper Tsum is between 3000–4000m, there is no real difficulty in planning, because the villages are very close together between Chhokang Paro and Nile/Chhule. Once acclimatised, the route is moderate.

According to officials, it is not permitted to head north from Mu Gompa, although groups and individuals have been doing this. Part of the problem lies with the fact that the local people trade extensively with Tibet through to the town of Kyirong. The Chinese are naturally wary of letting foreigners too close to the border and the traders do not want the border to be shut. You should seek local advice if planning to go to the border areas. If the situation allows foreigners to reach the Ngula Dhojyang pass, you will need to carry sufficient food, and in any case it will be necessary to camp on route.

> **Festivals**
>
> Being totally within the Buddhist zone of Nepal, the Tsum Valley inhabitants participate in all the regular Buddhist festivities; Losar, Buddha's birthday, Guru Rinpoche's birthday and the various Cham dances. A celebration called Panda occurs in the village of Yarcho above Chumling in February, while a version of Mani, similar to the one in Samagaon, is celebrated in Ripchet village during April. Ngungne is widely celebrated across Tsum in Nile, Chhule, Phurbe, Rachen, Mu and Piren Phu. The festivities of Nara (Khangsar Ladrang) are held in Chhokang Paro and at the isolated cliff-clinging monastery of Chi Phu.
>
> All the main monasteries have a festival in the early monsoon called Gumba Dhupa Chhe Ji. The riotous Dharchyang horse races are held in Upper Tsum in late September into October. Around the same time is the Gumba Ngile Ladrang. Also in the autumn, a celebration takes place at Milarepa's Cave that is unique to the valley, according to local homestay people. Nara Jhong takes place at Gonhgye monastery above Chhule in late November. The twin villages of Ngakyu-Leru hold the Nga Ladrang Nara in December.

Route description

The following description assumes that most visitors are using lodges or homestays for overnights. Campers will have more varied options. Trekkers heading into the Gumba Lungdang and Ganesh Himal area of Tsum so far need to camp for optimum comfort and achievability. Only the monastery of Gumba Lungdang can provide any lodgings at present. Options are sure to appear soon for lodgers, so check in Domje.

Tsum Valley Trek Summary	
Start	Bridge below **Lokpa** (est.1700m)
Finish	Below **Lokpa** (1700m)
Distance	approx 80km (50miles)
Time	6–14 days
Max. altitude	**Dhephyudonma** (4000m) or **Ngula Dhojyang Pass** (5093m)
Trekking style	Basic lodges, homestay or camping

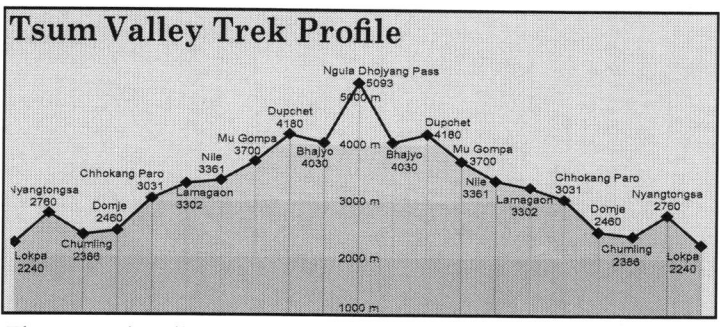

Tsum Valley Trek Profile

[Elevation profile chart showing: Lokpa 2240, Chumling 2386, Nyangtongsa 2760, Domje 2460, Chhokang Paro 3031, Lamagaon 3302, Nile 3361, Mu Gompa 3700, Bhajyo 4030, Dupchet 4180, Ngula Dhojyang Pass 5093, Dupchet 4180, Bhajyo 4030, Mu Gompa 3700, Nile 3361, Lamagaon 3302, Chhokang Paro 3031, Domje 2460, Nyangtongsa 2760, Chumling 2386, Lokpa 2240]

The stages described in the following routes correspond roughly to daily marches, but levels of acclimatisation could modify some days.

Jagat or Philim – Lokpa (6–7hrs)
Jagat – Philim – Chisopani – Lokpa

Reaching Lokpa from Jagat in one concentrated day is quite feasible. For comprehensive details of the route from Jagat to Philim and on to Chisopani, see the description for the Manaslu Circuit. The trail for Lokpa branches away from the main Manaslu Circuit route just before the Budhi Gandaki suspension bridge, about 2hrs from Philim. Apparently an old trail used to climb from Philim through Anga and Serjong to Lokpa, the first village in Lower Tsum. With only one lodge at Lokpa so far, and nothing else nearby, options are limited and so is space between the beds – a sting in the tail if it's overfull. However, Lokpa is a good place to catch up with descending trekkers and hear their recommendations and tales.

From the signboard 'Welcome to Tsum Valley' and junction, the path climbs steadily up through blue pines with a few narrow sections to excite the mood. Far below, the trail to Deng and the old route to Nyak can be viewed with some smugness, for this is the start of a big adventure off the main route. Higher up is a great view towards the Kutang Himal. Monkeys may watch your progress up here.

The trail zigzags up around the spur and reaches a concrete kani gateway, about 1hr from the turnoff. Soon the gradient eases and a lone house is reached. The forest is still dense ahead, but within 30mins the single building of **Lokpa** (2240m) is attained – the New Tsum Hotel & Lodge. It is not the most spacious residence, with creaky floors, a steep staircase and tiny bed-sized rooms, for which all are nonetheless grateful. The food is passable and there are twelve beds. Guides and porters do not seem to like this place, since they do not have good accommodation. The main settlement of Lokpa is higher uphill, lying on the old trail, and has limited agricultural land planted with potatoes, maize, beans and wheat.

The lodge has a soaring view of the delicate snow fluting of Ganesh II's outlier peaks of the Tewa and Lumbo Himal. Eastwards the dense forest is watched over by sheer cliffs and the narrow ravine of the Siyar Khola that looks like a dead end – a bit like Lokpa itself, really. The river might really be called the Shar Khola, since it comes from the east.

Lokpa – Chumling (4–5hrs)
Lokpa – Sardi Gorge – Sardi Danda – Gumlung – Chumling

This is a harder than expected day, as the route goes up and down steeply several times, on rough rocky trails high above the river. Look out for raptors circling above, searching for any unfortunate animal (or human) that has slipped to its death off the almost vertical slopes of the whole valley. Having crossed the final bridge, rest assured that it's all uphill now to Chumling! There are no tea shops before Chumling, so no lunch; take a chapatti or two from Lokpa.

Stage 1: Lokpa – Chhokang Paro

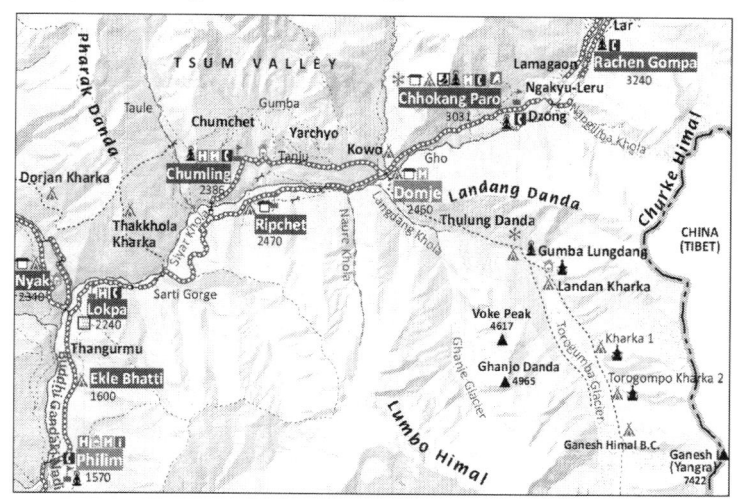

From Lokpa the trail slowly descends into ever danker and darker forest, but only for a while to a bridge. At a small junction, ignore the lower path that heads to a dodgy log bridge, and continue up right. Soon the way comes to the new bridge over the Sardi Khola (Sarti Khola). The Sardi Gorge is a forbidding canyon with soaring forests and menacing-looking cliffs all the way to the sky. It is roughly 40mins from Lokpa. The route descends to the Siyar Khola riverbank and becomes narrow as the defile eclipses all sunlight. A gaily painted Buddhist vision of heavenly mantras is seen across the river. There are a series of holes in the rocks, where the salt traders once used ropes for precarious progress along of this part of the route. Luckily today a new trail has been built. It is now cut from the sheer cliffs; soon begins what will turn out to be a never-ending, relentless climb upwards in the dense forest.

Chir pine, rhododendron, bamboo and all manner of dense forest trees, lichens, ferns and mosses enclose the path. The rhythm of the trek is becoming apparent – walk all day, doze all night, wake up smelly, go to bed smelly, eat occasionally, wash – never! The constantly climbing trail rises for roughly 500m and the path is always steep. There are a few stone plinths providing places for porter loads, thus giving hikers a few minutes of respite. Close to the top, where the trail goes over the vertical cliffs of the spur, it's necessary to be very careful, especially on the loose path stones. On one section, dubbed by us 'Damien's corner' (where we met a Belgian mountaineering philosopher friend), there is a rocky section with some exposure. Damien had been attempting to climb Ganesh, but the gods are pretty petulant on this mountain range for most assailants, as its highest summits have hardly ever been climbed. See box later.

Wide-winged vultures and Himalayan Griffons circle above these ghostly crags. Eventually a spectacular vista opens up – the southeast ridges of Shringi Himal. Spectacular waterfalls cascade down the lower ramparts of the mountain to the valley below. A very dangerous route on the northern side of this valley, once taken by our porter, Tenzing, has been all-but-abandoned due to its extreme exposure – it linked Chumling to Deng. No sooner is the summit of this climb reached than the path descends steeply again. The descent continues for about 1hr down to a stream and the bridge across the Siyar Khola. It takes 3–4hrs from Lokpa to here. The abandoned, ransacked and vandalised teashop will probably be re-established here at Gumlung. A signpost marks ways to Chumling left, 45mins, and Ripchet right, 1hr 45mins. The trail to Ripchet is steep, in poor condition and best saved for the way down for those with time. Ripchet also has much easier access from Domje, so at this stage of the trek, head across the bridge to Chumling.

The path climbs up the hillside on reasonably graded slopes and it does indeed take most hikers 45mins to reach lower **Chumling** (2386m). The village is spread across the hillside in clumps of dwellings. Almost blocking the path, the Tsum Ganesh Himal lodge is at present the only lodge. A beautifully fluted snow cone, part of the Ganesh II northwest ridge, is glimpsed high above from here. It turns a brilliant, bright red at sunset. However, before that there is time to explore the settlement.

Just before the suspension bridge along from the lodge a path leads up to the left, passing chortens. A few minutes up is a large chorten displaying some good, detailed paintings, including a Samantabhadra Yab-

Yum – that's the picture of the couple embracing on the right. A bearded wise sage is next to them, looking very much like the hero of Bhutanese Buddhism, the Shabdrung. A blue Mahakala guards the chorten and there are images of Buddha, Vajrapani and what appears to be a blue Medicine Buddha. Higher up the trail is a clump of houses with a small, closed gompa topping it off. Beware the 'dog patrol' here and across Tsum; most canines are chained up, but not all. A three-tiered beige-coloured chorten is imposing and the mansion-like house below in the field illustrates a degree of prosperity for those sustained by the rich, fertile nature of the agricultural land here.

Heading across the same bridge near the lodge and climbing up, there is another small gompa, but the dog patrol won't let anyone too close. Some way beyond central Chumling is another large beige-coloured stupa and monastery, but it is hard to visit, being far away and up ill-defined country paths. Chumchet, Gumba and Yaarchyo are isolated hamlets or single buildings seen from Chumling, miles up the hillsides and also hard to visit without a longer stay. One can image that a great view of Ganesh Himal could be had from somewhere above Chumchet. The slopes of Shringi Himal are sheer and imposing above Chumling and a strange gash has been cut across the south face by water and ice. The local hydro plant is set below these cliffs and rock walls. The settlement of Ripchet – locally known as Rhipche, meaning 'on the shady side' – can just be seen high on the opposite valley wall to the south, below dense forests.

Chumling – Chhokang Paro (5–6hrs)
Chumling – Tanju – Domje – Gho – Chhokang Paro

Today there should be tantalising views of Ganesh Himal, given good weather, including a sneak at Ganesh I. Ganesh Himal II (7118m) and Ganesh IV (7140) are some of the most spectacular in the whole Ganesh Himal range of summits, which numbers at least seven separate peaks. The trek today is quite hard, because of the long, unrelenting uphill to Chhokang Paro and the increasing altitude. There is only one refreshment stop en route at Gho. Chhokang Paro is still developing its two lodging options.

The suspension bridge at Chumling has been paid for by Gurkha Agricultural Aid and the Kadoorie Foundation of Hong Kong that has also built shelters in the Nar-Phu area amongst others. From the bridge the trail descends. Looking back, it is startling to see that the lodge is built almost on an overhang – good job we didn't see it before sleeping; we might have had a hangover this morning! Into pretty trees, the path passes a water-driven prayer wheel and contours nicely, high above the Siyar Khola. Views of Shringi Himal continue to impress and so do the drop-offs on the right – care in places again needed. The hay-making season is in full swing and so is the buckwheat harvest. Pancakes are very filling when made of buckwheat in Tsum.

The trail is fairly flat as it contours the hillside and then continues through lush forest. But the flat bit doesn't last long! In about 1hr the village of **Tanju** appears, with a small mini-monastery housing a prayer wheel. Beyond the settlement the trail is mostly through shady, sweet-smelling woodlands with a few ups and downs. Langurs abound and playful monkeys tumble through sparkling leaves dappled with sunlight. **Domje** (2460m) or Dumje, a spread-out place, is attained in another 45mins or so. A loose, unstable-looking cliff of sandy conglomerates provides the only hazardous zone, although the path above the river is narrow at times. Looking west, there are tantalising views of Baudha Peak. There is no sign of any bridge across the river here to Domje central. A sign here says that Rainjam is 45mins away, but the actual location of **Rainjam** is unclear.

Rounding the cliffs, the trail works into the side valley of the Sarphu Khola that drains the eastern face of Shringi Himal and the Syakpa Glacier. The side river is crossed on a new suspension bridge, with views south of the Gumba Lungdang valley showing off the great glacier-draped peak complex of Ganesh II, Ganesh IV (Pabil) and the rocky face of Ganesh I to their left. (With all these different Ganesh peaks, it's actually very hard to identify the peaks correctly). Apparently 'Lama Jhuysa', which means 'special place for high Lamas', is located here at the confluence of the three rivers – the Sarphu Khola, the Siyar River and the Lungdang Khola.

The trail climbs steeply for 25–30mins to reach a small hamlet called **Gho**, with an unusual-looking shrine. Above Gho is a set of chortens and then begins a relentless uphill stint. The path is very steep in places and of course a few short descents add to the mix. Pines, larch and birch cover the hillsides, but above the slopes are almost sheer. After 1hr up from Gho, a couple of large chortens provide a popular resting spot before the last push on up to Chhokang Paro. It doesn't look far, but it takes another 45mins to reach the three welcoming stone chortens seen for so long from below. A wide, mildly uphill, stone path leads to a kani gate and the five chortens that guard the fields of Chhokang Paro.

There are more chortens than people around Chhokang Paro, so it must be well-protected. In a few minutes the main part of **Chhokang Paro** village (3033m) is reached. The entrance chorten has some well-known Buddhist icons on display – Chenresig, Guru Rinpoche, Vajrapani, Yamantaka, a Green Tara and a White Tara. Eight more chortens are seen on the right side of the street. Many of the houses have their courtyards facing southeast to catch the morning sun. The name Chhokang Paro is used by the local people and it is said to be two villages, but they are so close as to be one in reality. Even together the settlement is quite small, despite being the administrative headquarters of Tsum region. The Nepalese name for the village is Chhekampar, which is confusing before a visit. The police permit check post here is currently the only control point within the Tsum Valley.

There are two lodges in Chhokang Paro: the Tashi Shop & Lodge has twin rooms, but at the moment the Tashi Delek Hotel has only dormitory beds. We continued to Ngakyu, where there is a delightful homestay in the house of Nima Zhangmu and Jhimi. Our homestay room was soon to be their puja chamber, with beautiful Tibetan carpets throughout. The great ridge of Churke Himal looms high above the route, sitting astride the Tibetan border. **Galdang Gompa** is situated on a hillside high above the Chhokang Paro fields. It is about a 2hrs climb from the village, with awesome surrounding views.

Chhokang Paro – the inside story

According to Sonam Lama and Lopsang Chhiring Lama (who have produced a coffee table book for Himalayan Map House), the retreat of local reincarnate, Lama Kunchyok, is situated just below Paro (Paaro) village, with its identifying red tin roof. Another Buddhist master, Rinzin Wangchuk, once lived on a hill here and he was later reincarnated in the east of Nepal, near Taplejung. Apparently both the reincarnated Rinpoches are currently studying at Kopan Monastery in Kathmandu. Kopan also supplies much of the funding for Rachen and Mu monasteries. Paro Gompa, situated below a large pipal tree, is famed for its riot of colourful masked dances during late spring.

We are also informed that there was once a cremation site at a nearby location called Tolankha. In years past locals used to chop dead bodies into small pieces for the vultures – a practice known as sky burial, common in Tibet. This practice was discontinued 30 years ago because of the lack of people who knew how to chop the dead bodies correctly! Strangely, herds of Himalayan Tahr are said to congregate at that former site – what do they know?

Another curious fact is that where juniper bushes are found near springs, the local people have designated those spots as holy places, so it is forbidden to cut any trees around here. At the Nuru Lhakang, local women pray diligently on every full moon (or as the local people say in their particular style of English, fool moon!).

Upper Tsum

Chhokang Paro – Nile or Chhule (4–5hrs)
Chhokang Paro – Kaye – Ngakyu-Leru – Burji – Phurbe – Pangdun – Chhule – Nile

With no substantial hills to climb, the going is much easier. There is a wealth of interest all the way to Nile, with so many settlements, chortens, mani walls and gompas. The main attraction is the Piren Phu Cave retreat of Milarepa, although it is not always accessible if the guardian is out. Don't forget also to visit the Gonhgye monastery above Chhule; Lama Sherap is a mine of information and it's a beautiful spot. Long mani walls, often with carvings of Milarepa on the stones and not the usual Om Mani Padme Hum, run in tandem with the trails.

Stage 2: Chhokang Paro – Mu Gompa

In fact a maze of chortens leads the path out of Chhokang Paro. Over to the right is the small hill on which **Jhong** (or Dzong) is located. It's best to visit it on the way back in order to keep left of the mani walls that dot the path up and down. A sign says it will take 15mins to Kaye. It could be longer if you stop to count all the chortens en route – there are 22 at least. **Kaye** is no more than a large school ground (the Chhekam primary school) and from here one needs to keep left of the long, long main wall. However, it could lead you astray if you want to stop in Ngakyu, which is the lower of the twin villages of **Ngakyu-Leru**. Both places have closely packed houses; the compound walls are stacked with firewood and prayer flags dominate the skyline of the villages. This productive area is heavily cultivated, growing wheat, buckwheat, mustard and potatoes... and apple trees, yum yab yum! Apples are proving popular with fruit-starved tourists here.

The homestay house of Nima Zhangmu is located about half way along the narrow street of Ngakyu on the left (northwest side) opposite an alley that leads to some apple orchards. The house has red and blue window panels, but anyone can direct you to the right place for this welcoming homestay. The house is typical, with the living area on the first floor. We stayed in what will become the family puja prayer room. Food was delicious, if limited, and taken in the large kitchen – the warmest place. Electricity was available and charging batteries possible. Leru above Ngakyu is also building a lodge. Beware of dog patrols in the late evenings.

A trail leads from Ngakyu-Leru across the Siyar River to Rachen Gompa, but the monastery is best left for the return journey. **Lamagaon** village (3302m), also known as Nga, is a short walk from Ngakyu-Leru. There is a small shop here. Not long (15mins on the signpost) after leaving Lamagaon is the settlement of **Burji** with one new lodge that will have thick mattresses (we met the porters near Chumling taking these goodies up). Burji is easily bypassed by the trail, but is worth a look around. Burji is home to the guardian of the key to Milarepa's Cave (Piren Phu). The cave complex is just beyond the northern suburbs of Burji and one trail departs to it from some chortens.

The proliferation of mani walls continues below the gigantic rock walls of Langju Himal. Shortly above on the left is the retreat monastery of **Chi Phu**, but it too is often locked up. Also known as Tsephu Sange Chholing gompa, it is devoted to male monks and is one of the oldest in the region.

Ahead and across the Siyar river is the village of **Phurbe** (3231m). The alleys in the village are confusing; do not hesitate to ask the local people the way, as they are eager to meet visitors from beyond their isolated valley. Looking down

> ### Piren Phu – Milarepa's Cave
> The famous cave is up in the rocky foothills and is about a 50m climb above the chortens. The path, such as it is, from the chortens north of Burji zigzags up through the wild shrubs. A clump of prayer flags to the left sits adjacent to the route up from Burji village. A row of stupas are found near the retreat, which has two main chapels and two cave features. We unfortunately could not find the man with the key. One attraction is an impression of Milarepa's footprint, and it is his meditation place that has been made into the gompa. Apparently another visual image is a rock in the shape of an elephant. One chapel is devoted entirely to Milarepa and the other houses the popular Nyingma-pa deities of the region. Because part of this cave is used by snowcock pigeons, it is also known as *Piren Phu* or Pigeon's Cave. Offering butter lamps here is believed to give merit to all sentient beings. A fee may be charged to enter the shrines.

the valley to the south, Ganesh II and Churke Himal glint in the morning sun. Looking eastwards is the great wall and glaciers of the Kipu Himal. Not far gently on up is **Pangdun**, with a small gompa. The chamber has a large prayer wheel so typical of these mini-gompas of Tsum. Guru Rinpoche features prominently, along with the protectors and Samantabhadra. A sign suggests that Chhule is only 25mins north. The trail climbs easily to a small rise and ahead is an impressive stupa – the most picturesque and largest yet seen. Beyond it in view is Chhule and high above is Gonhgye Monastery.

The large round stupa has a doorway, but it cannot be accessed. The stupa eyes seem wary of the strangers who have begun to intrude into its domain. Shortly the striking, three-tiered kani gate of Chhule is at hand. A short descent leads to the village side-stream bridge and then it's best to head for Nile, which has a homestay. **Chhule** (3347m), literally meaning the 'shady side', is expected to develop accommodation soon.

> ## The demons of Chhule and the Poshyop Glacier valley
>
> Look east of Chhule and you see an intriguing, mysterious valley with a path discernible from the Gonhgye monastery; it also traverses around the picturesque waterfall on the south side. A formidable, treacherous glacier route in fact leads from Chhule to Kyirong in Tibet, but foreigners are forbidden to explore it. In fact it is also out of bounds for locals of other parts of Tsum and even those from Nile (for grazing, trade with Tibet or any other reason). This is because the demon of the Poshyop Glacier valley breaths fire when disturbed by outside devils and has done for centuries, such are the animistic and ancestral beliefs of the region. Some years ago some hydro engineers ventured into this astonishing-looking hanging valley to research for possible power plant sites. Shortly afterwards a great avalanche wrought devastation to parts of Chhule. Foreign feet may truly fear to tread here.

For Nile village, continue around the western edge of Chhule. A path cuts down to the Siyar Khola which, after a camping area, is crossed on either the old wooden cantilever bridge or the swish new concrete and steel one – the old one requires less uphill! That is important, because it's quite a steep drag up into **Nile** (3361m) and the paths are confusing. Keep left under the tree and then head up into a narrow alley. Follow this, watching out for any dog patrol, and go around to the right and then left to find the Tsumba Nile Lopsang Homestay (mobile 994640008). The new toilet block across the field is a giveaway in any case. The house is similar in style to the homestay in Ngakyu and indeed they are related family.

A typical 'foodings' menu at the Nile Homestay

Chapatti	Rs200
Pancake + tea	Rs280
Local florist (flour) chapatti	Rs230
Tibetan Bread	Rs300
Dal bhat set	Rs350–450
Noodle soup	Rs170
Veg fried rice	Rs280
Dhindo – mashed local grains Tsampa style+dal	Rs250
Tea list black, cup/small pot/big pot	Rs50/170/200
Coffee same	Rs70/270/320
Tibetan tea – that rancid buttery old favourite! (no big pot – it's too sickly even for Tibetans)	Rs90/300
Beer – Tuborg (more food value than most food!)	Rs400–450
Lhasa beer can/bottle (Chinese delights) (more water than comes out of any taps here!)	Rs150/250
Coke/Sprite (not bad for a remote area)	Rs150

For further life-sustaining energies – go to a monastery!

If time allows, Gonhgye Gompa, perched high above the village of Chhule, is well worth a visit; it has spectacular views. To reach the monastery from Nile, cross to the east bank of the Siyar Khola and look for a small steep path up on to the fields behind the chorten here. Continue between stone walls and locate a gap giving access to a path and the hillside ahead. Choose the best small path and zigzag up to find a wider track (15mins to here). Go right and follow the track and channel around until you meet the main path coming up from Chhule. Zigzag steeply on the easiest path heading left, uphill of course. The monastery is reached in 30mins from Nile this way. (You could have also gone left at the main track and then right where a good path leads less steeply to the monastery – it's a good route for the return trip but has fewer photo opportunities than the first option.)

Gonhgye Monastery

According to Lama Sherap at the monastery, who speaks good English, the complex belongs to the Kar-nying-pa sect. This is the same hybrid mix of old school Nyingma-pa and Kagyu-pa that exists all over Tsum and is sometimes referred to as the Kangin sect.

The upper chamber houses prayer books and has a central stupa as its main feature. On each side are Buddha and Chenresig. Above are local deities: Nyingma, Vajrasada and Nyima Lungchepa, with a red hat and looking like Tsong Khapa of the Gelug-pa sect. (The Gelug-pa sect has no presence in the Tsum Valley or around Manaslu). Apparently lay people do much work for the monastery, teaching yoga and conducting some rituals and ceremonies, since there are not so many monks in the valley. Most of the gompas in the Tsum Valley are nunneries. The books are significant, for there are 100,000 Tantra texts held here and they are collectively called the Nyingma Chubum. (Some of the above names might be misspelt in translation.)

The lower chamber is believed to date back 700 years and it houses the Buddha of the future, Maitreya. Large butter urns stand aside the entrance and there are two prominent protector masks of Mahakala and Yamantaka. Otherwise the chamber has all the usual colourful paintings of the main Nyingma-pa and Kagyu-pa icons. A two-day festival occurs here in October with Cham masked dances performed. The Tsum Valley is known locally as the blessed valley (Kyimalung).

Lama Sherap has an interesting history, for he studied in Rumtek monastery in Sikkim where the sect is Karma-pa/Kagyu-pa. He then spent time in retreat (in meditation) at Namo Buddha close to Dhulikhel, a few kilometres east of Kathmandu. Later he briefly spent some time in Scotland studying and teaching Buddhism, and has also travelled to Buddhist centres in much of South and South East Asia. Lama Sherap is not often in residence at Gonhgye, since his jurisdiction covers the whole of the main Tsum Valley and the Gumba Lungdang valley.

Nile or Chhule – Mu Gompa (2–3hrs)
Nile – Chho Syong – Mu Gompa – Dhephyudonma

This is a fantastic day, starting gently but topped off with a short, steep and breathless climb to Mu Gompa. Adding in Dhephyudonma is no walk in the park either, but every struggling step to this breathtaking sanctuary is worthwhile when you reach it, and soon forgotten after taking a welcome cup of tea with the nuns. The sun doesn't last long in this narrowing valley and it can get very cold and windy in the afternoon, so dress warmly. Take snacks and water if going for a day trip from Nile or Chhule. The round trip walking time is about 4hrs, but adding a visit to Dhephyudonma and exploring Mu will add another 2–3hrs. The altitude will begin to tell up here and the side trip to Dhephyudonma means climbing to over 4000m. However, no one should come to Tsum and miss these two attractions. Given time, it is worthwhile to stay at Mu Gompa and perhaps explore the trail towards Kalung. Just remember that sleeping well at a higher altitude needs better acclimatisation.

From **Nile** descend to the riverbank and cross either bridge. Continue north on the east bank of the river, as the path climbs gently through pastures with a few mani walls and small chortens. The pastures are locally called **Sengum**, but there is no regular habitation here. **Rholmi** is another such area. Yak herders and local people are encountered coming and going, herding their livestock, sometimes to trade with Tibet or in very late spring to look for Yarsagumba. Behind you, down the main valley, the views are ever more enticing as Ganesh II starts to appear in all its glory, with those incredibly extensive glaciers and ice fields tumbling from its pointed cone-shaped summit.

About 1hr from Nile the trail switches to the west bank of the Siyar Khola, now a much-diminished flow of water. On the west side there are views skywards of the almost overhanging glaciers of Langju Himal. Sadly we never really got a good view of the Langju Himal peak (apart from a distant glimpse from Salleri after Jagat on the Manaslu route). A stiffer climb begins around the hillside to a landslide area and a wooden bridge over the side stream before continuing on up. Across the valley, weird erosion features can be seen on the barren sandy mountains. The eastern Phuchun valley opens out and it's not surprising to see herders heading up into the great bowl. Apparently also in the area is the Chho Syong Tal (lake), about 2–3hrs walk uphill, but it is not indicated on any map.

Approaching Mu you can see the Dhephyudonma retreat high on the hillside. Rikang Gompa is also high up, on a plateau-like area on the other side of the Siyar Khola. A signboard soon welcomes trekkers to Mu and from here a small steep path on the left leads up to the monastery gates (2–2½hrs from Nile).

The Mu gompa building is not large, but it has a considerable number of bedrooms, making it a significant retreat. The monastery has undergone restoration since 1998. In fact there were hardly any monks or nuns here in late November. Rooms at the gompa are supplied with good mattresses and perhaps blessings from on high.

To reach Dhephyudonma from Mu, a trail leaves in a south-westerly direction from behind the Mu Gompa courtyard, through a red tin doorway. Initially the route is rather loose, exposed and precarious. Care is needed, as the slope is slipping away. Once clear of this, the narrow and sometimes-exposed route climbs around the tantalising hillside. At each new corner one expects to see the gompa, but eventually as the path gets steeper a chorten is seen.

From here the way is less severe, but then a spectacular ravine and waterfall seemingly bar the way. However, the path drops below a crag to cross the raging white torrent on a small bridge. A juniper tree marks the arrival at the retreat (45mins–1hr from Mu Gompa). On the return trip to Mu there is a direct, very steep, zigzagging shortcut down to the welcome sign. Nepalese guides will delight in this challenge, but tourists with dodgy knees might want to avoid it and retreat via Mu.

Mu Gompa

Mu Gompa (3700m) is the highest and most northerly permanent human settlement in the Tsum Valley. The monastery is situated at an altitude of 3700m. Although a little over 100 years old, Mu is one of the larger complexes of Tsum and was established in 1895.

Lama Sherap Dorje Drukpa Rinpoche heads the establishment. The connection of Mu to the Drukpa is commemorated by the occasional visits of various Bhutanese Lamas. The monastery stores many religious books, including the Kangyur. The central lifesize statue is Chenresig, seen here as the eleven-headed version called Avalokiteshvara in Sanskrit. Guru Rinpoche sits on the left and two Buddhas (Amitabha Buddhas perhaps) on the right. Milarepa sits on the top right with his trademark hand to ear. Tara, Lokpa Rinpoche and the Dalai Lama are given prominence, although the Dalai Lama is of the Gelug-pa sect.

The monks of Mu perform regular meditations, annual rituals and alternate fasting. At one time there were said to be 500 monks and nuns in Mu and Dhephyudonma. However, these days only a few nuns remain. The monastery is overseen by Lama Sherap and it too conforms to the unusual Tsum Valley blend of Nyingma-pa and Kagyu-pa. There are two special festivals celebrated in this monastery: Ngyungne, which occurs in September/October with fasting for world peace, and Yaarney, which involves the reading of sacred texts and some rituals being performed.

If you're young and fit, Make the most of it. If you're old and slow, Mind how you go!	Whatever you do Remember the rule: Don't mix attitude With altitude!

Dhephyudonma Monastery

Also sometimes written Dhephu Donma, Dhephudoma or Dephyudonme, the name means 'place of the birth of the light.' It is one of the oldest monasteries in the Tsum Valley, probably dating back 815 years. As mentioned, the history of this monastery is directly associated with 'the birth of Buddhism' in the valley. It is said that nomads who had migrated to the Tsum Valley requested a lama from Tibet to establish the gompa.

Today Dhephyudonma is often manned by a couple of student nuns through the winter period. The small gompa has two urns of butter each side of the main door. Inside, the important icons are Sakyamuni Buddha with Guru Rinpoche central and Chenresig on the right. This image of Guru Rinpoche is rather fearsome. Twenty-one Tara images grace the upper level as well as thirty-five Buddha images. The whole entourage of the Kagyu-pa – Milarepa, Gampo, Marpa, Nilopa and Tilopa – are also in residence here. Mahakala and a Yab–Yum couple are of note, and another image is that of Kharying, of whom we know nothing!

There is a fabulous view from the monastery to the south of Ganesh II, and a slither of Ganesh IV–Pabil. Across the valley, closer to the southeast, is the exquisitely decorated and fluted peak of Langpo (6648m) in the Kipu Himal, high above the Poshyop glacier. Looking east, there is a great panorama of the Phuchun valley encircled by dark, forbidding barren mountains. The high ridge behind the retreat obscures any views to the north.

Side Trip: Mu to the Tibetan border

The following section is included for reference, but be sure to check with the locals and check posts if the area is open to outsiders. We have heard that foreign trekkers have been putting up Free Tibet flags on their excursions to the border and the Chinese are enraged by these politically hot misdemeanours. Since the valley entrepreneurs depend on trade with China for supplies of Lhasa beer and cheap shoes, among other more important products, they are fearful that the border will close. Local people ask foreigners not to antagonise the Chinese authorities. According to the homestay at Nile, seven Chinese PLA soldiers were seen in Chhokang Paro in October 2012, so the threats about border tensions are real enough. This Chinese incursion was also said to be in response to someone placing Free Tibet paraphernalia at the border.

Mu – Bhajyo (est 3–4hrs)
Mu – Kalung – Bhajyo

Most of the notes on the trails beyond Mu have been based on information supplied by Sonam Lama and Lopsang Chhiring Lama.

The trail north if permitted can be accessed by skirting around the Mu Gompa hillside from the welcome sign. The path passes the helipad and continues above a camping area. After a chorten the route contours around to a landslip area which requires care, since the exposure level is constantly changing. This area of steep mud and rock slides called **Phrang** is particularly slippery during and after the monsoon. This difficult part of the trail is 20mins from Mu Gompa.

There is a large birch forest across the river and locals report that the protected Himalayan Musk Deer can often be seen there. The trail passes through an area known locally as **Mijam**. Ahead is the confluence of the rivers that drain from the Thapla pass and the Ngula Dhojyang. The path ascends to **Kalung** (est. 3900m), with large deserted terraces that were once used for agriculture. There are fabulous views from Kalung of the Ganesh Himal range and the upper Tsum Valley. Marmot burrows are common here, but there is little vegetation apart from small thorny bushes. Many yaks, naks and chauris graze in the area.

The Ngula Dhojyang pass to the east is commonly used by the locals for trading with the nearby villages of Sya and Ghun, as well as the larger town of Kyirong – all in Tibet. On the way to Bhajyo is **Chhanchhu** (1½hrs), where you may encounter the local yak herders. **Bhajyo** (4030m) is the name of the confluence of the Yamdro and Siyar Kholas; from here you can see the Ngula Dhojyang pass. This whole region is above the tree line, with snow and small glaciers.

Bhajyo – Ngula Dhojyang Pass rtn (est 8–9hrs)
Bhajyo – Thongbu – Pama – Ngula Dhojyang Pass – Bhajyo

The trail from Bhajyo crosses the Yamdro Khola, ascends to a flat area and then climbs to the **Ngula Dhojyang La** pass (5093m), which is covered in snow. Mani walls act as sacred signposts for travellers to find the trail when it is snowbound. The wild landscape supports herds of blue sheep and has some good grazing. From the pass, you can see the high rolling steppes of the Tibetan plateau and the village of Moon. It takes 5hrs to ascend to the pass from Bhajyo and about 3hrs to return.

Other High Passes to Tibet

The Thapla pass to the west of Kalung is located at an altitude of 5104m; it is partially covered by snow and a glacier. A summit cairn marks the pass, while a small Tibetan village can be seen far below, delineated by a small zone of greenery set beside a barren ridge. Another high col is the Yangdol (5326m) pass, north of Kalung along the Yangdol Khola. The trail from Kalung to the Yangdol pass is apparently hardly discernible high up, according to one Israeli trekker who explored this normally off-limits area. These two passes are rarely used, as they present significant dangers to traders. Yaks cannot cross the highest passes and in any case they would only be usable in high summer.

Bhajyo – Mu (est. 3hrs)
Bhajyo – Kalung – Mu

From Bhajyo the return trek down to Mu can be done relatively painlessly the next day – unless you have over-extended your energy on the excursion to the Ngula Dhojyang pass.

Mu – Rachen (3–4hrs)
Mu Gompa – Chhule – Pangdun – Phurbe – Lar – Rachen

This is a pleasant amble down the main valley from Mu or Nile to Rachen. Enigmatic Rachen is a rather peculiar place; it's a huge complex. For trekkers it offers good beds and electric charging facilities, but it has crummy toilets and eating choices. There is no 'middle path' when it comes to paying the bill! The superior status of the place makes it quite expensive, especially for the Nepali staff. Don't be taken in by the religious aspects of the place; charity, it seems, is for others.

It takes around 1½hrs to return to Nile if on a day trip. The route is the same to **Pangdun** (40mins). Note the wind vane and three chortens on the east side, and some deeply cut water channels in the cliffs of Langju Himal. Continue to **Phurbe** (20mins). If you come here late in the day, say from Mu or after the day trip to Mu, you might catch a fabulous sunset on the Kipu Himal peaks, east of the village. Head up left next, just after Phurbe under a tree, and then go almost level all the way to Rachen Gompa. En route, 15mins from Phurbe is **Lar** village, with a homestay called Sherab's. Currently it has only one dormitory room though. In Lar is the Buddha primary school, the first school in Tsum built after the visit of King Birendra. The sturdy houses of Lar have relatively large compounds for their livestock. Well-built stone walls protect their fields from the wind, while thorny bushes keep the livestock out. Just over 15mins from Lar is **Rachen Gompa** (3240m), with its red tin roof, on the left just after a chorten.

Rachen Gompa

The gompa is set in a vast area enclosed by walls that form the outer residential rooms for the nuns. The original monastery is a small building in the southwest corner (close to any rooms that seem to get offered to passing trekkers in need of a place for the night). There are separate areas for retreat. There is a certain air here that gives the nunnery a feeling of peace and harmony. Although we arrived just after dark and were given a nice room, we are not really sure how welcome trekkers are at the gompa. You will have to rely on the grapevine for news about the accommodation options here. A double room cost Rs650 so it does not come cheap; however, the mattress thickness is 10cm, so a comfortable night can be expected. Power is available for those tiresome camera and torch batteries. As for food, there is a massive kitchen hall but no one seems to be able to cook much. Expect tea and instant noodles for easy eats. Presumably when more nuns are in residence the quality of cooking improves.

Rachen Gompa (nunnery) was established in 1905. It houses approximately 90 nuns, apparently belonging to the little known Ngak-pa sect, which does not allow animal slaughter. In winter many of the nuns leave for lower climes as we witnessed en route down to Chhokang Paro. The main Lama is Zopa Rinpoche.

The inside walls of the old nunnery are decorated with the same terracotta images already seen in Tsum, in particular at Mu. These are 1000 moulded clay statues of Chenresig/Avalokiteshvara – the compassionate one. A complete set of Kangyur block prints from Tibet, printed on both sides is housed in the building. The central lifesize icon is Chenresig (Avalokiteshvara) in eleven-headed form. A stupa made of gold and silver alloy sits on the right and two images on the left. One is the red hat lama of the Kagyu-pa and the other was said to be Najurma, an icon about which we have no idea. Other images are Vajrapani, Guru Rinpoche, Sakyamuni Buddha and the Buddha in mudras, with hands in one of the many positions. Much of the interior is richly painted with murals depicting Buddhism and its history. The ceilings and beams are decorated with images of dragons, birds and other animals.

Outside, painted on the entrance walls, are an elephant and the vehicle of Guru Rinpoche, the chained tiger. A picture similar to Mi Tsering, the old man, is present, as is a fearsome Mahakala. On the right are three of the four usual monastery guardians (see glossary for details of them). The fourth guardian has been banished perhaps, or couldn't afford the lease on his space here! Each month, on the day of the full moon, tormas (pyramids of dough) decorated with butter and flower petals are offered in the monastery. Deities such as Phola, Khola and Chusin are worshipped. Tara is worshipped from September to November, when the nuns are also invited into the villages for ceremonies.

Rituals and folk dances are performed in the courtyard in front of the main chapel. A brand new monastery lhakhang is being built with the aid of outside donations.

Rachen – Chumling (6–7hrs)
Rachen – Jhong – Chhokang Paro – Gho – Domje – Tanju – Chumling

This is quite a long day, but with only Chhokang Paro in between as a stop of any significance, it makes sense to head on down after the wonders of Tsum have been explored. There are a few sights to check out on the return journey, so it will not all be a big slog down.

As you drop down from Ngakyu to Jhong, there is a great view towards the west of Baudha and Himalchuli, especially if you leave the trail just above all those chortens and head left to some grassy knolls set above a dense pine forest. Chhokang Paro sits neatly below the frame of Himalchuli, to add interest to the scene. Take a diversion to the left to reach Jhong, where the small gompa is well worth the effort.

Jhong Monastery
The monastery, administered by Nga Ladrang, was renovated in 2005–6 and painted a bright gold and red colour. There is a big prayer wheel and some lavish paintings. At least seven Mahakala images adore the interior, as well as Buddha, Guru Rinpoche, Chenresig and a stupa image. Near the door is a fine flamboyantly painted image of Palden Lhamo, the Tibetan female 'temptress and witch' for want of a better description. The Red Hat lama appears again, as do the four harmonious friends – the Elephant, Monkey, Rabbit and the Bird, representing harmony for peace. Apparently the lama is in retreat at the seemingly inaccessible, isolated building seen high up in the forest to the southeast.

Chhokang Paro is less than 25mins down from Jhong. The long descent from Chhokang Paro is much less effort going down, but since the trail is narrow and sometimes exposed, care must be taken. The steepness is surprising and explains why this stage seemed so hard on the way up (especially hard for old codgers like us!). After the Sarphu Khola bridge and just down around the corner is another small mini gompa, sitting forlornly in a field overlooking Domje. It is painted a silver colour and boasts a few terracotta images, books and a small altar with Guru Rinpoche. The local people called the gompa Tinso Tsechen Chholing. Apparently there is sometimes a small clinic in Domje run by nuns from Gumba Lungdang. In an ideal world it would be great to stay in Domje – see below. From here to Chumling is a pleasant amble, being mostly undulating.

Chumling – Lokpa – Deng (7–8hrs)
Chumling – Siyar Khola Bridge – Lokpa – Deng

That daunting trek up from Lokpa to Tsum, filled with anticipation, is soon remembered as you drop to the Siyar Khola and then begin the never-ending climb over the sheer-sided canyon of the Siyar Khola.

On the descent be especially careful of 'Damien's Corner', where the loose small stones on the steeply dropping path could launch you into freefall over the sheer cliffs. Having crossed the Sardi Khola gorge bridge, it's a short hop and a skip back up to the Lokpa lodge. After tea or drinks, it's worth pushing on down to the Budhi Gandaki bridge and making for Deng – for those on the Manaslu trek. It is probably also worth going on to Philim (or Chisopani) for those returning by way of Arughat to Kathmandu.

Alternative route: Domje – Lokpa via Ripchet (1½ days)
Domje – Ripchet – Lokpa

For those with time, it may be worthwhile to take the alternative trail to Lokpa via Ripchet. It is a beautiful, traditional-looking village with quaint houses that might be overlooked by many trekkers. Ripchet sits on a shelf high above Chumling on the south side of the Siyar Khola. Its meadows are surrounded by dense forests of rhododendron, oaks and all the temperate species of tree found at around 2500m. There is apparently a designated homestay, but it might also be necessary to ask at one of the many houses that sit in these fertile fields.

We have not done this route, but it can be seen heading up into the trees from Domje across the Siyar Khola. The trail climbs steadily in thick forest and bridges a deep ravine on an airy suspension bridge. From here the way is up to the plateau of **Ripchet** village (2470m). We estimate it will take around 2hrs to reach Ripchet from Domje. Those who have been to Ripchet thoroughly recommend this alternative, since the village is so untroubled by modernity. The trail to Lokpa continues high and then drops for 400m to the Siyar Khola bridge at Gumling on a steep and difficult trail. That said, the beautiful forest is sure to be a delight.

Side Trip: Gumba Lungdang and Ganesh Himal Base Camp

We did not explore this deeply incised valley but the valley's pleasures are well worth the effort, given plenty of time. The following is an outline. Until decent lodgings are established in Domje, it will be hard for independent trekkers to enjoy the valley's attractions without some discomfort. The monastery at Gumba Lungdang is the only place offering shelter at present. The height gain from Domje is considerable, so it should be left for any return journey when altitude acclimatisation is optimum. It is much easier to explore this valley for those equipped to camp. That said, it is probably possible to find a willing householder in Domje to provide some kind of overnight facility. In this case taking the time to walk a few hours up the valley would be rewarding, as the views of Ganesh Himal are better.

Domje - Gumba Lungdang (5-6hrs)
Domje - Lapche - Gumba Lungdang

Take a packed lunch and enough drinking water for this day. The Gumba (Gompa) Lungdang valley hosts surprisingly lush pine forests for most of the way. En route it is apparently easy to get lost in the dense forest. From the mani walls known as Lapche, there is a scenic view over lower Tsum. The roaring sound of the Lungdang River pierces the deep silence. There are some sheds and much of the trail to the gompa is in oak forest (about 5hrs from Domje). The Gumba Lungdang monastery

(3200m) is home to around 20 nuns and older people come to meditate here. This serene nunnery has a big courtyard, with the main building facing south, where the majestic Ganesh Himal ranges seems to grow out of the monastery. Camping places can be found 30mins walk from here. High up in the valley there are views west to Himalchuli, Ngadi and Manaslu.

Ganesh Himal Base Camp
Gumba Lungdang – Ganesh BC – Gumba Lungdang

Very few climbers have attempted to climb Ganesh Himal from this side. However, a day-hike (5–7hrs) to Ganesh Himal base camp illustrates the variety of flora and fauna as well as superbly displaying the mountains. Close to the glacier it's best to climb up on to the top of the moraine to enjoy the clear view of Ganesh Himal to the northeast and Shringi Himal to the west. **Ganesh Base Camp** is around 4000m, so it is a low starting point for climbers. The north side of Ganesh Himal is characterised by massive glaciers and snowfields, since it spends so much of the day in the shadows. The views here are reputed to surpass even those of the Annapurna Sanctuary, with a great cirque of fluted peaks and a more intimate ambience. Return to camp early along the same trail; it will take about 3hrs.

Typical lodge kitchen in the Tsum Valley.

Ganesh Himal

With seven summits comprising the great range of Ganesh Himal, it is surprising that these peaks have rarely been climbed. Paldor, the eastern outlier peak, is regularly assaulted by Trekking Peak groups, but the main tops of Ganesh remain supremely untrodden.

The range was reconnoitred by H. W. Tilman and his party in 1950, followed by a first attempt in 1953. Ganesh I (7422m), also called Yangra, was attempted initially by the Japanese team who were chased away from Manaslu in 1954, but it was not summitted then. It was a year later, in 1955, that Raymond Lambert led a mixed Swiss and French team via the the Southeast Face and Ridge. Unusually for that time, a female climber, Claude Kogan, was a member of the party. Lambert, Kogan, and Eric Gauchat finally reached the summit, but sadly Gauchat fell to his death on the descent. In 2012 an international commercial expedition run by Altitude Junkies attempted the first ascent of Ganesh I from the Nepalese side, but failed to find a route across the immense crevasses and seracs. The gods of Ganesh do not intend to share the summit!

The glistening white fluted western summit of Ganesh IV (Pabil – 7118m) was first conquered by a Japanese team in 1978, fully twenty-five years after Everest. It was attained via the south and southeast ridges.

As far as we know Ganesh II appears to be a virgin peak thus far. Does anyone claim success on it?

Other treks

Lower Manaslu Region

The region known as Lower Manaslu encompasses the hilly tracts around the main town of Gorkha. The area includes the villages and hillsides west and northwest of Gorkha, east and northeast of Gorkha, including the Dharche Danda ridge and Rupina La pass. South of Gorkha towards the Manakamana temple and beyond are the endless rolling hills and ridges stretching as far as the eye can see towards India. These hazy blue ridges are a beautiful sight, not to be missed, from the numerous vantage points in the region. Himalayan panoramas include Annapurna, Baudha, Himalchuli and Ganesh Himal. The villages of Laprak and Barpak were devastated by the first earthquake and rebuilding will take some time, so check with trekking agencies for the latest information.

Apart from the trek to Dharche Danda, which Bob did in 1980 and we partially checked out in 1988, the following information comes to us with the kind help of 'Jit' Sane Gurung from Gumda, and Sunar Gurung and Harka Gurung from Laprak, all north of Gorkha town.

Currently five treks in Lower Manaslu are proving increasingly popular. These are the Gorkha Pilgrimage Trail, the Gorkha Cultural Trail, the Lower Manaslu Trek, the Dharche Danda Trek and the Rupina La Pass Trek. Most of these routes are community-based eco-trails, but camping and self-catering is necessary in some places. Halfboard in homestays currently costs around Rs1000 per person. Be sure to sample the local barley *dhindo* and organic vegetable *tedo*.

Gorkha Pilgrimage Trek
Kathmandu – Manakamana – Baskot – Gorkha

This short 4–5 day mini-trek packs its punches in quick succession and is ideal for a short sojourn into the middle hills that offers fabulous panoramic views. On a clear day the arc of peaks stretches from the Annapurna massif through Himalchuli/Manaslu to Ganesh Himal and even Langtang to the east. A guide is necessary since few foreigners come this way and, if you want to savour the scenery in comfort, add a porter to the equation. As a rule, the best time of year for viewing the sweeping panoramas is late October through to mid December. Spring may be hazy and hotter. Fully supported camping is one self-contained option, but independent hikers can find basic lodges and homestays are available.

The trek begins with the exciting bus journey from Kathmandu to the Manakamana cable car station, about 100km from the capital (3+hrs bus ride). The novelty value of taking a cable car ride in Nepal has not worn off with the local people and it's a busy spot every day, especially at festival times. The 10min ride up invariably takes passengers through the morning mists and out again to another world, to the clear air of Manakamana some 1000m above. **Manakamana** (1304m), temple of the wish-fulfilling goddess of the same name, has been a sacred pilgrimage place for Hindus for centuries. The temple complex hosts a couple of impressive Newari-style pagoda shrines and is thronged by colourful crowds and yellow-robed sadhus.

From the hurly-burly of the temple shrine, the trail heads northeast along the ridges parallel to a dirt road. En route the path climbs to the Bakyeshwori temple. According to legend, when the goddess Parvati died, her husband Shiva toured the world with her on his back, as he could not bear to let go of her. Her tongue fell off at this temple, and thus it is worshipped by those with speech impediments. Nearby is the cave of the martyr Lakhan Thapa, who was the first anti-Rana martyr, hanged in 1933. After crossing the Tinmane Bhanjyang to **Pipalchhap** (1130m), the trail continues to **Baskot** (1170m). This village has several homestay options. Sunsets and sunrises are sure to reveal that exquisite willowy light that captures the very essence of the Himalaya. After Baskot is the Himalaya Devi shrine, devoted to a stone deity with a large antique bell.

The trail descends to the saddle at **Kaulebangar** (990m), home of the martyr Lhakan Thapa, whose statue stands in the village. It then contours around the sweeping terraced hillsides to Rampur. The small col of **Dhungagade Bhanjyang** provides a short workout and soon the busy bazaar hilltop town of **Gorkha** (1060m) is attained. Gorkha town provides plenty of interest for visitors, with the famed palace of Prithvi Narayan Shah above the settlement and superb views north from the hills above. The markets are awash with hill traders and boisterous market sellers. There is a plethora of overnight lodgings. Regular bus services link Gorkha with Kathmandu and Pokhara. Gorkha town also has a museum housing a collection of weapons, coins and personal belongings of Prithvi Narayan Shah. A suggested itinerary is given in the general route planning section of the appendix. To make this trek longer, continue on the Gorkha Cultural Trail described below.

Gorkha Cultural Trail
Gorkha – Barpak – Laprak – Gumda – Machha Khola – Arughat

This trek north and northeast of Gorkha town takes 6–7 days and displays the very best of the Lower Manaslu region without the need to follow any 'gruesome trails' or to cross any high and wild passes. The traditional, barely changed hill villages of Barpak, Gumda and Laprak are top-notch attractions for those wanting to discover the true lifestyles of the hill-farming communities. The grand finale is the spectacular vista and dramatic descent into the mysterious gorges of the Budhi Gandaki, the gateway to Upper Manaslu and the Tsum Valley. Currently most groups trekking here are fully supported campers, but the villages are enthusiastically embracing the new homestay concept, where villagers set aside space within their homes for passing trekkers.

The trip starts in Gorkha after a half-day bus journey from Kathmandu, so there is plenty of time to explore the magnificent Durbar Palace above the town. Campers can enjoy a superb panorama from the field camp close to the palace. From Gorkha it's necessary on the normal itinerary to take a jeep (or bus) on the newly constructed dirt road along the Dorandi Khola valley, almost all the way to Barpak. Purists could trek the whole way via Saangu, Bhaluswara, Chanaute, Sirudanda, Matthar and Ghyanchowk, but this could easily add 3–4 days of walking.

(Sirudanda is unusual in that it has a gompa and a Sherpa community.) The Dorandi Khola valley will be quite hot and humid for most of the trekking season, so think carefully about this option.

From the large Gurung settlement of **Barpak** (1915m), with its distinctive stone roofs, the trek begins a strenuous forested climb to the **Pusu (Bhosu) Kang pass** (2800m) – a rather rude awakening! You are strongly urged to prepare at home with some pre-trek training, since this ascent is formidable for a first day. Perhaps that purist walk is not such a bad plan after all; besides, you could start in any of the places en route by taking a jeep part of the way. Chanaute is one place to commence the trek, since the dirt road and the trail diverge there. Those sitting on the Pusu Kang pass will now at least have the pleasure of a descent to **Laprak** (2100m) to follow their exertions.

Laprak is another magnificent Gurung village, with shingle roof houses and two welcoming lodges. From here the trek to Gumda is only a half day to recover from that punishing previous introduction. (Another route from Laprak goes via the Dharche Danda back to Gorkha.) **Gumda** (1800m) is a fine, typical country hill village. The Ganesh Himal peaks are to the east high above the Budhi Gandaki valley. The normal route from Gumda is to head down the ridges to **Machha Khola**, some 1000m below. Other trails appear to offer shorter but steeper options to **Lapubesi**, again in the deep canyon of the Budhi Gandaki. Once in Machha Khola, with its new trekkers-style lodges and good food, the trek follows the Budhi Gandaki downstream to **Soti**, where the dirt jeep track enables visitors to access **Arughat** more quickly. For details of the sometimes exposed route, with its tiring ups and downs between Machha Khola and Soti, see the Manaslu Circuit trek in reverse.

From Arughat a choice of rough jeep/bus routes via Gorkha or Dhading can be taken to Kathmandu.

Lower Manaslu Trek
Kathmandu – Manakamana – Khanchowk – Dharche Danda – Laprak – Barpak – Gorkha

The trek into the Lower Manaslu area and the Dharche Danda ridge is a combination of the two treks above, with a variant via the Dharche Danda ridge's forested hillsides and panoramic viewpoint. The trek requires at least ten days and a couple of extra days would be highly worthwhile. A week is plenty if you are just doing the Dharche Danda trek separately, starting and finishing in Gorkha (a trek Bob did back in 1980). Camping is still the most popular option, although the lower villages are quickly developing homestays.

The traditional route taken by trekkers on the Lower Manaslu route begins in **Manakamana**, reached by road from Kathmandu followed by 10mins in the cable car. Time spent watching the temple throngs is a joy before the real business begins. From here the route follows the ridges to **Pipalchhap** and **Baskot** for a gentle introduction.

A longer day's march follows, as the trail heads through **Kaulebangar**, **Rampur** and then diverts from the Gorkha path northeast to **Taple Bazaar** and **Khanchowk** (930m). Much of the way is along the ridges offering great views of Baudha, Himalchuli and Ganesh Himal. At **Ghyampesal** a small col divides the valleys of the Khanchowk Khola and the Jarang Khola.

The trail now winds its way up and around in a dizzying manner at times to the settlement of **Tallo Thotnery,** via the Kharchok Bhanjyang close to a cave shrine known as **Sita Cave**. This cave is 250m off the trail, and a visit inside is very exciting, with long caverns, narrow tunnels and claustrophobic holes to squeeze through. Legends recount that Sita hid here when her husband Rama accused her of adultery.

From here the path enters beautiful forest with plenty of rhododendron (an attraction in itself in springtime). Nyauli Kharka is a good spot for campers to rest before the climb up to the Dharche Danda viewpoint (3220m). The spot is considered sacred, and no killing, cutting trees, drinking alcohol or making excessive noise is allowed. A small temple graces the summit. Given clear weather, the panorama includes Annapurna South, Machhapuchhre, Annapurna II, Lamjung, Baudha (with Himalchuli almost hidden behind it) and Ganesh Himal. However, the vast, unending blue-tinged ridges to the south are as startling as the main Himalayan summits. India is far to the south – well out of reach, say some!

Continuing northwards, the route drops to **Sambe Kharka** and, again keeping to the high ridges, eventually reaches **Laprak**. Allow enough time to explore the Gurung village, as it's one of the most picturesque on the route, well away from modern intrusions for the most part. Following a reverse route to the Cultural Trail already described above, this trek option heads west to **Barpak**; alternatively, you could head east to Machha Khola.

The route chosen from the large settlement of Barpak will, as already discussed under the Gorkha Cultural Trail, depend on how much time you have available or whether a dirt road option to Gorkha better suits your timeframe or mood. Either way, **Gorkha** demands your attention for several hours, with all its fine tourist sites.

Dharche Danda Trek
Gorkha – Taple – Khanchowk – Kharchowk – Nyauli Kharka – Dharche Danda – Gorkha

From the viewpoint at Dharche Danda, Ganesh Himal rises like the giant elephant head that its name suggests. Peak after peak of Ganesh Himal line up like sentinels. Beyond are Langtang and the Gosainkund ridges, although not always in perfect view due to any haze. To the west the peaks of the Annapurna massif are utterly dominant, with the obvious pyramid of Machhapuchhre on display – showing off its unique fishtail shape in a different guise. To the north high above we can almost touch the lower flanks of Baudha and Himalchuli.

From **Gorkha** the route heads to Ahale, a prosperous settlement with shops, teahouses and basic lodges. Continuing down, the next village is **Taple**, a beautifully tidy and flower-bedecked area. There is a popular school nearby with a large catchment area. Some way down the hillside is **Khanchowk** (930m), a major crossroads. The trail heads northeast from Khanchowk, gaining altitude through a series of north–south ridgelines and climbing into very dense, pristine forest. The views from anywhere just out of the trees are fabulous.

From **Dharche Danda** a vast panoramic vista opens to the south, with views described above. Often the valleys below are blanked out by a veil of fluffy white clouds that burns off as the morning sun heats up. Poor old rafters far below have to wait for hours in winter for the clouds to lift – but high up on these ridges, it's heavenly.

Rupina La Trek
Gorkha – Dharche Danda – Diling Kharka – Rupina La – Nyak – Jagat – Arughat

The Rupina La Pass links the Lower Manaslu area to the higher trails of the Budhi Gandaki. At 4720m it's not a particularly high pass, but there are dangers. Heavy snow, avalanches, icy winds and wild, lonely high pastures characterise the route. Ideally trekkers need to carry ice axes as a minimum, since snow is common at any time. These windswept barren hills below Baudha have a reputation for weather problems. Crossing the Rupina La at the moment is a trek only for campers, since lodges have not yet been developed in the region and most of the route goes through wild, uninhabited country. However, with the dirt road already close to Barpak, it might just be a matter of a few seasons before such accommodation is built.

Rupina La Trek via Dharche Danda

The route begins in **Gorkha** and follows the same route described above to Dharche Danda and beyond towards Laprak. An overnight in **Laprak** (2100m) would allow time to explore the village's charms.

Heading north, the regular route follows the high forested ridges from Pusu Kang via **Humche** (2800m) to **Diling Kharka** (3100m). Continuing north again on the ridge lines and in dense untouched forest, the trail climbs through **Gai Kharka** (cow shelter) (2900m) to either a camp used at 3440m or to **Sumrang Kharka** (sheep shelter) (3800m). The camp chosen will depend on the altitude acclimatisation of the group or individuals.

With almost 1000m of ascent needed to conquer the **Rupina La pass** it is always going to be one of those days that begins with great, if nervous, anticipation. The snowy cone of Baudha dominates the pass and ahead lies the long glacial valley of the Chhilung Khola. This vast glacial network drains the east faces of Himalchuli, Baudha and Rani Peak to the north – a coronet-like ridge peak that is seen from the lower Tsum Valley near Chumling. Although the distance trekked today is not far, **Baudha Base Camp** (3600m) is the usual camping spot, because of the strenuous and sometimes harrowing crossing of the pass. Snowfall and icy winds combined with the effects of altitude are all guaranteed at some time during the day/season. It will probably take at least 8hrs to cross the pass.

Descending, with that joy that comes from getting over any high Himalayan pass, the route drops to **Jarong** (3420m) and then **Jhong Kharka** (2960m). By now the air is warmer and heads are clearer as the trail leaves the glacial moraines and rubble behind to gain the refreshing forest once more. Eventually, after two days of descending, the trail reaches the home comforts of **Nyak** (2340m), and from here on it's down into the balmy reaches of the Budhi Gandaki. In three days the weary explorer can be back in **Arughat** awaiting the bus for Kathmandu. Perhaps he or she would rather be back in those wild and exciting uplands than bumping and lurching all the way to Dhading or Gorkha!

Alternative route: Rupina La via Barpak

The classic approach to the Rupina La is via the Dharche Danda, but an equally inspiring route could start in Barpak. Jeeps for Barpak leave the Abu Khaireni – Gorkha road near Syauli Bazaar and from Gorkha town.

For much of the way the dirt road follows the banks of the Dorandi Khola. This valley is quite wide in its lower reaches and has its headwaters high up below Baudha. **Barpak** is a large, neatly laid-out village and is currently the roadhead for the Dorandi Khola valley. North of the village are high, wild foothills, mostly the haunts of herders and the occasional adventurous group of trekkers or mountaineers. The trail from Barpak heads north through **Jongong** (1440m) and climbs relentlessly to **Gai Kharka** (2900m) – meaning cow pasture – with some rough shelter. See above for the description of the route from here across the Rupina La pass and down to Nyak.

Manakamana Temple

Ganesh Region and Ruby Valley

Ganesh Himal Trek (Great Himalaya Trail)
*Syabrubesi – Gatlang – Somdang – Pangsang La –
Lapagaon – Mangral Bhanjyang – Tatopani*

Although not necessarily part of any venture to Manaslu or Tsum, the south side of the Ganesh Himal is on the designated Great Himalaya Trail (GHT) and geographically adjacent to the main routes of this book. Being so close to Kathmandu, it is surprising that the area is so far off the radar of most visitors. In the 1980s the Ganesh Himal trek was marketed with some success as a high-and-wild camping trek. It remains that way today, an enticing adventure below the snowy peaks seen from the rooftops of Kathmandu. This is a fully supported venture at present and you need at least 10–14 days to do it justice.

In outline, the east to west option along the GHT begins in Syabrubesi, Gatlang or Somdang, depending on the state of the mountain road. It's not ideal to start from Somdang since the first pass, the Pangsang La, is the highest. From the pass there are stupendous views across much of Central Nepal. Then the route descends to Tipling, Chalis and Shertung. Two options follow: either via Lapagaon or more ruggedly via Lapchet and Hindung. West of Khading the route traverses wild forest to Nauban Kharka and then heads northwest to join the main Manaslu trekking route at Tatopani.

Being enthusiastically promoted by TAAN and local agents is the **Ruby Valley Trek**. The normal approach is from Dhading along the Ankhu Khola valley but other access trails come from Syabrubesi and Betrawati (Singla Pass). From Shertung and Chalis a more adventurous route heads to Hindung below Ganesh IV and Ganesh III. A further climb leads to the mystical lakes – the Kalo (black) Kunda and the Seto (white) Kunda. The Ganesh Himal Tourism Development Committee has full details on www.rubyvalleytrek.com and www.rubyvalleytreks.com

For more details please see our trekking guidebook to Ganesh Himal, in the same series.

Lamjung Region

Although outside the Lower Manaslu region, the district of Lamjung lies just west of the Marsyangdi valley that trekkers from the Manaslu Circuit will use en route to the main road at Dumre. Those with sufficient energy left after the Larkya La crossing might consider taking the following short options to Pokhara from Khudi, Besisahar or Kalimati.

New routes (and dirt roads) are rapidly being developed in this area. The region is now encouraging moderate homestay trekking, so there is no reason why the area cannot be transited by hikers wanting to reach Pokhara from the Manaslu trek as a gentle winding down. Homestays with local families are being encouraged in order to spread the visitors' dollars into areas where, until now, only subsistence agriculture has sustained the way of life. Ironically these latest, increasingly fashionable, initiatives are a reinvention of the 'good old days' of early trekking, 40 years ago, when trekkers stayed in local houses. However when you 'travel back in time' you can't expect the level of luxury and standard of toilets that you found in Bimthang, for example. You still need your guide, as the trails are not yet marked. It gets quite hot in late spring in the lower foothills, so heading here after the Larkya La pass is better in late autumn and early December.

There are four routes to reach Pokhara from the Marsyangdi valley. The northern 'Gurung Heritage Trail' goes from Khudi to Gumle Bazaar. Another trail cuts from Khudi via the Baglungpani high ridge to Nalma and on to Pokhara. From Besisahar another option climbs to Lamjung Durbar, heads to Puranokot and then down via Neta to Ramgha before jeeps appear. The other route leaves the Marsyangdi at Kalimati, climbs to Chowk Chisopani then heads on three different trails to Ramgha. The routes offer fine scenery, tranquillity and equally spectacular views – Machhapuchhre, Lamjung and Annapurna II dominate the region. Across the Marsyangdi Valley, the views offer a different perspective on Baudha, Himalchuli, Ngadi Chuli and Manaslu. Almost nothing remains of the 15th-century settlements, which had historic links to the ruling Shah dynasty.

Gurung Heritage Trail (4–5 days)
Khudi – Ghalegaon – Bhujung – Pasagaon – Nagidhar – Gumle

This easy-to-moderate option visits the regions below Annapurna II and Lamjung where the Gurung culture is displayed in villages such as Bhujung – places that have rarely been heard of, until now. The trek utilises homestay accommodation. The trek is within the ACAP area, but this is not an added expense for Manaslu Circuit hikers. The authors have not done this route, so timings are estimated.

The path from **Khudi** heads to **Simpani**, the village of temples, used by devotees of a local deity, Thani Mai, and Mahadev, as well as by followers of Ganesh, Krishna and his consort Radha. Further on through uninhabited forest the trek reaches Ghalegaon (3–4hrs). **Ghalegaon** (2092m), once the dominant fiefdom of the region, is a beautiful Gurung settlement. There is a side trail to Ghan Pokhara, a hilltop village with panoramic views.

After Nayan there are no facilities; the trek is through isolated country to Bhujung (3–4hrs). This aesthetically pleasing traditional village is currently notable as being the largest Gurung village in Nepal. Bhujung now has the benefit of electricity and homestays are available.

From **Bhujung** (1625m) is necessary to descend on the famous Gurung stone staircase trail into the wide valley of the Midim Khola. The next usual overnight stop (4–5hrs) is **Pasagaon** (1652m), with its Buddhist kani and monastery. The trail follows the ridges and descends to the Rudi Khola valley and eventually reaches **Nagidhar** (1260m). From here the trail descends to **Gahate** and then down to the sweaty Madi Khola River to **Gumle Bazaar** (7–9hrs). Buses or jeeps take roughly 2hrs and depart when full from Thumsikot/Gumle Bazaar for Pokhara.

Khudi – Pokhara via Baglungpani (3–4 days)
Khudi – Baglungpani – Nalma Phedi – Begnas Tal – Pokhara

Those with masses of time can follow tracks or trails linking Khudi to Pokhara, via the high ridge of Baglungpani (take a guide).

A rather never-ending climb up close to the Boran Khola eventually leads through forest for much of the way to Baglungpani (1595m), where there is a lodge. The views from this high col are worth the stiff climb, with panoramic scenes of the Annapurnas, Himalchuli, Ngadi and Manaslu. Alas, the path down is as equally demanding as the ascent was – all the way to Nalma Phedi. Down here it's hot, humid and hard going, but at least new jeep routes are making the journey to Pokhara much quicker. The valley route follows the Midim Khola to Karputar, crosses the saddle of Sarka Bhanjyang and drops to Begnas Tal and Pokhara.

Besisahar – Ramgha – Pokhara (3–4 days)
Besisahar – Puranokot – Thuloswanra – Neta – Ramgha

The star attraction of Puranokot, apart from the superb ambience, is the new climbing wall, so some may wish to overnight here. Although a historical site, little remains of Thuloswanra's past glories; however, the views of the mountains – Lamjung and Annapurna II – are magnificent.

The trail climbs steeply from Besisahar to **Lamjung Durbar**, a substantially intact, Newari-style former fiefdom palace. The route continues along the wooded ridges and around terraced rice fields to **Puranokot** (1750m), a large village. The people in Puranokot call themselves the Duras, a Mongoloid group from the Dura Danda Ridge, but there are also Gurungs. The trail heads across the Manage Danda area to **Thuloswanra** (1600m) in around 4–5hrs.

From Thuloswanra a complex series of ridges and valleys that typify the area lead by well-routed trails to **Neta** (1100m). After Neta is **Tandrangkot**, another former hilltop fortress that has long since fallen into ruins. From here the track heads down to **Samibhanjyang**, set on a small saddle, and into the valley of the Midim Khola. The temperatures soar and it gets muggy walking down to **Ramgha** (6–7hrs). Rough dirt roads run from Ramgha to Karputar, then over the Sarka Bhanjyang to Begnas Tal and thus on to Pokhara.

Kalimati – Chowk Chisopani – Pokhara (4 days)
Kalimati – Chowk Chisopani – Sundar – Thulung – Neta – Ramgha

The main attraction of this option to Pokhara is that it is so far utterly untouched by tourism. The tranquil rural environment of the villages and the stunning panoramas are an added bonus. The arc of Himalayan giants stretches east from Baudha, Himalchuli, Ngadi and Manaslu, to Lamjung, Machhapuchhre and as far west as Annapurna South. Homestay is still being developed, so you need to check their status before planning an overnight stay. A guide (and porter) is essential across this entire region, both for safety and to avoid getting lost. Bandipur, a beautiful hill town near Dumre, is also worth a visit en route between either Pokhara or Dumre and Kathmandu. The Old Inn is a very atmospheric haunt to stay in – it's not haunted as far as we know!

The suggested routes go from Chowk Chisopani via Sundar Bazaar to Okhlepani, Thulung, Neta and Ramgha to Pokhara, or via the Raipali pass to Kuncha and then to Okhlepani.

Chowk Chisopani can be accessed by jeep from Kalimati (approx 22km from Dumre) or by hiking (2hrs walk uphill). The village is noted for the presence of Newari people who have migrated to the hills from their ancestral home in the Kathmandu Valley. A well-stocked shop, a large school and two temples (devoted to Lakshmi, Narayan and Shiva), are located here. The family of Sohan Shrestha has a beautiful, traditional Newari house south of the temples, with typical mud-plastered walls and delicately-carved wooden windows and doorways. It is planned to become a homestay. For more details see updates on www.expeditionworld.com or contact Sohan Shrestha at sohan_kgh@hotmail.com. Rural Heritage (http://rural-heritage.com/), who already operate The Old Inn in Bandipur, are planning a new development in the village as well.

From the northeast end of the school, a trail heads down to Paundi or Sundar. The path descends steeply and crosses a small 'tractor' track (5–10mins). At an intersection, go left for **Sundar Bazaar** (3hrs approx). A guide is vital for this section of the route. From Sundar Bazaar erratic transport should be available to Khatri Thanti and beyond towards **Chanapata** or **Okhlepani**. However, you might end up walking, so be prepared, taking water and snacks. From either of the two villages it is easy to access the Puranokot to Ramgha route – well, it is if you have a knowledgeable guide.

Alternative: Chowk Chisopani – Ramgha (4 days)
Chowk Chisopani – Bayapani – Okhlepani – Neta – Ramgha

A more direct link to Thuloswanra and Ramgha is to take a trail from the temple area of Chowk Chisopani to the **Raipali Bhanjyang** pass (1hr) and west to **Bayapani** (2hrs). The route then descends from here to Ruksepani and down to a dirt road near **Kuncha** (4hrs from Chowk Chisopani). After crossing the Paundi Khola, the trail climbs to **Okhlepani**, (at least 6–7hrs). It then goes on to **Tulung** via **Neta** and **Samibhanjyang** to **Ramgha** from where jeeps go to Pokhara, with luck.

The last word

For most people Himalayan trekking begins as a dream, one of those ideas that will be planned one day. The reality will invariably be laced with some trepidation and much anticipation. It may take years for that dream to come true, but anyone drawn to mountains will eventually want to explore this fantastic range. A trek in Nepal will rarely be a luxurious affair – all those ghastly buses, the brutal ascents, grungy dog patrols, the knee-shattering steps, midnight loo stops, hard beds and that relentless exhausting breathtaking pass but ... soon all that privation is forgotten – the Himalaya might easily become an addiction.

It's the beginning that's the worst, then the middle, then the end. But in the end, it's the end that's the worst.
Samuel Beckett

Have a safe and happy trek!

Approaching Namrung

Appendices

Appendix 1:
Trek summaries and suggested schedules

Grading
The degree of difficulty is defined in the following grades. The grades are relative but remember that there's hardly a flat area in Nepal. Easy (A) – still requires effort with sections of steep ups and downs. Moderate (B) is harder, including higher altitude, and Strenuous (C) involves steep climbs and exposed paths with some at altitude. All treks listed require trekkers to be in good physical shape beforehand.

Note: Jeep or bus journeys are indicated as approximate. Elsewhere timings are split for jeep + trek time etc.

Trekking routes		Time	Alternatives	Time
Manaslu Circuit Trek (B/C)				
Day 1	Kathmandu – Arughat (bus)	7–8hrs	Kathmandu – Gorkha (bus)	5–6hrs
Day 2	Arughat – Machha Khola	2+6–8hrs	Gorkha – Khanchowk/Arughat	3–4hrs
Day 3	Machha Khola – Jagat	6–8hrs	Arughat – Lapubesi	2+4–5hrs
Day 4	Jagat – Deng	7–8hrs	Lapubesi – Dovan	7–8hrs
Day 5	Deng – Ghap	4–5hrs	Dovan – Philim	6–7hrs
Day 6	Ghap – Lho	6–8hrs	Philim – Deng	5–7hrs
Day 7	Lho – Samagaon	3–4hrs	Deng – Namrung	7–8hrs
Day 8	Samagaon – Pungyen return	5hrs	Namrung – Shyala	6–7hrs
Day 9	Samagaon		Shyala – Samagaon	1–2hrs
Day 10	Samagaon – Samdo	4–5hrs	Samagaon	
Day 11	Samdo		Samagaon – Samdo	4–5hrs
Day 12	Samdo – Larkya Phedi	4–5hrs	Samdo	
Day 13	Larkya Phedi – Bimthang	6–10hrs	Samdo – Larkya Phedi	4–5hrs
Day 14	Bimthang – Kharche	3–4hrs	Larkya Phedi – Bimthang	6–10hrs
Day 15	Kharche – Tal	6–7hrs	Bimthang – Tilje	5–6hrs
Day 16	Tal – Jagat	5–6hrs	Tilje – Tal	3–4hrs
Day 17	Jagat – Bahundanda	5–6hrs	Tal – Chamje – Besisahar (jeep)	1+3hrs
Day 18	Bahundanda – Besisahar	5–6+1hrs		

Trekking routes			Time	Alternatives	Time
Tsum Valley Trek (B/C)					
Day 1	Kathmandu – Arughat		7–8hrs		
Day 2	Arughat – Machha Khola		2+6–8hrs		
Day 3	Machha Khola – Jagat		6–7hrs		
Day 4	Jagat – Lokpa		6–7hrs		
Day 5	Lokpa – Chumling		4–5hrs		
Day 6	Chumling – Chhokang Paro		5–6hrs		
Day 7	Chhokang Paro – Nile		4–5hrs		
Day 8	Nile – Mu Gompa		2–3hrs	Nile – Mu – Rachen	5–7hrs
Day 9	Mu Gompa – Bhajyo		3–4hrs	Rachen – Chumling	6–7hrs
Day 10	Bhajyo day hike to Tibet		8–9hrs	Chumling – Philim or Deng	6–7/7–8hrs
Day 11	Bajyo – Mu		3hrs	Philim – Dovan	6–7hrs
Day 12	Mu – Rachen		3–4hrs	Dovan – Lapubesi	7–8hrs
Day 13	Rachen – Chumling		6–7hrs	Lapubesi – Arughat	3 + 2hrs
Day 14	Chumling – Philim/Deng		6–7/7–8hrs	Arughat – Kathmandu	7–8hrs
Day 15	Philim – Dovan		6–7hrs		
Day 16	Dovan – Lapubesi		7–8hrs		
Day 17	Lapubesi – Arughat		3 + 2hrs		
Day 18	Arughat – Gorkha		3–4hrs		
Day 19	Gorkha – Kathmandu		5–6hrs		

Trekking routes	Time	Alternatives	Time

Lower Manaslu Region

Gorkha Pilgrimage Trek (A)

		Time
Day 1	Kathmandu – Manakamana	5hrs
Day 2	Manakamana – Baskot	5–6hrs
Day 3	Baskot – Gorkha	6–7hrs
Day 4	Gorkha – Kathmandu	5–6hrs

Gorkha Cultural Trek (B/C)

Day 1	Kathmandu – Gorkha	5–6hrs
Day 2	Gorkha – Barpak	7–8hrs
Day 3	Barpak – Laprak	6–7hrs
Day 4	Laprak – Gumda	3–4hrs
Day 5	Gumda – Machha Khola	5–6hrs
Day 6	Machha Khola – Soti	6–7hrs
Day 7	Soti – Arughat	2hrs
Day 8	Arughat – Kathmandu	7–8hrs

Trekking routes		Time	Alternatives	Time
Lower Manaslu Trek (B)				
Day 1	Kathmandu – Manakamana	5hrs		
Day 2	Manakamana – Pipalchhap	4–5hrs		
Day 3	Pipalchhap – Khanchowk	7–8hrs		
Day 4	Khanchowk – Tallo Thotnery	5–6hrs		
Day 5	Tallo Thotnery – Sambe Kharka	6–7hrs		
Day 6	Sambe Kharka – Laprak	4–5hrs		
Day 7	Laprak – Barpak	5–6hrs		
Day 8	Barpak – Sirandanda	6–7hrs		
Day 9	Sirandanda – Gorkha	1 + 5hrs		
Day 10	Gorkha – Kathmandu	5–6hrs		
Dharche Danda Trek (B)				
Day 1	Kathmandu – Gorkha	5–6hrs		
Day 2	Gorkha – Khanchowk	6–7hrs		
Day 3	Khanchowk – Tallo Thotnery	5–6hrs		
Day 4	Tallo Thotnery – Dharche Danda	5–6hrs		
Day 5	Dharche Danda – Sita Cave	4–5hrs		
Day 6	Sita Cave – Taple	7–8hrs		
Day 7	Taple – Gorkha	4–5hrs		
Day 8	Gorkha – Kathmandu	5–6hrs		

Trekking routes		Time	Alternatives	Time
Rupina La Trek (C)				
Day 1	Kathmandu – Gorkha	5–6hrs		
Day 2	Gorkha – Khanchowk	5–6hrs		
Day 3	Khanchowk – Tallo Thotnery	5–6hrs		
Day 4	Tallo – Sambe Kharka	6–7hrs		
Day 5	Sambe Kharka – Humche	5–6hrs		
Day 6	Humche – Diling Kharka	5–6hrs		
Day 7	Diling Kharka – Gai Kharka	5–6hrs		
Day 8	Gai Kharka – Sanrung Kharka	4–5hrs		
Day 9	Sanrung – Rupina – Baudha BC	8–9hrs		
Day 10	Baudha BC – Jhong Kharka	5–6hrs		
Day 11	Jhong Kharka – Nyak	4–5hrs		
Day 12	Nyak – Jagat	5–6hrs		
Day 13	Jagat – Machha Khola	5–6hrs		
Day 14	Machha Khola – Arughat	6–8+2hrs		
Day 15	Arughat – Kathmandu	7–8hrs		

Ganesh Himal Trek (B/C)

Notes: Times given are only an indication or estimate

*Alternative trail route possibility is unverified – help! Since there is a bridging point over the Budhi Gandaki below Liding, it might be possible to trek from Yarsa to Liding & Soti, making the trek even shorter by one day at the end – more help please!

Trekking routes		Time	Alternatives	Time
Day 1	Kathmandu – Nuwakot	5hrs		
Day 2	Nuwakot – Syabrubesi	3hrs	Kathmandu – Syabrubesi	6–8hrs
Day 3	Syabrubesi – Gatlang	5–7hrs		
Day 4	Gatlang – Somdang	6–7hrs		
Day 5	Somdang – Pangsang La Phedi	6–7hrs		
Day 6	Pangsang La Phedi – Tipling	6–7hrs		
Day 7	Tipling – Chalis	4–5hrs		
Day 8	Chalis – Lapchet	5–6hrs		
Day 9	Lapchet – Nauban Kharka	6–7hrs		
Day 10	Nauban Kharka – Yarsa	4–5hrs		
Day 11	Yarsa – Kerauja	5–6hrs		
Day 11	Kerauja – Machha Khola	5–6hrs	Kerauja – Tatopani	5–6hrs

Trekking routes	Time	Alternatives	Time

Gurung Heritage Trail (B)

Day 1	Ghalegaon – Bhujung	3–4hrs	
Day 2	Bhujung – Pasagaon	4–5hrs	
Day 3	Pasagaon – Nagidhara	4–5hrs	
Day 4	Nagidhara – Gumle Bazaar	3–4hrs	
Day 5	Gumle Bazaar – Pokhara	2–3hrs	

Khudi – Pokhara via Baglungpani (B)

Day 1	Khudi – Baglungpani	6–7hrs	
Day 2	Baglungpani – Nalma	6–7hrs	
Day 3	Nalma – Pokhara	3–4hrs	

Besisahar – Ramgha (A/B)

Day 1	Besisahar – Puranokot	4–5hrs	
Day 2	Puranokot – Neta	5–6hrs	
Day 3	Neta – Ramgha	5–6hrs	
Day 4	Ramgha – Pokhara	3–4hrs	

Trekking routes	Time	Alternatives	Time

Chowk Chisopani – Pokhara (A/B)

Day 1	Kalimati – Chowk Chisopani	2hrs
Day 2	Chowk Chisopani – Okhlepani	4–6hrs
Day 3	Okhlepani – Neta	3–4hrs
Day 4	Neta – Ramgha – Pokhara	4–5hrs+3–4hrs

Alternative: Chowk Chisopani – Pokhara via Bayapani (A/B)

Day 1	Kalimati– Chowk Chisopani	2hrs
Day 2	Chowk Chisopani – Okhlepani	6–7hrs
Day 3	Okhlepani – Neta	3–4hrs
Day 4	Neta – Ramgha – Pokhara	4–5hrs+3–4hrs

Appendix 2:
Bibliography

Anderson, Mary. **Festivals of Nepal** George Allen & Unwin 1971
Berger, Fritz. **In the Shadow of Gauri Shankar: Dolakha 1973–2011** Himal Books 2014
Bista, Dor Bahadur. **People of Nepal** Ratna Pustak Bhandar 1987
Blum, Arlene. **Annapurna: A woman's place, first female on Annapurna** 1978, republished 1998
Bonington, Chris. **Annapurna South Face** Cassel 1971, Pilgrims reprint 1997
Bonington, Chris. **Everest the Hard Way** Hodder & Stoughton 1976
Boustead, Robin. **Nepal Trekking and the Great Himalaya Trail** Second edition Trailblazer 2015
Bowman, W E (Bill). **The Ascent of Rum Doodle** 1956 (www.rumdoodle.org.uk – a great skit on the big mountaineering expeditions of the past, written long before they became in vogue)
Chorlton, Windsor and Wheeler, Nik. **Cloud-Dwellers of the Himalayas** Time-Life Books 1982
Dalai Lama. **An Introduction to Buddhism and Tantric Meditation** Paljor Publications 1996
Durkan, David. **Penguins on Everest** Second edition Swami Kailash 2014
Fisher, James F. **Trans-Himalayan Traders** Univ. California Press 1986
Fleming. **Birds of Nepal** reprints by Indian publishers only
Gibbons, Bob & Pritchard-Jones, Siân. **Kathmandu: Valley of the Green-Eyed Yellow Idol** Pilgrims 2004
Gibbons, Bob & Pritchard-Jones, Siân. **Annapurna: A Trekkers' Guide** Cicerone 2013 (second edition 2016)
Gibbons, Bob & Pritchard-Jones, Siân. **Mount Kailash: A Trekkers' Guide** Cicerone 2007
Gordon, Antoinette. **The Iconography of Tibetan Lamaism** Munshi Ram M Delhi 1978
Govinda, Lama Anagarika. **The Way of the White Clouds** Rider and Company, London 1966

Hagen, Toni. **Nepal: The Kingdom of the Himalayas** Kümmerley and Frey 1980

Herzog, Maurice. **Annapurna** Jonathan Cape 1952

Hillary, Edmund. **High Adventure** Hodder & Stoughton, London 1955

Hunt, John. **The Ascent of Everest** Mountaineers Books, London 1953

Kalsang, Ladrang. **The Guardian Deities of Tibet** Winsome Books India 2003

Kawaguchi, Ekai. **Three Years in Tibet** 1909 reprints

Kind, Marietta. **The Bon Landscape of Dolpo** Peter Lang AG 2012

Krakauer, Jon. **Into Thin Air** Anchor Books/Doubleday, New York 1999

Lama, Sonam & Lama, Lopsang Chhiring. **Manaslu and Tsum Valley** Himalayan Map House 2013

Lachenal, Louis. **Carnets du Vertige** Editions Guérin 1996

Landon, Perceval. **Nepal Vols I and II** Pilgrims 2007

Lhalungpa, Lobsang P. **The Life of Milarepa** Book Faith 1997

Lonely Planet **Nepali Phrasebook** Frequently published

Mierow, Dorothy and Shrestha, Tirtha Bahadur. **Himalayan Flowers and Trees** Prakashan/Pilgrims

Messner, Reinhold. **Annapurna** The Mountaineers, 2000

Noyce, Wilfred. **Climbing the Fish's Tail** Heinemann, 1958, reprinted by Book Faith/Pilgrims Publishing, 1998

O'Connor, Bill. **Adventure Treks: Nepal** Crowood Press 1990

Pauler, Gerda. **The Great Himalaya Trail** Baton Wick 2013

Peissel, Michel. **Mustang: A Lost Tibetan Kingdom** 1964, reprints

Pritchard-Jones, Siân and Gibbons, Bob. **Kailash and Guge: Land of the Tantric Mountain** Pilgrims 2006

Pritchard-Jones, Siân and Gibbons, Bob. **Ladakh: Land of Magical Monasteries** Pilgrims 2006

Pritchard-Jones, Siân and Gibbons, Bob. **Himalayan Travel Guides – Manaslu & Tsum Valley; Dolpo; Ganesh Himal; Langtang; Everest; Rolwaling & Gauri Shankar; Nepal Himalaya; Mustang** Himalayan Map House 2013–16

Pritchard-Jones, Siân and Gibbons, Bob. **Earthquake Diaries: Nepal 2015** Expedition World/CreateSpace (Amazon) 2015
Pritchard-Jones, Siân and Gibbons, Bob. **In Search of the Green-Eyed Yellow Idol** Expedition World/CreateSpace (Amazon) 2015
Reynolds, Kev. **Abode of the Gods** Cicerone 2015
Reynolds, Kev. **Trekking in the Himalaya** Cicerone 2013
Roerich, Nicholas. **Altai Himalaya** 1929, reprinted by Book Faith India 1996
Sakya, Karna. **Dolpo: The Hidden Paradise** Nirala 2007
Snellgrove, David. **Buddhist Himalaya** Oxford 1957
Snellgrove, David. **Himalayan Pilgrimage** Oxford 1961
Stevenson, Andrew. **Annapurna Circuit** Constable 1997
Tilman, H W. **Nepal Himalaya** Cambridge University Press / Diadem Books–The Mountaineers 1983
Tucci, Giuseppe. **Shrines of a Thousand Buddhas** Pilgrims, Varanasi 2008
Venables, Stephen. **Higher Than the Eagle Soars** Random House 2007

Films

A wonderfully evocative film about the people of Dolpo in Nepal, **Himalaya** (first released as **Caravan** in Nepal) portrays the life of traditional village yak herders in the remote regions. Good background is **Seven Years in Tibet**, about Heinrich Harrar's life as a fugitive from World War II and his life in Lhasa close to the Dalai Lama. A recent release is **Himalaya Bhotia**, a French-made film about the people of northern Nepal.

Music

There are a lot of new CDs on Himalayan themes. A few are folk songs, others are amalgams of Tibetan chants, songs and 'Western Oriental'. These tunes resonate with calming and meditative music. Some are **Tibetiya, Sacred Buddha, Karmapa: Secrets of the Crystal Mountain, Journey to Tibet, Sacred Chants of Buddha**, sound track of the film **Himalaya, Nepali Folksongs**. All these can be found in Kathmandu.

Appendix 3:
Glossary

Religious and other terminology

Significant Buddhist deities

The **Dhyani Buddhas** face the four cardinal directions; they are often found on stupas and chaityas (small stone chortens). The Dhyani Buddhas were created from the wisdom of the Adi (first) Buddha, the primordial Buddha. **Vairocana** is the first Dhyani Buddha and resides in the stupa sanctum; Vairocana is the illuminator, to light the way. **Akshobhya** faces east; **Amitabha** faces west; **Amoghasiddhi** faces north, with a seven-headed serpent behind him; **Ratna Sambhava** faces south (these are the Sanskrit names).

The following are some other important deities; Sanskrit names are shown first.

Sakyamuni (Sakya Tukpa) The mortal Buddha, Gautama Siddhartha, born in Nepal.

Avalokiteshvara (Chenresig) Bodhisattva having renounced Nirvana, the end of the cycle of rebirth. He embodies compassion (karuna) and remains on earth to counter suffering. The Dalai Lama is considered to be his earthly representative.

Amitayus (Tsepame) Buddha of Boundless Life, an aspect of Amitabha; he is associated with longevity.

Vajrapani (Channa Dorje) Spiritual son of Akshobhya. He carries a *dorje (vajra)* and is a powerful, wrathful protector. He has monstrous Tantric powers and wears a snake around his neck.

Hayagriva (Tamdrin) Wrathful emanation of Chenresig, guards many shrines. Blood red with a small horse sticking out of his head, he wears a garland of skulls.

Manjushri (Jampelyang) God of wisdom, who carries a sword to cut through ignorance. Worshipping Manjushri gives intellect and intelligence.

Yamantaka (Dorje Jigje) 'Slayer of death', a wrathful emanation of Manjushri; a Gelug-pa deity with a buffalo head.

Tara (Drolma) Sacred to both Buddhists and Hindus, representing the maternal aspect, symbolising fertility, purity and compassion. With 21 versions, Tara appears in different colours: red, green, white and gold, and as Kali, dark blue, representing different aspects of her nature.
Maitreya Buddha (Jampa) The future Buddha.
Medicine Buddha Engaged for healing the sick, often a blue colour with four hands.
Mahakala Linked to Shiva with his trident. He tramples on corpses and is a wrathful Avalokiteshvara.
The Four Harmonious Friends
Found in many monasteries, depicting four animals, one on top of the other: the Elephant, Monkey, Rabbit and the Bird. These represent harmony for peace and the removal of conflict.
The Four Guardians Seenat monastery entrances. Dhitarashtra is the white guardian of the east, holding a flute. Virupaksha guards the west; he is red with a stupa in one hand and a serpent in the other. Virudhakla is guardian of the south, holding a blue sword. Vaisravana guards the north, holding a yellow banner and a mongoose, usually seen vomiting jewels.
Padma Sambhava (Guru Rinpoche) The most famous icon of Buddhism, an Indian Tantric master who went to Tibet in the eighth century. He established the Nyingma-pa Red Hat sect. His consort Yeshe Tsogyal recorded his teachings to be revealed to future generations.
Milarepa Tibet's poet, magician and saint – a historical figure, associated with many legends. He meditated in caves as a hermit before achieving realisation.

Significant Bon deities

Bon has four main peaceful deities, the 'Four Transcendent Lords': **Shenlha Wokar, Satrig Ersang, Sangpo Bumtri and Tonpa Shenrap Miwoche.**
Others include: **Kuntu Zangpo** (similar to the primordial Adi Buddha of Buddhism); **Kunzang Gyalwa Gyatso** (very similar, and perhaps a precursor to the 1000-armed Avalokiteshvara); **Welse Ngampa** (a nine-headed protector representing 'piercing ferocity' and crushing the enemies of Bon); **Sipai Gyalmo** (a protectress called the 'Queen of the World').

Other definitions

Arhat Original disciples of Buddha who have managed to become free from the cycle of existence (samsara). Arhats are not often seen as icons, but when they are, their faces have moustaches and beards.

Bharal Species of blue sheep.

Bhatti Small rural dwelling.

Bodhisattva Disciple of Buddha who has delayed the attainment of Nirvana in order to teach.

Bon Pre-Buddhist religion of Tibet.

Chang Home-brewed barley wine/beer, sometimes made with other grain.

Chorten Similar to a small stupa (see below) but does not normally contain relics.

Dakini Female deity who can fly.

Dorje/Vajra Thunderbolt: it destroys ignorance. A complex figure-of-eight-shaped metal object found at many temples and shrines.

Dzong Fortress, castle.

Gompa Tibetan name for a monastery.

Gonkhang Small, dark and somewhat forbidding chamber housing the protecting deities: Yamantaka, Mahakala and Palden Lhamo, among others.

Kani Entrance archway to settlements.

Kharka Herders' shelter and meadow.

Kora Circular pilgrimage trek around a sacred mountain or lake.

Lama Religious teacher and guide, male or female.

Lhakhang Temple chapel within a monastery.

Losar Tibetan New Year festival.

Mandala Circular pattern made of many colours, often a square or squares within a circle. Represents 'the divine abode of an enlightened being.

Mani stone Rock covered with engraved Buddhist mantras, sometimes painted.

Mani wall Long wall made of flat stones engraved with Buddhist mantras; may also contain prayer wheels. You should always keep these on your right.

Palden Lhamo Fearful Tibetan female goddess, always on horseback.

Prayer flag Seen in five colours, on which prayers are printed; these flutter in the wind, sending prayers direct to heaven. The colours represent the five elements: earth, fire, air, water and ether.

Prayer wheel Engraved cylinder with Tibetan script and containing prayers. Generally fixed into a wall, or hand held and spun while walking; the spinning action activates the prayers.

Puja Ceremony offering prayers.

Rakshi Nepalese alcoholic drink, not always healthily prepared.

Rigsum Gonpo Three chortens seen above kanis and elsewhere, representing the three deities who offer protection to villages. The red chorten represents Manjushri, giving wisdom; the white chorten represents Avalokiteshvara, offering compassion; and the blue, black or grey chorten represents Vajrapani, to fight off evil. They ward off many spirits found in the three worlds: sky, earth and underworld.

Sadhu Self-proclaimed holy man/ascetic.

Sago Namgo Seen in the northern regions, these strange objects give protection against bad omens. They relate to the 'Mother Earth spirits' and translate as Earth Door and Sky Door. Made from ram skulls, wood or fabric.

Sky burial Form of burial where the body is cut up and fed to the vultures and large birds.

Stupa Large monument, usually with a square base, a dome and a pointed spire on top. The spire represents the levels towards enlightenment. A stupa may often host the remains of a revered lama or teacher.

Tantra Oral teachings and Buddhist scriptures, describing the use of mantras, mandalas and deities in meditation and yoga. It is commonly associated with physical methods of striving for enlightenment but equally applicable to meditation methods using the energies of the mind.

Thangka/tangka Religious painting, usually on silk fabric. They are often seen in all monasteries, hanging on walls or pillars.

Tsampa Traditional Tibetan food: roasted barley mixed with butter tea, it is made into a sort of porridge.

Vajrayana Buddhism 'Diamond' branch of the religion found in Tibet and associated with Tantric ideas.

Yab-yum Depiction of two deities, male and female. The male represents compassion and the female wisdom. Deities depict the spiritual union and higher awareness.

Yidam A personal tutelary deity used in meditation practice.

Appendix 4:
Nepali language hints

Useful words and phrases

Hello/Goodbye	*Namaste*
Goodnight	*Suva ratri*
How are you?	*Tapailai kasto chha?*
Very well	*Ramro chha*
Thank you	*Dhanyabad*
Yes (it is)	*Ho*
No (it isn't)	*Hoina*
Yes (have)	*Chha*
No (don't have)	*Chhaina*
OK	*Tik chha*
What is your name?	*Tapaiko naam ke ho?*
My name is Bob	*Mero naam Bob ho*
Please go slowly	*Bistaari jaane*
Where is a lodge?	*Lodge kahaa chha?*
What's the name of this village?	*Yo gaaunko naam ke ho?*
Which trail goes to Lho?	*Lho jaane baato kun ho?*
Where are you going?	*Tapaai kahaa jaane?*
I don't understand	*Maile buhjina*
I don't know	*Ta chhaina*
Please give me a cup of tea	*Chiyaa dinos*
How much is it?	*Kati paisa*
Where is the toilet?	*Chaarpi kahaa chha?*
Where is there water?	*Pani kahaa chha?*
I want to rent a pony	*Malaai ghoda bhadama chaainchha*
I need a porter	*Ma kulli chaainchha*
I am sick	*Ma biraami chhu*
I have altitude sickness	*Lekh laagyo*

Other useful words

what	*ke*
where	*kun*
when	*kaile*

how much	*kati*
good	*ramro*
bad	*naramro*
cold	*jaaro/chiso*
hot	*garam/tato*
trail	*baato*
steeply up	*ukaalo*
steeply down	*oraalo*
flat (Nepali flat!)	*terso*
dangerous	*aptero*
river (small)	*khola*

Food

food	*khanaa*
bread	*roti*
rice	*bhaat*
noodle soup	*thukpa*
eggs	*phul*
meat	*maasu*
yoghurt	*dahi*
sugar	*chini*
salt	*nun*
water	*pani*
boiled water	*umaalekho pani*
black tea	*kalo chiyaa*
hot water	*tatopani*
cold water	*chiso pani*

Numbers

1	*ek*	11	*ekhaara*
2	*dui*	12	*baara*
3	*tin*	15	*pandhra*
4	*char*	20	*bis*
5	*paanch*	30	*tis*
6	*chha*	40	*chaalis*
7	*saat*	50	*pachaas*
8	*aath*	100	*ek say*
9	*nau*	500	*panch say*
10	*das*	1000	*ek hajaar*

Appendix 5:
Useful contacts

Tour operators in Nepal
Alliance Treks www.rubyvalleytreks.com
Ama Dablam Adventures www.adventure-himalaya.com
Asian Trekking www.asian-trekking.com
Beyond the Limits www.treksinnepal.com
Dream Himalaya www.dreamhimalaya.com.np
Explore Dolpo www.exploredolpotrekking.com
Friends Adventure Team www.friendsadventure.com
Himalayan Encounters www.himalayanencounters.com
Himalayan Rock www.himalayanrock.com
Nepal Nature dot com Travels www.nepalnaturetravels.com
Off the Wall www.offthewalltrekking.com
Sacred Himalaya www.sacredhimalaya.com
Sherpa Adventure Travel www.sherpaadventure.com
3 Sisters Adventure Trekking www.3sistersadventure.com
Trinetra Adventure www.trinetra-adventure.com
The authors have either worked with these providers or know them from experience; many more can be found online.

Tour operators overseas
Classic Journeys www.classicjourneys.co.uk
Exodus www.exodus.co.uk
Expedition World www.expeditionworld.com (travel site run by the authors)
Explore www.explore.co.uk
Intrepid Travel www.intrepidtravel.com
KE Adventure Travel www.keadventure.com
Mountain Kingdoms www.mountainkingdoms.com
Peregrine www.peregrineadventures.co.uk
Sherpa Expeditions www.sherpa-walking-holidays.co.uk
The Adventure Company www.adventurecompany.co.uk
Trekking Team Poland www.trampingi.pl
Walks Worldwide www.walksworldwide.com
Wilderness Travels USA www.wildernesstravels.com
World Expeditions www.worldexpeditions.co.uk

Online information

www.gov.uk/foreign-travel-advice – travel advice and tips
www.himalayanrescue.org – rescue information
www.info-nepal.com – general background
www.nepalimmigration.gov.np – immigration department for visa and permits
www.kmtnc.org.np – conservation themes
www.mnteverest.net/trek.html – list of trekking companies
www.nepalmountaineering.org
www.taan.org.np – Trekking Agencies Association of Nepal
www.visitnepal.com – travel information
www.welcomenepal.com – tourist information
www.ekantipur.com – news
www.nepalnews.net – news
www.nepalnow.com – news
www.stanfords.co.uk – maps
www.themapshop.co.uk – maps
www.tsumvalley.org
www.tsumvalleyhomestay.com
www.manaslucircuittrek.com
www.manaslutrailrace.org
www.trekkingpartners.com – to find a trekking partner

Important phone numbers

Fire Brigade	101
Police Control	100
Telephone Inquiries	197
Tribhuvan International Airport	4471933

Hospitals

B & B Hospital	5533206
Bir Hospital	4222862/63
Ishan Childrens Nursing Home	4381962
Kanti Children's Hospital	4427452
Norvic Hospital	4258554
Patan Hospital	5522266
TU Teaching Hospital	4412505

Police

District Police Office, Kathmandu	4261945
District Police Office, Lalitpur	5521207
Emergency Police Service	4226999

Embassies

Australia, Bansbari	4371678
British, Lainchour	4411590
China, Baluwatar	4411740
France, Lazimpat	4418034
India, Lainchour	4414990
Japan, Panipokhari	4426680
Thailand, Bansbari	4371410
USA, Maharajgunj	4411179

Please note that all phone numbers are likely to change.

Maps

Heaven forbid that there should be an earthquake powerful enough to make the map correct!
Ramond de Carbonnieres *said of a Pyrenean map in the 19th century*

Maps change and so has the Kathmandu Valley (Boudhanath stupa in 1975)

TIBET
(CHINA)
INDIA
Scale 1:5000000
0 50 100 150 200
Lapche Bhanjyang 5018
Chang La 5293
Sarpe Bhanjyang 5012
Chhunsa Lake
Gorakh 6088
Simikot
Api 7132
Saipal Himal 7031
Darchula
Danphesail 6103
Chainpur
Gamgadhi
Baitadi
Martadi
Rara Lake
Kora La 4660
Dhadeldhura
Sanphebagar
Marim Bhanjyang
Phoksundo Lake
Dipayal Silgadhi
Mangalsen
Manma
Jumla
Lo Manthang
Mahendranagar
Dailekh
Muktinath
Jugu La
Dunai
8176
Jomsom
Thorung La
Yandol Bhanjyang 5325
Dhangadi
Jajarkot
Khalanga
Dhaulagiri
Tilicho Lake
Birendranagar
Musikot
Annapurna 8091
Chame
Manaslu 8163
Ganesh 7429
Langtang Ri 8201
Gaulariya
Salyan
Liwang
Beni
Phewa Lake
Tulsipur
Pyuthan
Baglung
Besisahar
Tilman Pass
Nangpa La
Cho oyu
Sagarmatha (Mt. Everest) 8848
Kushma
Pokhara
Gorkha
Dhunche
Nepalgunj
Ghorahi
Tamghas
Syangja
Renjo La
Ghan La 5752
Arghakhanchi
Damauli
Trishuli
Kodari
Lhotse
Makalu 8463
Tansen
Dhadingbesi
Bidur
Chautara
Cho La
West Col
Kangchenjunga 8586
Butwal
Bharatpur
KATHMANDU
Bhaktapur
Taulihawa
Bhairawa
Parasi
Lalitpur
Dhulikhel
Charikot
Salleri
Lumbini
Sunauli
Hetauda
Manthali
Khadbari
Taplejung
Chiya Bhanjyang 3139
Okhaldhunga
Diktel
Sindulimadhi
Terhathum
Phidim
Birgunj
Bhojpur
Kalaiya
Raxaul
Malangawa
Dhankuta
Ilam
Gaur
Jaleshwor
Gaighat
Siraha
Dharan
Kakarbhitta
Janakpur
Rajbiraj
Inaruwa
Chandragadhi
Biratnagar
Protected Areas
1 Api-Nampaa Conservation Area
2 Sulkla Phant Wildlife Reserve
3 Khaptad National Park
4 Rara National Park
5 Bardiya National Park
6 Banke National Park
7 Shey-Phoksundo National Park
8 Dhorpatan National Park
9 Annapurna Conservation Area
10 Manaslu Conservation Area
11 Chitwan National Park
12 Parsa Wildlife Reserve
13 Langtang National Park
14 Shivapuri National Park
15 Gauri-Shankar Conservation Area
16 Sagarmatha National Park
17 Makalu-Barun National Park
18 Makalu-Barun Buffer Zone
19 Kangchenjunga Conservation Area
20 Koshi Tappu Wildlife Reserve

THAMEL/CENTRAL KATHMANDU

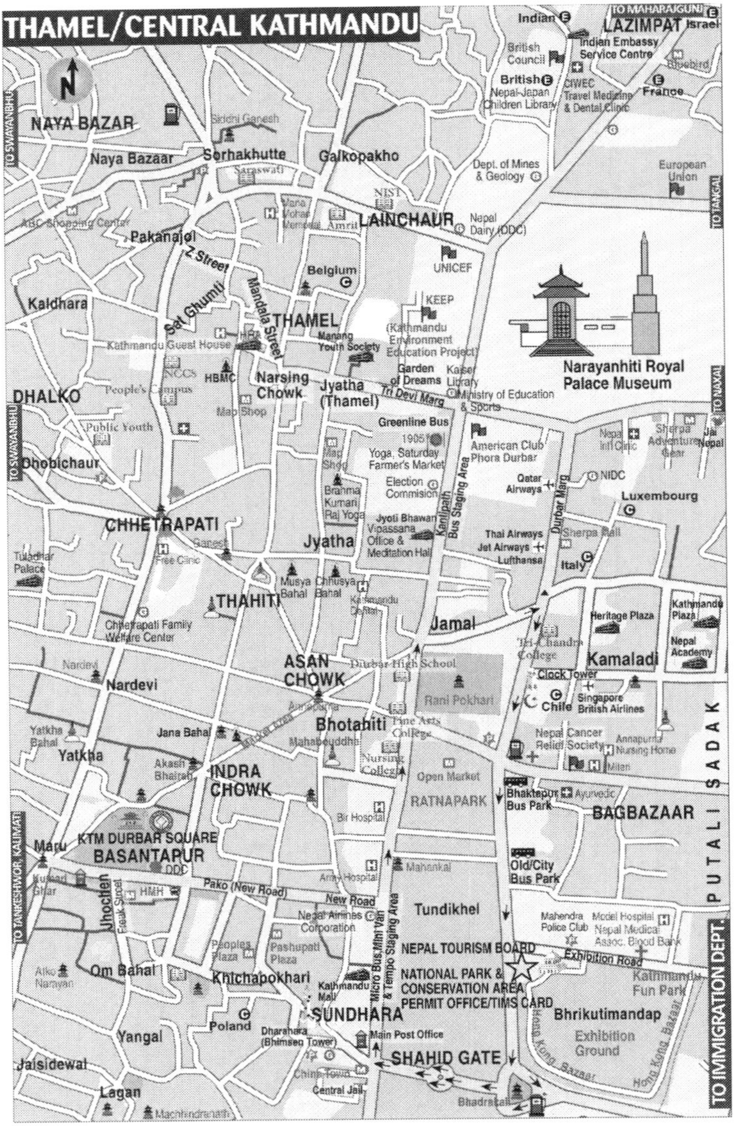

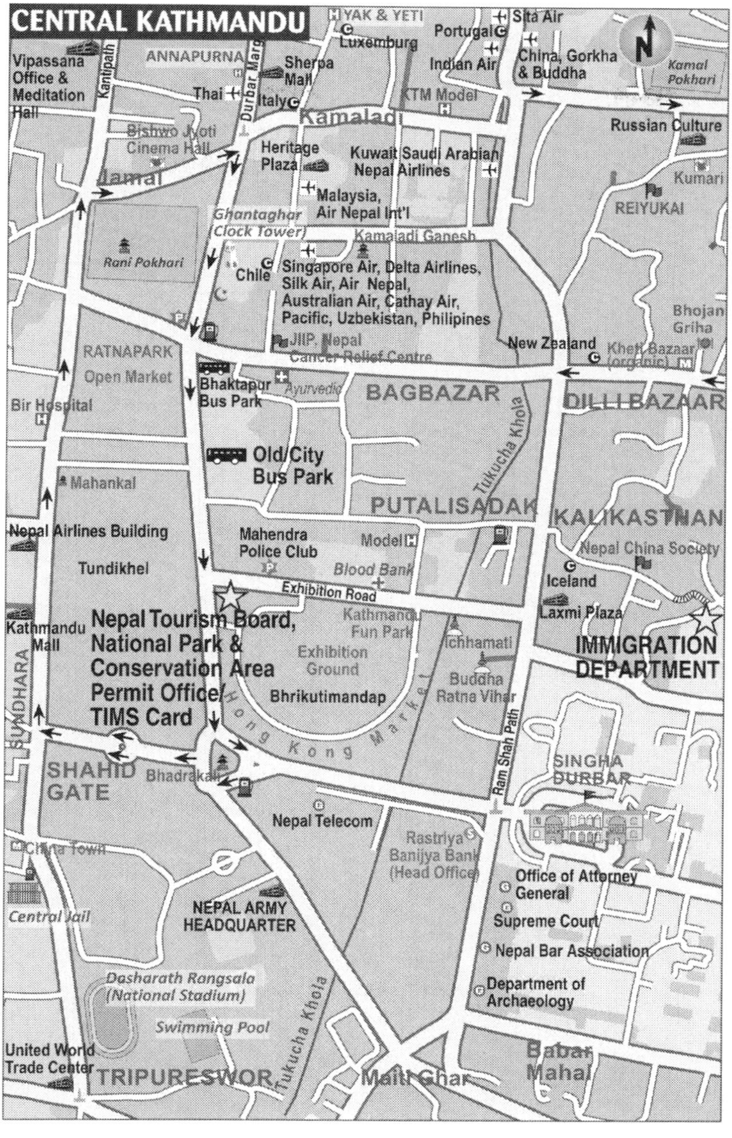
CENTRAL KATHMANDU
YAK & YETI
Sita Air
Luxemburg
Portugal
Vipassana Office & Meditation Hall
Kantipath
ANNAPURNA
Durbar Marg
Sherpa Mall
Indian Air
China, Gorkha & Buddha
Kamal Pokhari
Thai
Italy
KTM Model
Kamaladi
Russian Culture
Bishwo Jyoti Cinema Hall
Heritage Plaza
Kuwait Saudi Arabian Nepal Airlines
Jamal
Malaysia, Air Nepal Int'l
Kumari
REIYUKAI
Ghantaghar (Clock Tower)
Kamaladi Ganesh
Rani Pokhari
Chile
Singapore Air, Delta Airlines, Silk Air, Air Nepal, Australian Air, Cathay Air, Pacific, Uzbekistan, Philipines
Bhojan Griha
RATNAPARK
JIIP, Nepal Cancer Relief Centre
New Zealand
Kheti Bazaar (organic)
Open Market
Bhaktapur Bus Park
Ayurvedic
BAGBAZAR
DILLI BAZAAR
Bir Hospital
Tukucha Khola
Old/City Bus Park
Mahankal
PUTALISADAK
KALIKASTHAN
Nepal Airlines Building
Mahendra Police Club
Model
Nepal China Society
Tundikhel
Blood Bank
Iceland
Exhibition Road
Laxmi Plaza
Kathmandu Mall
Nepal Tourism Board, National Park & Conservation Area Permit Office/ TIMS Card
Kathmandu Fun Park
Exhibition Ground
Ichhamati
IMMIGRATION DEPARTMENT
SUNDHARA
Buddha Ratna Vihar
Bhrikutimandap
Hong Kong Market
Ram Shah Path
SHAHID GATE
Bhadrakali
SINGHA DURBAR
Nepal Telecom
China Town
Rastriya Banijya Bank (Head Office)
Office of Attorney General
NEPAL ARMY HEADQUARTER
Central Jail
Supreme Court
Nepal Bar Association
Dasharath Rangsala (National Stadium)
Department of Archaeology
Swimming Pool
Tukucha Khola
United World Trade Center
TRIPURESWOR
Maiti Ghar
Babar Mahal

Manaslu

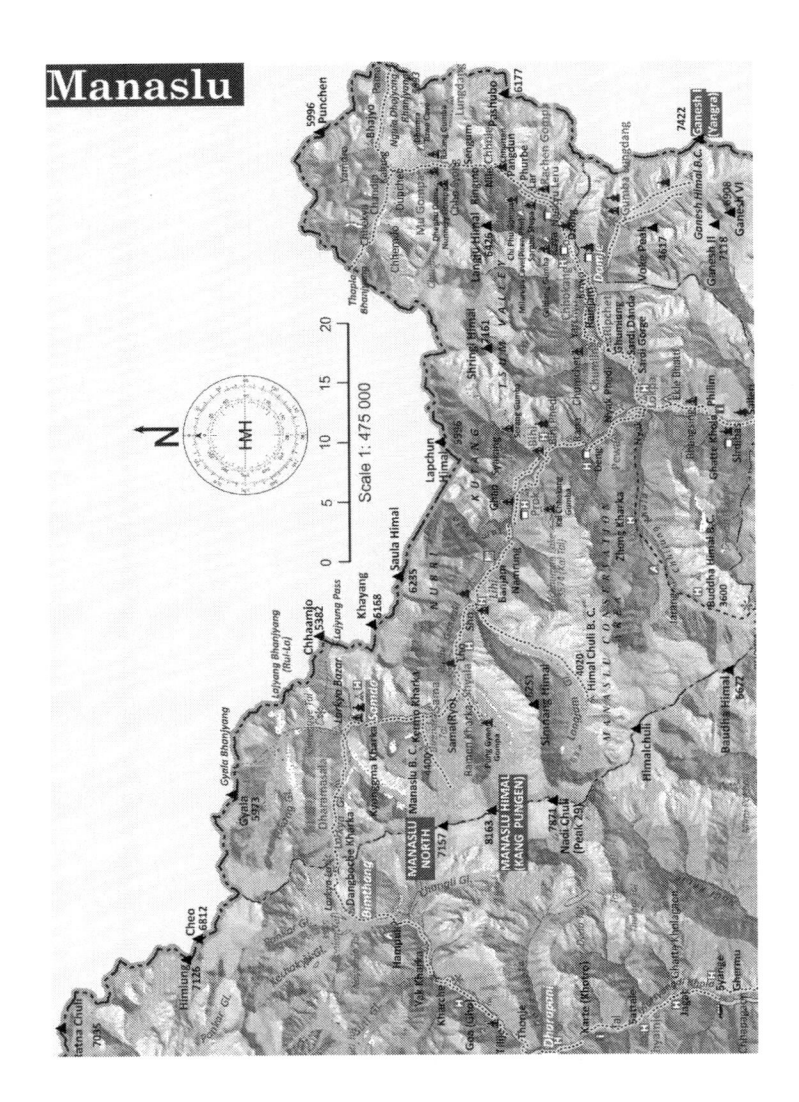

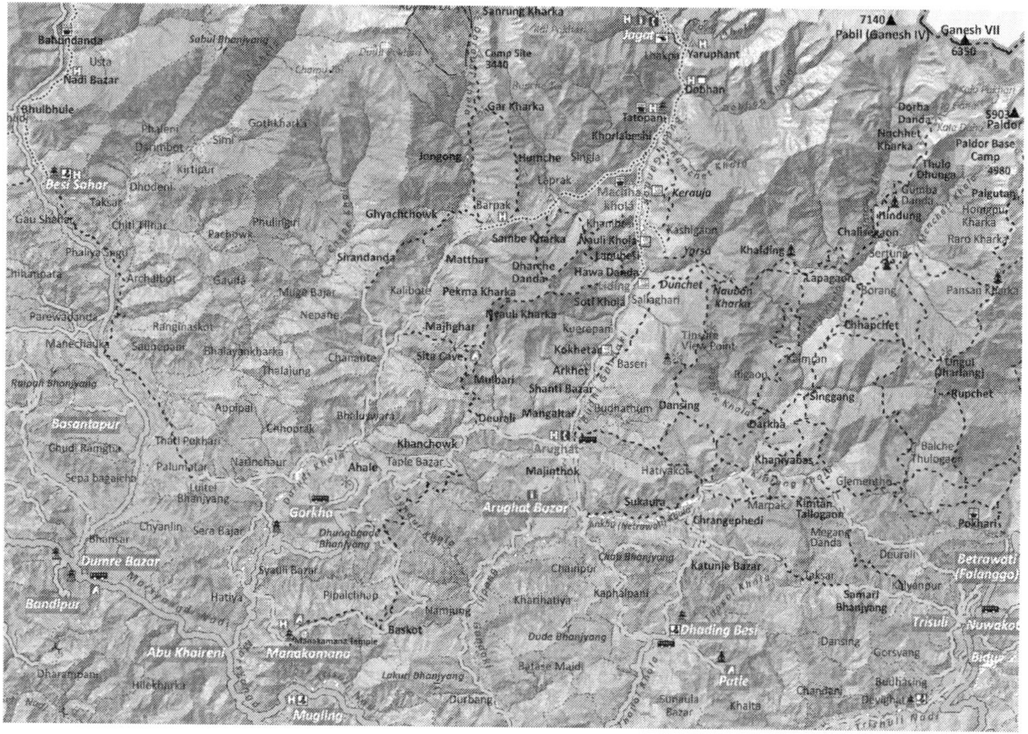
Sanrung Kharka
Jagat
Yaruphant
7140
Pabil (Ganesh IV)
Ganesh VII
6350
Bahundanda
Sabul Bhanjyang
Usta
Nadi Bazar
Camp Site
3440
Dobhan
Bhulbhule
Gar Kharka
Tatopani
Dorha Danda
5903
Paldor
Phaleni
Gotikharka
Simi
Khorlabeshi
Nachhet Kharka
Paldor Base Camp
4980
Dhanbot
Jongong
Hunche
Singla
Thulo Dhunga
Kirtipur
Besi Sahar
Dhodeni
Laprak
Macchha Khola
Kerauja
Gumba Danda
Paigutang
Taksar
Hindung
Hongpu Kharka
Gau Shahar
Chiti Tilhar
Ghyachchowk
Barpak
Phulinjuri
Pachowk
Khamber
Kashigaon
Challsegaon
Raro Kharka
Sambe Kharka
Nauli Khola
Phaliya Sagu
Jambeshi
Yarsa
Khafding
Sertung
Sirandanda
Matthar
Dharche Danda
Hawa Danda
Chihanpata
Archalbot
Gaudu
Dunchet
Naubon Kharka
Lapagaon
Muge Bajar
Kalibote
Pekma Kharka
Borang
Pansan Kharka
Sotl Khola
Sallaghari
Parewadanda
Nepane
Chhapchet
Majhghar
Kuerepani
Ranginaskot
Tin Sire View Point
Manechauka
Saunepani
Bhalayankharka
Kokhetar
Charante
Sita Cave
Baseri
Kimlon
Tingul (Dharlang)
Thalajung
Arkhet
Rigaon
Mulbari
Raipali Bhanjyang
Shanti Bazar
Singgang
Rupchet
Appipal
Dansing
Budhathum
Bhaluswara
Basantapur
Mangaltar
Darkha
Chhoprak
Deurali
Arughat
Balche Thulogaon
Ghudi Ramgha
Thati Pokhari
Khanchowk
Khaniyabas
Narinchaur
Palumatar
Taple Bazar
Ahale
Majinthok
Hatiyakot
Sepa bagaicha
Luitel Bhanjyang
Glementho
Gorkha
Arughat Bazar
Sukaura
Marpak
Kimtan Tallogaon
Pokhari
Chyanlin
Sera Bajar
Chrangephedi
Bhansar
Dhanagaunda Bhanjyang
Megang Danda
Deurali
Betrawati (Falanggo)
Dumre Bazar
Katunje Bazar
Chauripur
Syauli Bazar
Taksar
Hatiya
Pipalchhap
Kharihatiya
Kaphalpani
Samari Bhanjyang
Bandipur
Namjung
Trisuli
Nuwakot
Baskot
Dhading Besi
Manakamana Temple
Dude Bhanjyang
Dansing
Abu Khaireni
Manakamana
Gorsyang
Bidur
Batase Majdi
Patle
Dharampani
Hilekharka
Lakuri Bhanjyang
Buddhasing
Chandani
Devighat
Durbang
Sunaula Bazar
Khalta
Mugling
Trisuli Nadi
Budhi Gandaki

Tsum Valley

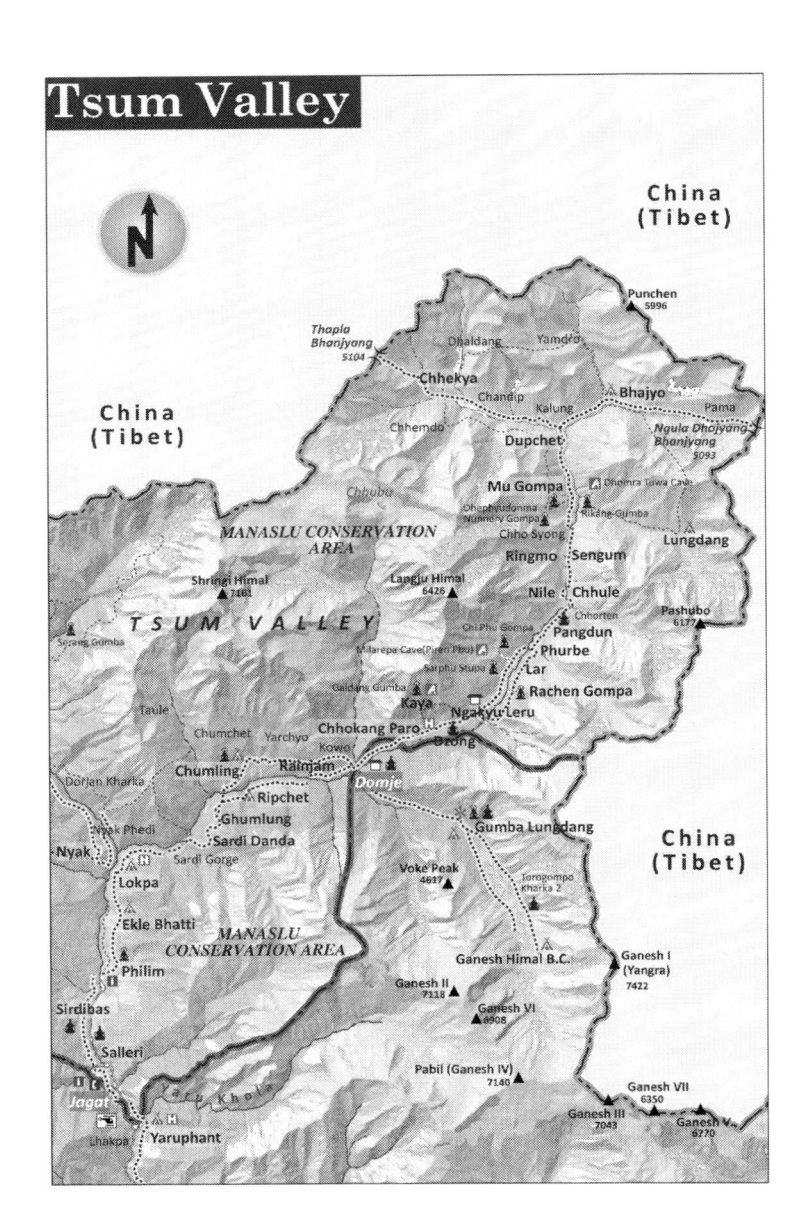

Ganesh Himal
Dupchet
Gompa
Dhephyudonma Nunnery Gompa
Chho Syong
Lungdang
MANASLU CONSERVATION AREA
Nile
Chhule
Pashubo
6177
Ghap
TSUM VALLEY
Rachen Gompa
Bihi Phedi
Chhokang Paro
Langpo
6648
Rana
Chumling
Deng
Domje
Ripchet
GUMBA LUNGDANG
Nyak
Landan Kharka
Lokpa
China
(Tibet)
Bangsing
Ekle Bhatti
GANESH HIMAL B.C.
Ganesh II
(Lapsang Karpo)
7118
Ganesh I (Yangra)
7429
Philim
Sirdibas
Salleri
Ganesh IV (Pabil)
7052
Ganesh VII
6350
Jagat
Ganesh III
(Salasungo)
7110
Ganesh V
6986
Yaruphant
Kalotuppa
4705
Dovan
Paldor
(Bhrange)
5896
Tatopani
Kharka
Dobra Danda
Paldor Base Camp
Khorlabesi
Kerauja
Nojet Kharka
Machha Khola
Yangjo
Lari
Tatopani
Gomba Danda
Thugman
Lingjo
Khanibesi
Thambuchet
Yarsa
Khading
Shertung
Somdang
Gatlang
Lapubesi
Tipling
Budhi Gandaki
Lapa Gaon
SHYABRU
Soti khola
Nauban Kharka
Magne Goth
Borang
Pang Sang Pass
3850
Keurenipani
DHUNCHE
Singla Pass
4045
Trishuli Ganga River
Ganga Jamuna
Rigaon
ARKHET BAZAR
Singgang
Rupchet
Boka jhunda
Dangsing
Gongga
LANGTANG NATIONAL PARK
Mathillo Mulabari
Phulkharka
Darkha Phedi
Bhalche Thulogaon
GRANG
Kimtang Tallogaon
Hatiyakot
Archale
Parchyang
Chisapani
Marpak
Pokhari
Charangge Phedi
Katunje Bazar
Megang Danda
DEURALI
BETRAWATI
Saramthali
Kaphalpani
SAMARI BHANJYANG
TRISULI BAZAR
Halle
Narjamandap
DHADING BESI
Dansing
NUWAKOT
Charghare
Sundaripani
Khanigaon
PATLE
Gorsyang
BIDUR

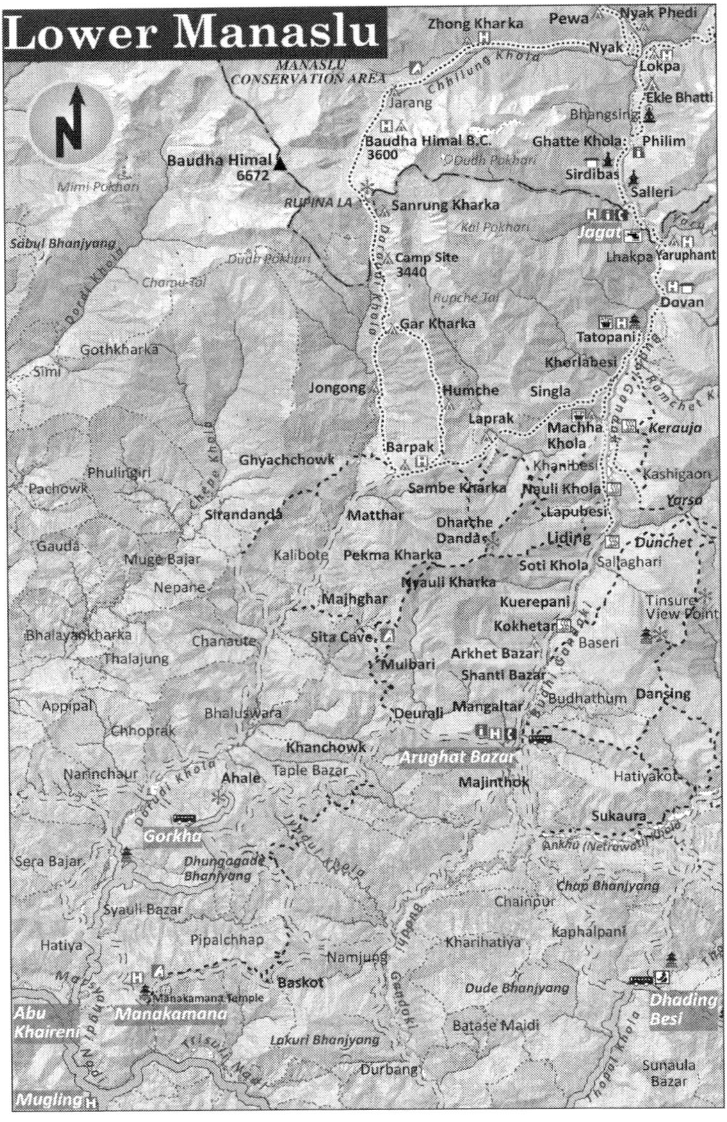
Lower Manaslu
MANASLU CONSERVATION AREA
Zhong Kharka
Pewa
Nyak Phedi
Nyak
Chhilung Khola
Lokpa
Jarang
Ekle Bhatti
Bhangsing
Baudha Himal B.C.
3600
Ghatte Khola
Philim
Baudha Himal
6672
Dudh Pokhari
Sirdibas
Salleri
Mimi Pokhari
RUPINA LA
Sanrung Kharka
Kal Pokhari
Jagat
Sabul Bhanjyang
Dudh Pokhari
Camp Site
3440
Lhakpa
Yaruphant
Charpu Tal
Dovan
Runche Tal
Dordi Khola
Daraudi Khola
Gar Kharka
Tatopani
Gothkharka
Khorlabesi
Simi
Jongong
Humche
Singla
Laprak
Machha Khola
Kerauja
Barpak
Ghyachchowk
Khanibesi
Phulingiri
Kashigaon
Pachowk
Chepe Khola
Sambe Kharka
Nauli Khola
Sirandanda
Matthar
Yarsa
Lapubesi
Dharche Danda
Liding
Gauda
Dunchet
Muge Bajar
Kalibote
Pekma Kharka
Soti Khola
Sallaghari
Nepane
Nyauli Kharka
Majhghar
Kuerepani
Tinsure View Point
Bhalayankharka
Chanaute
Sita Cave
Kokhetar
Baseri
Thalajung
Mulbari
Arkhet Bazar
Shanti Bazar
Budhi Gandaki
Budhathum
Dansing
Appipal
Bhaluswara
Deurali
Mangaltar
Chhoprak
Khanchowk
Arughat Bazar
Narinchaur
Daraudi Khola
Ahale
Taple Bazar
Majinthok
Hatiyakot
Sukaura
Gorkha
Ankhu (Netrawati) Khola
Sera Bajar
Dhungagade Bhanjyang
Chap Bhanjyang
Syauli Bazar
Chainpur
Budhi Gandaki
Kaphalpani
Hatiya
Pipalchhap
Kharihatiya
Namjung
Marsyangdi Nadi
Baskot
Dude Bhanjyang
Manakamana Temple
Abu Khaireni
Manakamana
Dhading Besi
Batase Maidi
Lakuri Bhanjyang
Trisuli Nadi
Thopal Khola
Durbang
Sunaula Bazar
Mugling

about the authors

Siân Pritchard-Jones and Bob Gibbons met in 1983, on a trek from Kashmir to Ladakh. By then Bob had already driven an ancient Land Rover from England to Kathmandu (in 1974), and overland trucks across Asia, Africa and South America. He had also lived in Kathmandu for two years, employed as a trekking company manager. Before they met, Siân worked in computer programming and systems analysis, but was drawn to the Himalaya en route from working in New Zealand.

Since then they have been leading and organising treks in the Alps, Nepal and the Sahara, as well as driving a bus overland to Nepal. Journeys by a less ancient (only 31-year-old) Land Rover from England to South Africa provided the basis for several editions of the Bradt guide Africa Overland, including the sixth edition published in April 2014. Visiting the fantastic boiling lava lake of Erta Ale in the Danakil desert of Ethiopia, and Somaliland was their last African research trip.

In Kathmandu they work with Himalayan Map House and previously worked with Pilgrims Publishing, producing cultural guides – Kathmandu: Valley of the Green-Eyed Yellow Idol and Ladakh: Land of Magical Monasteries – and a historical look at the Guge Kingdom, Kailash: Land of the Tantric Mountain.

In 2007 they wrote the Cicerone guide to Mount Kailash and Western Tibet, as well as updating the Grand Canyon guide. During 2011 they returned to Tibet, this time driving the same old Land Rover back from Kathmandu to the UK overland via Lhasa, through China, Kazakhstan, Russia and Western Europe. Their Annapurna trekking guide for Cicerone was published in January 2013, with a 2nd edition in 2016. In 2015 they published Earthquake Diaries: Nepal 2015 and their autobiography In Search of the Green-Eyed Yellow Idol.

For Himalayan Map House they are writing a new series of trekking guidebooks: Himalayan Travel Guides. Titles so far published include Manaslu & Tsum Valley; Upper & Lower Dolpo; Ganesh Himal & Tamang Heritage Trail; Everest; Langtang, Gosainkund & Helambu; Rolwaling & Gauri Shankar; Nepal Himalaya; and Mustang.

Printed in Great Britain
by Amazon